P9-DVX-728

THE
PATROL

THE
PATROL

SEVEN DAYS IN THE LIFE OF A
CANADIAN SOLDIER IN AFGHANISTAN

RYAN FLAVELLE

FOREWORD BY DAVID J. BERCUSON

HARPERCOLLINS PUBLISHERS LTD

To Bravo Company II PPCLI and all those I walked with.
And to Darcy, who has been with me every step of the way.

CONTENTS

FOREWORD

CANADIANS AND THEIR COLONIAL PREDECESSORS have been at war on and off since Samuel de Champlain and his arquebusiers killed three Iroquois chiefs in 1609. Before and after Confederation, wars have defined Canada, and although many would deny it, they have defined Canadians as well. Most of these wars have entered the realm of history; patriotic Canadians remember that Vimy Ridge came to define us in the First World War, that the British burned the White House in 1814, or that we landed on Juno Beach in 1944. But few Canadians pause to reflect that we are currently fighting another war, one that differs greatly from other wars but is as real, bloody, and "hot" as they were.

The Canadian war in Afghanistan began in the fall of 2001 with great popular support. Canada, after all, was helping the United States respond to the mass atrocity of the Twin Towers and the Pentagon on September 11, 2001. The Canadian public wanted revenge no less than the Americans did. In early 2002, a Canadian battle group arrived at Kandahar Airfield to campaign under U.S. command, hunting the Taliban and al-Qaeda through the mountains that surround Kandahar City. Those troops were withdrawn in the summer of 2002 when their six-month mandate ended. But in the late summer of 2003, Canadian soldiers went back to Afghanistan, first to patrol Kabul, and later (in early 2006) to secure

Kandahar Province against a rising insurgency fought by a resurgent Taliban.

As the war in Kandahar dragged on and Canadian casualties began to mount, popular support for the war began to wane. The Afghan mission became controversial, and a very large number of Canadians wanted to wash their hands of this war, and perhaps of all war.

These events are the stuff of the history that has and will be written to tell the story of how Canada got involved in Afghanistan, what Canada did or did not accomplish there, and how command decisions were made, battles fought, and formations manoeuvred. We know, for example, that in terms of length and numbers of soldiers deployed, Afghanistan has become Canada's third-largest war, surpassing Korea. And, unlike Korea, it is a war fought in the information age; just about every aspect is being recorded by both observers and soldiers. All this raw material will eventually tell the history of Canada's part in the war in Afghanistan.

But there is a massive gap between war as historians and other observers write about it and the experience of war itself. Only those who have actually experienced war can truly know what it is. This is why war memoir literature is such an important contribution to understanding warfare. Ryan Flavelle's book will, among other things, contribute to our collective understanding of this war, and of all war.

In a perceptive book entitled *The Soldiers' Tale: Bearing Witness to Modern War* (1997), Samuel Hynes, a veteran of the Second World War in the Pacific, wrote, "If we would understand what war is like, and how it *feels,* we must turn away from history and its numbers, and seek the reality in the personal witness of the men who were there." I don't believe Hynes was denigrating history when he wrote those words; he was instead drawing a sharp distinction between the observation of war, contemporary or historical, and knowing it through experience.

This doesn't mean that all war memoir literature succeeds in explaining, or even tries to explain, what it was like to be there. In fact, most war memoir literature fails to convey a sense of time and place in war, and of the unique human experience that it is. Yet some notable works have succeeded. Those who would truly know the First World War on the western front must read Robert Graves's *Goodbye to All That* or Siegfried Sassoon's *Memoirs of an Infantry Officer.* Similarly insightful memoirs of the Second World War would include E.B. Sledge's *With the Old Breed at Peleliu and Okinawa,* George MacDonald Fraser's *Quartered Safe Out Here,* Murray Peden's *A Thousand Shall Fall,* or Farley Mowat's *And No Birds Sang.*

I believe Ryan Flavelle's book will one day stand on its own in the same category. It is the first book I have read that gives me a feeling for what this war is like, recounted from the point of view of one soldier who fought it. It is a monumental Canadian literary achievement by a young man who has seen the face of this par-ticular war up close and who has the gift of being able to convey through his writing what he saw and what he felt. That is a rare gift.

Ryan is by no means the first combat veteran I have ever met. I have worked for, talked to, and recorded the impressions of hundreds of Second World War, Korean, and Afghanistan veter-ans. When the reserve formations for which I was an honorary lieutenant-colonel (33 Field Engineer Squadron and 41 Combat Engineer Regiment) began to send young soldiers to augment the regular force in Afghanistan in 2007, I began to realize that Canada was producing a new generation of veterans. What is so different about these people is that they are young, much younger than I am and considerably younger than the other veterans I had known through much of my life.

In some ways Ryan personifies these young Canadians. He has long experience with this new generation of soldiers, both in

Canada and in Afghanistan. Their generation has a new language to describe this war, and new means with which to do it. Militaries have always been cultural entities, and this army and this war are no different. Flavelle's work affords the reader new insights into that culture. Acronyms like FOB, KAF, TIC, and phrases like *ramp ceremony* are entering our collective consciousness. Songs like "Soldier Side," which Ryan forced me to listen to, are describing and defining their war and giving it its own symbols. The opium poppy, the grape field, the LAV, and the Highway of Heroes are invoked when we characterize this war.

Modern communications allow our soldiers to be far more aware of the world around them than my dad's generation, who fought the Second World War. Many of these young kids use technology only for social networking, merrily LOLing and WTFing their experience at war. But others, like Ryan, can expand their horizons much farther and more quickly than was possible in the past. I admire that, but the gap between us boomers and them seems very wide at times. Their music, their language, their culture are largely alien to me. Most of them go to war playing video games, shooting computerized insurgents and listening to iPods in between patrols. Don't think they are soft just because they bring their electronic toys with them; after all, soldiers in the Second World War hauled their record players with them. Don't imagine life has gotten that much easier because they eat foil-packaged food in self-heating containers instead of stale compo rations. War is still war, the pain of loss is still deep, and the terrible sight of destroyed bodies is still horrifying.

There is a greater immediacy to Ryan's war than to the Second World War or even to Korea (which was largely ignored by the folks at home), because it is an instant war, one where soldiers update their Facebook status with postings like "RIP Terry Street 1984–2008." My dad's generation said goodbye to wives and sweethearts for years, communicating only through letters, often infrequent.

Ryan's generation phones home with regularity or connects with e-mail. Thus every death in Afghanistan seems more tragic and immediate than the mass losses Canada suffered in at Vimy Ridge or in Normandy.

When I first met Ryan, I could not easily grasp the reality that this bright and articulate young man had been a soldier, outside the wire, in Afghanistan; that he had volunteered to lay his life on the line as surely as any of the old veterans who had fought in Canada's other wars. Like them, Ryan had chosen to go to war; he had not stumbled into combat as some of Canada's peacekeepers had in the Balkans or in Cyprus. And yet he, like many of the young reservist veterans I know, did not strike me as some battle-hardened "professional." He played his music, he played his games, he smoked almost as a hobby—but when the time to kit up and move on came, he went. Now I think that when my dad's generation fought their war, they were probably very much like Ryan and his comrades-in-arms.

This is a war memoir built on Ryan's experience on a single patrol in the western reaches of Kandahar Province, along the south bank of the Arghandab River. It is his personal journey into the heart of darkness and back from it. Throughout the story of the patrol, he weaves his vivid recollections of the sights, sounds, smells, fears, and adrenalin rushes of his personal war and explains why he went, while telling what modern war and army life are like.

He places those stories into the larger experience of a young Canadian man's life in this plugged-in world of technical connectedness. He confronts the dirty and primitive existence of the universal infantry soldier—hot, dusty, dangerous, and yet compelling in a very strange and unique way. He told me that he originally wanted to title the book *One Patrol: The Nintendo Generation Goes to War*. The contrasts that emerge are challenging. Here are Ryan and his fellow soldiers, with all the technological advances of modern war at their fingertips, trudging through the torrid days of an Afghan summer, living like primitive beings on a remote planet revolving around a distant star, gaining a bit of relief in the merely hot darkness of nights that were sometimes as menacing and surreal as the Transylvanian nights of Bram Stoker.

It is important that Canadians know the history of the war in Afghanistan and Canada's part in it. But it is even more important for Canadians to understand what that war was like for the soldiers who fought it. We are fortunate that Ryan Flavelle has the skill and the talent to give us a glimpse of what life and death were really like for the men and women who experienced it from the "sharp end."

Dr. David J. Bercuson, OC, FRSC
Director of the Centre for Military and Strategic Studies,
University of Calgary

ACKNOWLEDGEMENTS

SO, HERE YOU HAVE IT. You are reading the first lines of my first book, the culmination of all my efforts to get a book published. First of all, I would like to thank you for reading this book—unless you stole it or are reading the Google Books "preview"—in which case, go buy my book. I'm a poor graduate student/reservist.

Derek MacIssac, who has a master's in anthropology and was also in my unit, put the idea of writing this book firmly in my mind. We had just finished viewing *Watchmen* and were talking about the value of narrative. He told me that I had an obligation to write down my experiences so that they wouldn't be lost, and the conversation really stuck with me. My friend and then-roommate Cindy Strömer (I remembered the umlaut) gave me an opportunity to speak at the Strategic Studies and Security Consortium (S3C) conference in 2009, and that speech made me realize that I could actually say something meaningful about this war.

Dr. David Bercuson at the University of Calgary is truly an amazing guy. I don't think many grad students call their advisor a "friend," but in my case it is the only word that applies. Dr. Bercuson has guided me through my graduate degree and consistently passes on his many years of experience and wisdom to me. Although some of the things he says make me blush (which I no longer thought was possible), I'm glad that we drink beer together and talk as friends.

Dr. Bercuson introduced me to my agent, Linda McKnight, the best in the business. Without her there would be no book. As well, my editor, Jim Gifford, has done a excellent job of polishing the roughest parts of the book. He has made the process infinitely more enjoyable than it otherwise would have been.

All of my friends in the infantry and in the army have been helpful and interested in the progress of this book. Specifically I would like to thank Casey Balden, Troy Leifso, Chris Nead, John Stegmeier, Randy Gorden, and Joe Lammerhirt.

A few people read earlier drafts of the manuscript and made excellent suggestions for changes, specifically Jeff Obermeyer, Katelyn Dykstra Dykerman, and Caleb Snider. Rylan Broadbent also took a look at an earlier version and helped me with the map and the photos.

Eric Cameron with DND is a good guy. He has a cool moustache and has forgotten more about public affairs than I could ever hope to learn.

My parents had to resign themselves to my decision to go to Afghanistan, and bit their nails the whole time I was there. I know how hard this was for them, and I am blessed that they have always supported me in everything I've done. A guy couldn't have better parents.

My wife, Darcy, has supported me in every conceivable way before, during, and after my deployment. She rocks.

Although I kept a journal while I was in Afghanistan, it can best be described as patchy and incomplete. I have relied upon my admittedly faulty memory for the majority of the material for this book, and no doubt some of the details are transposed from other conversations and events. The key parts of this book will forever be etched in my mind, but many of the details, especially the conversations I record, are the product of an imprecise recollection. The patrol kept me busy, and I had little time to record my thoughts or impressions as it progressed. I was also too busy to take a lot of pictures; those that appear in this book—except where identified—were taken before or after the patrol. If any zealous reader or former comrade finds anything that they believe to be inaccurate within this text, the fault lies solely with me.

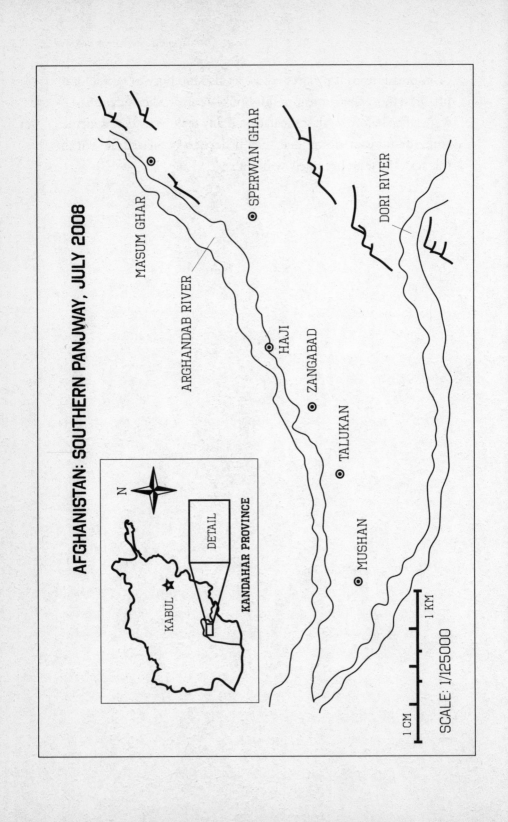

AFGHANISTAN: SOUTHERN PANJWAY, JULY 2008

KANDAHAR PROVINCE

DETAIL

N

KABUL

MASUM GHAR

SPERWAN GHAR

DORI RIVER

ARGHANDAB RIVER

HAJI

ZANGABAD

TALUKAN

MUSHAN

1 KM

1 CM

SCALE: 1/125000

PROLOGUE

IT IS ALMOST A MONTH since I returned from Afghanistan, and I am awake in the middle of the night at my parents' house in Calgary. I have just woken up from a dream of getting too far in front of my LAV. I need to smoke. I put on my army sweatpants and a T-shirt before opening the door quietly. As I sneak down the stairs, I make sure to step over the creaky floorboard that I've known about since I was a kid stealing cookies. All of a sudden, I am walking carefully on moondust, watching for IEDs under the starry Afghan sky. I am looking for boot prints on the newly vacuumed carpet of my suburban childhood home. It is only safe to step in boot prints.

I sit in the back of a Light Armoured Vehicle (LAV, pronounced "lav," not "L-A-V") in Shilo, Manitoba. We have been in the field for three weeks, the longest consecutive amount of time I've spent in the field for my military career. I am a reservist, a part-time soldier who trains on weekends and in the summer, each year completing another course that teaches me a skill set the military wants me to have. I did my basic training in 2001, before 9/11. I did my trades course in 2003, my advanced trades course in 2004, my leadership course in 2005. In 2006 I taught basic, and in 2007 I am preparing for war. *Normal career progression* the army might call it. I am a signaller, a Canadian

1

soldier responsible primarily for installing and maintaining radio and communications systems.

It is a hot summer day in Shilo; when I go outside I can hear the incessant noise of insects, and the sun beats down onto a field of grass that has been crushed by the tires of armoured vehicles. In the back of my LAV, I sit reading a copy of Anthony Swofford's *Jarhead*. The headset that I use to talk on our radio net is halfway on my head, allowing me to listen to the conversations in the command post (CP), a tent that we set up off the back of our vehicle, and to the two radio nets I'm responsible for. I am engrossed in Swofford's account of life as a marine, but at the same time I'm keyed up to hear "2"—my call sign. When it comes over the radio I replace the bookmark, put the book on the seat beside me, and respond by using the Press To Talk (PTT) switch on my headset (the army has such clever names for things like that).

"2, this is 0, what is 29er's current location?"

"2, he is collocated with my call sign at this time." (He is standing outside my LAV.)

"0, roger, inform him that we will be contacting him via Lima Lima." (Telephone.)

"2, wilco, out."

I poke my head outside the LAV, inform the company commander that 0 will be giving him a call, sit back down, take out Swofford's book and find my place again.

I am working with the infantry—B Company Second Battalion PPCLI, to be precise. The regular force, the Patricias, hard as fuck.

The old guys, those who were in for the last tour in 2006, tell stories about combat in hushed tones, as if they were afraid that someone was going to overhear them. They've earned their stories and they relish them. Over the past few weeks, when I'm not on shift, or when we are standing around smoking, waiting to shoot a range, I listen wide-eyed to tales of fighting against RPG-armed insurgents, pulling people out of burning vehicles, and getting "lit up" for hours or days or weeks. The infantry are very careful with their stories, and most tell them only when they are separate from the higher ranks, the officers, or those who have not gone to war. I feel privileged to listen in silence, taking slow drags on my cigarette and sipping bottled water.

The first half of the field ex is complete, and the last ranges are being conducted this morning. Sections assault plywood villages and play "Don't Shoot the Baby," while LAVs rise up behind them and fire 25mm shells over the heads of the advancing infantry. It is taken as routine work, just another day in the field.

But today is a special day. We are going to be "issued" beer for the first time since deploying to the field. Two beers per man, perhaps. Over the course of the week, talk of a buddy's failure to distinguish between civilian targets and insurgents at the range has dropped off. Now we talk about the beers. Will we get to have more than two? What will the first one taste like? The army has been dangling them in front of us for almost a week, and we are starting to feel like Tantalus, the booze always just out of reach. The company "smoker" will involve competitions like throwing rocks into tiny holes to see who is the best at throwing grenades, flipping truck tires down a road to see who is the most powerful soldier in the company, and playing section-level tug-of-war to see which is the strongest section. The "canteen," a battle box full of goodies, will sell cigarettes, pop, and chocolate bars. We will wait in line for a half-hour for our beers. This is our afternoon's vacation from training to go to Afghanistan.

After another chapter of Swofford's book, I get the message over the radio. The last troops are packing up and moving back to my location. The smoker is on.

I am part of the headquarter's tug-of-war team, and we win four competitions in a row. I feel happy even as my hands become blistered. We chain-smoke cigarettes as we toss our rocks, and I don't do too badly. It reminds me of playing horseshoes. Maybe I'm starting to fit in with the infantry. Then the circle I'm standing in closes off as someone turns their back to me. Maybe not.

I wait in line for my beers and watch fistfights break out around me. A big, tall infanteer beaks off a shorter guy who has never been overseas. They are shoving each other in a matter of seconds. Later they will probably drink beer together. I feel like a kid at Christmas as I watch the line slowly advance and the veterans butt in with their friends. After we've drunk our two beers I stand at the side and watch them scream lines from the movie *300*.

"Patricias! What is your profession?"

"*Aaaoooo!*" is the response. Loud.

Someone suggests a game of joust and volunteers are canvassed. Soon they have gathered up two stretchers, two boots, a roll of duct tape, and two long plastic poles. Six guys stand beside each stretcher, with one kneeling on it. I volunteer to be the one kneeling because I want to prove myself. Two infantry soldiers are selected instead. On the signal, the stretchers are lifted onto the shoulders of the six, and the two groups of men run at each other. The soldiers kneeling on the stretchers wear helmets and body armour. They hold the poles, each with a boot duct-taped to the end of it, and lean forward like medieval knights. When the two groups charge at each other, one of the "knights" is struck in the mouth by his opponent's pole, which knocks out two teeth. He lies sprawled out on the ground in a pool of blood. I'm glad that I wasn't accepted as a volunteer. We agree on the story that he took an elbow while playing rugby, and a medic is found. While he waits, the toothless infanteer drinks beer, which mixes with the blood in his mouth. Someone else finds his teeth and gives them to him. He is already telling the story, and a group of soldiers gather around him and pat him on the back.

I retreat to the CP, manage to get another two beers, and eat a barbecued hamburger off a paper plate. The patty came out of a box, and I smother Heinz ketchup and mustard all over it. A typical army smoker. We listen to music off a laptop and drink our beer slowly. I have been up for at least 18 hours every day for the past three weeks. I am extremely tired. I can hear the party going on behind our CP; a bonfire has been started and the smoke rises over us. It is a cool Manitoba summer evening, but I am warm and content in my fleece. I go to my tent, which is separated from those of the rest of the company. I read a few pages of Philip K. Dick's *Do Androids Dream of Electric Sheep?*, which I'd left beside my cot. I pass out with my headlamp still turned on, music blaring outside my tent.

Before I started training for the tour, I studied history at the University of Calgary; I drank a bit too much beer with my friends and argued about *Star Wars* (Han obviously shot first) and the Progressive Conservative Party (an oxymoron?). I joined the reserves when I was still in high school, a 17-year-old kid who knew everything there was to know about the world. Eight years after I joined, I decided it would be a good idea to deploy to Afghanistan. Even though I was a full-time university student and part-time soldier, I always identified with the military. And when there is a war on, soldiers are meant to fight in it, not to drink too much beer with their friends and talk about things they think they understand.

I spent seven months in Afghanistan, deploying shortly after my twenty-fourth birthday in February. I've now spent ten years in the Communication Reserve.

Signalling is an unglamorous job. I like to think that we have harnessed the power of lightning, that we are warriors of the electromagnetic spectrum. But mostly we just drink coffee and press buttons. We are seldom mentioned in any historical document, despite our presence on every Canadian battlefield since the First World War. We are a living means to an end; we are the army's tongue. "746 Communication Squadron: you can talk about us, but you can't talk without us"—this is the unofficial motto of my unit.

When I decided to volunteer for an overseas deployment, I had no idea where I would end up. Unlike in almost every other trade, signals reservists can augment any formation, from the lowliest infantry company to the command of Task Force South itself. The simple fact is the army needs radios, and wherever there's a radio there's a signaller.

On this rotation, five soldiers from my home unit deployed, and we were flung to the Afghan winds. I was attached to the infantry, Bravo Company II PPCLI specifically. My friend Allan would be attached to 1 Combat Engineering Regiment (1 CER). Allan is a good signaller and a good friend. He is one of the funniest people I have ever met, and he covers his loathing for the world in general with a wry humour that brightens the lives of those around him. He would spend the majority of the tour with me in Patrol Base Sperwan Ghar, the first time two signallers from my unit would be engaged in combat together in recent memory. He is still in the military, running marathons and climbing mountains by himself for fun.

With the exception of Allan, I would not see a single one of the men from my unit throughout my deployment. But when we reunited in Calgary after seven months overseas, we didn't skip a beat. We had all suffered and sacrificed more than we could have imagined. Our normal reservist training cycle back home would never be the same.

I knew from the moment I signed my contract what being attached to an infantry company meant: fighting. The next 18 months of my life would be like nothing I could have imagined. I lived and worked with the infantry non-stop for that entire period. I took part in live-fire ranges, was issued the best equipment available to the Canadian Forces, and came to know every radio system in the army inside and out. When I deployed, I was a fully prepared signaller; as it turned out, this would not be enough. The fickle nature of the radio system that forms the backbone of the Canadian army resulted in the need for a signaller to accompany patrols. I, a lowly communications reservist, would spend a considerable portion of the next seven months patrolling with the infantry, attached at the hip to the company commander. Looking back, I realize that I had no idea what was in store for me. By the end of my tour, I was a completely different person. I left behind a lot of what was good about me in the grape fields of Panjway, but I brought a lot of experience home.

This is the story of one patrol in Afghanistan. This patrol will never enter the history books, except possibly as a half-sentence in an official history. Even then it will be noticed by few but the most ardent students of Canada's military past. Similar patrols are carried out by many different nationalities every day in Afghanistan. Their common nature is epitomized by the hardship and the camaraderie that make up the personality of this new conflict. It is the story of the patrol during which I discovered more about myself than I could have thought possible, so much so that I still have trouble navigating through the memories, the emotions, and the feelings. It is a patrol that haunted me at night for almost a year after it was over, until I would wake up and remember that I was in Canada and that everything was okay. This patrol served as the focal point for my broader Afghan experiences. It was the hardest thing I have ever done. It defined how I see myself as a man, and how I see men. This is the story of how I earned my stories.

I do not claim to have done as much as others on my tour. I spent the majority of it sitting in an air-conditioned room, monitoring radios and passing information on as quickly and accurately as I could. I do not claim to be a hero, nor even to have acted heroically. I do not even claim to have been in as much danger as many in my company. I know soldiers who have jumped in front of machine gun bursts for their friends. I know of a group of sleeping soldiers who had a rocket-propelled grenade (RPG) pass through their tent and lodge itself in a rucksack. That RPG had "*22*" written on the back of it, the call sign of the platoon that it almost wiped out. (We figured that the Taliban had begun calling their shots.) Instead, I merely claim to have been there, and to have recorded what I experienced.

This book does not address many of the questions raised by Canada's mission in Afghanistan. It is not about whether we should be there, and it is not about how we got there. Instead, I write with a singular purpose: I want the public to understand what we are doing and how we are doing it. I want our sacrifices and our triumphs to be more than a poorly registered blip on the evening news. I'm tired of the misconceptions and arguments built on foundations of poorly understood truth. Canadian soldiers are being asked to do an immensely difficult task. I merely try to explain what this task entails, and how we are going about doing it.

After I returned, a lot of people asked whether I thought we should be in Afghanistan. My honest answer was and is that I don't know. In fact, I think that I understand the war less now that I have returned from it than I thought I did before I departed. But now I understand how and why I do not understand; I have seen with my own eyes the quagmire that this conflict has engendered. I am forced to view questions of honour and morality through the lens of experience, yet I'm not sure that questions of this type even mean anything anymore. I have not returned a hero, as some might have you believe; rather, I have returned convinced that heroism is a quality best relegated to the imagination and one that bears little foundation in reality. We all did our jobs to the best of our abilities, and some people's abilities and experiences led them to do extraordinary things. A new chapter in the annals of our military history is writing itself, enshrining the deeds being done every day in the name of our country. These deeds are being performed, not by heroes but by well-trained professional soldiers.

The majority of popular accounts about Afghanistan have been written by embedded journalists. Although I can't challenge their bravery or eloquence, the result is often a story framed by a narrative of heroism. The reality is that heroism is an ethereal element, conspicuous by its absence as often as by its presence. The truth is far dirtier and more mundane than is usually reported. This is the story of one such dirty and mundane patrol, warts and all.

David Bercuson once told me that Afghanistan is becoming "Canada's second forgotten war" (the first being Korea). Recently I noticed that a story about methamphetamine consumption took greater priority on the CBC website than a story about a Canadian soldier killed overseas. I guess that the public has become numb to these fatalities, viewing them as unfortunate circumstances that happen in a faraway country, to be taken in as dinner is prepared. The lives of the soldiers whom the public so conveniently forgets are so much more than a two-minute sound bite. They are worth remembering.

CHAPTER 1
SPERWAN GHAR
14 JULY 2008

Oh, weren't they the fine boys! You never saw
  the best of them,
Singing all together with their throats bronze-bare;
Fighting-fit and mirth-mad, music in the feet of them,
Swinging on to glory and the wrath out there.
—ROBERT SERVICE, "TIPPERARY DAYS"

I ONCE READ THAT, due to the affordability and availability of the Walkman during the Gulf War, it was the first conflict ever to have its own soundtrack. Some journalists were even able to predict the outbreak of the ground invasion by the large purchase of batteries that preceded it. Everyone wants to escape into a melody. Reality takes on a whole new reality when it's punctuated with loud music.

I'm sitting in Sperwan Ghar, Afghanistan, on a warm Monday afternoon, but days of the week no longer hold any significance. *Ghar* is Pashto for "mountain," and our fortress looks like something out of a cartoon. We have nicknamed it "Castle Grayskull," and we discuss the feasibility of using dynamite or C-4 to reshape our beloved hill into a skull with glowing eyes. That would give the Taliban something to look at.

Music is blaring from every iPod, and most people are rocking out to hard metal as they pack their kit (the army word for equipment; especially nice or hard-to-acquire pieces of kit are known as *shiny* or *Gucci*). *Saw III*, a horror movie, plays on our TV as we pull everything that we need together, check it, recheck it, pack it, and repack it. This is no small task, as each of us is carrying nearly 70 kilos of kit. Last-second additions and subtractions are made. Water purification tablets and packs of crystallized Gatorade are added, and radio checks are conducted. All told, packing takes about two hours.

By the time that I start packing, everyone else in my room is putting the finishing touches on their kit. I am one of three company signallers, and as such it is my responsibility to pull an eight-hour radio shift every day that I'm in camp. This basically amounts to sitting in an air-conditioned command post (CP), listening to three speakers and writing down everything that comes out of them.

Today I'm let off shift at 1300, right after lunch. The headquarters section commander issued orders about the patrol in the morning. I missed them. Although I work at the nerve center of the company's operations, I am less informed than anyone else in headquarters as to what we are going to be doing on this patrol. A paper copy of our orders sits on the table in our room, under the constant supervision of at least one person. I sit down and try to read them, but the data refuses to sink in.

Military operational orders are encrypted by a twofold mechanism. First, they are uniformly printed in 8-point font, so one has to squint to read them: like this. Second, every important aspect contained within the orders is shrouded in a nearly impenetrable veil of acronyms. For example, "Bravo Company will conduct a Cordon and Search of suspected compounds near the village of Zangabad" becomes "IAW SoM, B Coy will conduct a dism C&S of CoI CM1001, CM1002, CM1003, CM1004 and CM1005 IVO Gr 12U QQ 1234 5678." One of the highlights of my tour was spending the entire day sending in written reports without using a single acronym. I sometimes had to call people to ask what their acronyms stood for.

Although I've learned to translate military newspeak into English, I just don't seem to have the strength right now. Instead, I chat up a few guys sitting around the picnic table outside, and try to get the actual situation from them. I sit beside our section commander and ask him what's going on:

"Hey, I missed orders, what's the deal with this patrol?"

"We're going to go out dismounted through all the Combat Outposts (COPs) with 4 and 9 Platoon. OC wants you to come along. We're going to hump to Zangabad, stay the day, and then hump to Mushan. When we're there, we are going to cordon and search in Mushan, stay overnight, come back to Zangabad and try to find the fuckers who've been mortaring them. We might push north of the river from Zangabad. We're leaving at last light tonight. We should be back in five days, but plan for two weeks."

And just like that I have the plain pragmatic clarity that I've come to expect from infantry non-commissioned members (NCMs). We will be going out with two platoons of infantry, one from our company and one from Charlie Company, attached to us for the length of the mission. My heart sinks a little bit, and I can feel nervousness turn into fear as my section commander talks to me. I work hard to control my expression. I'd heard through the grapevine that a hard patrol was coming up, but this was the first time I'd gotten any details. Now I know that we are going to be embarking on a long dismounted patrol through outposts that have been attacked every day for the last month. Our goal is to root out and destroy anyone who puts up a fight, and to find any and all of the equipment they are using to do it. There are no longer any qualms or quibbles—we are going to fight.

I've managed to spend four months in-country patrolling with the infantry without getting into a major firefight. It looks like that is all about to change. The unspoken implication lies heavy in my heart: there is a good chance some of us won't come back.

"Oh and, Flavelle, keep your shit muckled up." I never did find out exactly what *muckle* means.

My first thought is to e-mail my girlfriend, Darcy, tell her what's going on and that I love her. Unfortunately, the veil of operational security doesn't allow me to even tell her that I'm going out. I also have more pressing concerns.

It might be useful at this point to outline the situation on the ground in my little corner of Panjway at the time that these events are taking place. We are sitting in one of the southernmost prov-inces of Afghanistan, Kandahar. The majority of Canadian soldiers deployed to Afghanistan are based there, specifically just north of the province's capital, Kandahar City, in a base called Kandahar Airfield (KAF). KAF is famed for its numerous creature comforts such as a Tim Hortons, a Burger King, multiple shopping outlets, a weekly bazaar to buy souvenirs, and over five separate kitchens serving everything from burgers and fries to Nepalese-style curry. Everybody who resides on a semi-permanent basis outside of KAF despises it and everyone inside for being good-for-nothing WOGs (not even sure what that stands for; Without Guns? Waste of Groceries?). We band together in our hatred for how easy their lives are, despite the fact that many of the KAFers would willingly trade places with us. The reality is that most soldiers do not choose where they are going to be deployed overseas. Some, like me, could have just as easily spent their tour shopping for the perfect carpet at the weekly bazaar. What we in Sperwan Ghar do not see is the mind-numbing boredom and routine of life on KAF; instead, we focus on the glittering opulence of Burger King and the outdoor concrete hockey rink. Many in KAF want to be warriors and to test themselves against the Taliban; instead, they have to let their salty tears mingle with their iced cappuccinos.

About 40 kilometres southwest of Kandahar City is Forward Operating Base (FOB) Ma'sum Ghar (MSG). This mountain had been taken by force during a previous rotation, and it was the site of numerous battles involving Canadian soldiers. By the time we deployed, it had calmed down substantially, and basically marked the end of friendly territory. It is home to the Lord Strathcona's Horse (Royal Canadians), an armoured regiment. They are newly outfitted with Leopard C2 tanks, probably the best tank available in the world. We also hate them, but less than we hate those in KAF.

About 10 kilometres west of MSG is my home sweet home for seven months, Patrol Base Sperwan Ghar (PBSG). When a previous rotation of soldiers (ROTO) took it over from the Taliban, they found it outfitted with a Russian-built concrete compound, left over from the last war. What that means to us is a comfortable room with clean beds sheltered from the dust and sandflies outside. We also have functional shower facilities, and Canadian cooks who work harder than anyone else on camp to ensure that we are fed and our morale is high. There is even a library of books ranging from fantasy to self-help.

Everything to the west of Sperwan Ghar is basically Taliban territory. On TF 3–07, the ROTO before ours, the Van Doos (Royal 22nd Regiment) had established three police substations (PSSs) named after the villages they were situated in: Haji, Zangabad, and Talukan. At the end of the line there is one Afghan National Army strongpoint (SP), Mushan, with a company of ANA soldiers and only three Canadians. When the fighting season started, these outposts had been attacked every day, and the Afghan National Police (ANP) were pulled out and replaced by ANA. At that point we renamed the PSSs as combat outposts (COPs). The result is a line of outposts, stretching fourteen kilometres west of Sperwan Ghar, are under almost daily attack by the Taliban. Each one of these outposts, with the exception of Mushan, has about 40 Canadian soldiers and a roughly equivalent number of Afghan soldiers. It is along this line that we are to patrol and to try to disrupt the enemy's activities.

To our south are the Reg Desert and the Dori riverbed. To all intents and purposes, the world ends there, as no one ventures into the Reg except for nomadic tribesmen and camel herders. To our north is the Arghandab riverbed, a mostly dried-out expanse of sand and gravel sown throughout with improvised explosive devices (IEDs).

The villages on the north side of the Arghandab have already earned their place in Canadian military history; they are Taliban Central. Every time we've gone near them we've been attacked. A large part of the fighting that has taken place over the last five years, including Operation Medusa and the Battle of the White School, was over these tiny villages. This is the situation we find ourselves in on July 14, 2008.

I sit, smoke, and lay out my kit. I drink bottled water and what we call *Squiggle Coke*—Coca-Cola that has Arabic writing on one side. I'm packing an American backpack that I bought the last time I was in KAF over a month ago.

Into this pack I stuff a 117F radio (pronounced "one seventeen foxtrot"), the best man-portable radio available in the world. It has a simple user interface and the ability to conduct short-range very high frequency (VHF) communications as well as air-ground-air (AGA) ultra high frequency (UHF) and satellite comms. What that means in English is that it can communicate with basically anything on the battlefield, so long as a competent operator is using it. This radio is almost impossible to find in Canada, and is a very Gucci piece of kit indeed. It has a removable faceplate that you can plug a wire into, and I've run this wire through my pack and put the faceplate into a pouch attached to a shoulder strap. This way I can program, change, and work on my radio without actually having to take my pack off. It's the little things that help. The radio comes complete with three antennas and one handset that I can talk into or pass off to the company commander.

The first time most people try to drive a stick shift, they stall. Understanding that the clutch has a sweet spot and exactly how and when to let it out takes practice. The only way to learn is to develop the appropriate muscle memory, to teach one's leg muscles when exactly the clutch is going to disengage, through mostly unconscious repetition. I find that now the only time that I stall is if I think about how to clutch on a steep hill. If I do it unconsciously, I always succeed.

In the same way as one develops the ability to drive stick, one learns how to perform the duties of a soldier. Basic drill, which teaches a soldier how to march, stand at attention, salute, and fall into formation, can be learned properly only when you're not focusing on the individual movements. Your conscious brain has to be removed from the equation. On a boiling hot parade square in Dundurn, Saskatchewan (come for the dirt, stay for the cows), I stood bewildered as my instructors desperately and vocally tried to push me into the appropriate position and get our entire platoon to walk in step—a completely foreign concept. Every day for two months, we were marched everywhere, always under the watchful eye of our instructors, who would point out any faults. By the end of my time on that parade square, all of my responses were automatic. When called to attention, I didn't think, I just put my heels together. By the end of the summer, when two or more people in our platoon went out, even on our three days off, we would find ourselves walking in step without thinking about it. After the course was over, I was amazed to find that I would try to get into step with my friends in high school. My actions had become completely unconscious, and it took time to reassert my mind's control over such things as walking speed. The military had imprinted itself on my mind; like a tattoo, or learning to drive a stick shift, once there it can never be fully removed.

The skill set needed to succeed on patrol in Afghanistan is gained in a surprisingly similar fashion. The key is muscle memory and automating one's responses. By constant repetition, soldiers learn exactly how their kit is organized and laid out, how to quickly tie their boots in the morning, where and how magazines are stored in the tactical (tac) vest, how to access each pouch on their kit without looking at it. All of these movements become mostly unconscious. The habits I learned on a training exercise in Shilo became the habits I perform while walking through a grape field in Afghanistan. By the time that I'm preparing my radio for this patrol, I can program it without looking. I have simply performed the task so many times that it is firmly entrenched in my muscle memory.

In the end, this skill set is the only reason that I'm going on this patrol: I'm a signaller (or "radio donkey"), and I'm coming along to act as a living cell phone and secretary for the commander. Mind you, my position is the most sought-after of all the signalling jobs; it's far more exciting than sitting in an air-conditioned office listening to radio traffic.

I check and recheck my frequencies and settings, load fresh batteries, and find spares to carry with me. Finally, I conduct a radio check.

Beep. "2, this is 2 pronto, radio check, over." *Click.* Radio operators are known by three nicknames: *pronto, jimmy,* and *sigs fag. Pronto* is our official nickname, taken from the signallers' Bible (alternatively known as the ACP 125 CANSUP Foxtrot), which outlines the *only* acceptable way to speak on a radio; *jimmy* is our name for Mercury, the god of communications (I don't know why); and *sigs fag* stings just a little bit. I don't think there is any malice intended; working with the infantry reminds me of being in a high school locker room.

(On my first-ever exercise in Wainwright, Alberta, in 2001 someone poked their head into my tent and said, "Hey, I need a jimmy." I looked around and said, "Sorry, there's no Jimmy here, I'm Ryan and that's Marc.")

I push my radio as close to the back of my pack as I can. It is important to get as much weight as possible close to your centre of gravity. This helps to maintain balance, which has been a problem for me on previous patrols. On the other side of my radio I put two CamelBaks, each of which holds 2.5 litres of water. One is reserved only for use in a TIC (troops in contact), as previous tours have found that running out of water during a firefight can have dire consequences. I also put four frozen 500ml bottles of water into my pack; they will be my only source of cold water for the duration of the patrol. (Of course ice melts, so I have cold water for only one day.) I also bring eight granola bars (rocky road flavour) and two packages of flavoured almonds that my mom bought at the farmers' market in Calgary. She mailed them in a care package that I received recently, together with letters and comics from the *Calgary Herald*. I bring one spare pair of underwear and four pairs of socks. I may get a chance to wash some clothing in the buckets they have available in Zangabad and Talukan. I bring one spare pair of pants, because I figure that if I rip my shirt it won't be a big deal, but if something happens to my pants I'm screwed. On top of this I carry two packs of water purification tablets, my journal, a spare pen, electrical tape, and two infrared glow sticks (invisible to the naked eye, but visible to night vision goggles). Finally, I break down a carton of cigarettes and place the smokes strategically throughout my pack. I know that my pack will take a beating over the next couple days, and it is important to have my cigarettes in multiple locations. If one pack gets crushed, I can deal with it. If the entire carton is squished, I will be a very unhappy signaller.

I take my ranger blanket, a newly issued, thin CADPAT (Canadian Disruptive Pattern, the computer-generated digital camouflage pattern used by the CF) sleeping bag. I wrap it around the camping mattress I bought in Winnipeg before I left. This mattress is thin and light, and it looks like a big egg carton. When I bought it, one side was bright orange, not a fit with army camouflage, so I have spray-painted that side black. Once the mattress and ranger blanket are rolled up I take two loops of Bungee cord to hold them together, and strap them to the side of my pack. In the top pouch, I put in a Ziploc bag of 12 fresh AA batteries, and two spare memory batteries for my radio. Into this pouch I also stuff a length of cord, two more glow sticks, a pack of cigarettes, and three "toilet bags"—sealable bags used to poop in the field (they come with toilet paper). I lift up my pack to test the weight and shake it around. Heavy but stable.

I move on to my fighting kit. For the first half of the tour, I'd carried the issued Canadian tac vest. After patrolling for three months, I found it wasn't able to carry the amount of kit that I needed it to, so I ordered a new harness known as a *chest rig* from a company online. I'd borrowed a chest rig from a guy who was on leave for an earlier patrol, and I'd really liked it. The pouches are much larger and easier to gain access to than those of the tac vest, and there is a large zippered compartment in which I can hold notes, cheat sheets, orders, smokes, and water. Into this rig I pack nine magazines, which hold about 250 rounds of ammunition, my night vision goggles, two fragmentation and two smoke grenades, my backup weapons sight (if my sight falls off at least I won't be completely screwed), one litre of Gatorade, one litre of water, communications equipment cheat sheets, a notepad and pen, a compass, and a letter from my girlfriend. One side pouch contains all of my first aid gear, including a tourniquet (useful if I am bleeding excessively from a limb), QuikClot (a powder designed to instantly cauterize a wound), and an Israeli bandage, which is basically a piece of sterile cloth with a clip on the side that allows it to be easily tightened. This pouch is marked with a large first aid cross that I drew with a black Bic marker. Although I've mostly overcome my innate fear of grenades, carrying them is somewhat of a concern, as I don't trust the pouches that come with the chest rig. Instead, I decide to duct-tape the spoons (safety handle) onto the bodies of the grenades and put them into the other side pouch. I also stuff in two more IR glow sticks, and another package of nuts for some quick calories when I need them. Finally, I use Zap Straps to attach my bayonet to the bottom of my rig. I'm not lost in some fantasy where I'm going to be fighting hand-to-hand with the Taliban, but if I find myself in a minefield, I'm going to need a bayonet to probe my way out of it. Plus, you just never know. On the very slim chance that we get ordered to fix bayonets (which has happened on previous tours), I don't want to be the idiot without a pointy gun.

Putting on the chest rig is a two-person procedure, as it has shoulder straps that cross over my back and is held into place by a plastic clip that runs along the bottom. First I throw it on, and then I ask someone nearby to sort out the straps in the back. Once it's on, however, it's immensely comfortable.

After I've finished putting my chest rig in order, I move on to maintaining my personal weapon. I take it apart, clean it, and put it back together again. I make sure that the bolt is well lubricated. My weapon is the standard-issue C7A2 assault rifle. It holds a magazine of 30 rounds, and I've carefully put on an infrared laser sight (for use at night) and a Maglite that seems brighter than the surface of the sun. Each has a rubber toggle switch attached to the front-hand grip by Velcro, the cables being held in place by elastic bands and electrical tape. I've put a lot of effort into my weapon, and I'm proud of it, but not as proud as the infantry around me are of theirs.

I take a look at my flak vest, a Kevlar vest with two ballistic plates in the front and back that are designed to stop an AK round. Attached to my flak vest are two Kevlar shoulder pads, which we have been forced to wear by those above. We also have the option of getting Kevlar arm protectors (which we call *water wings*), and even a neck protector. But I feel I already have enough weight to deal with.

I recheck my helmet, which I've lined with a padding system formally called BLSS Kit ("bliskit" to soldiers). The padding cost about $200 and I had to stay on hold on the phone with an American company for an hour, but it was worth it. I ripped out the issued leather and Styrofoam strap that dug into my head every time I wore my helmet, and replaced it with pure bliss. I don't think it's possible to pay enough for a comfortable head while patrolling. The only problem with the bliskit is that the pads absorb water, so I have to wring them out every time I stop on patrol, leaving a tiny puddle of my own sweat on the ground. On my helmet is my NVG mount, an infrared light designed to be seen by those behind and above me, and my issued goggles, for protection against the dust and wind storms.

One major problem that I have while patrolling is that I'm basically as blind as a bat without my glasses. During a routine physical in Sper prior to redeployment, the medics asked me the standard questions: height, weight, are you a smoker, and so on. When they asked my vision category I responded "V4" (on a scale of 0 to 4, 0 being good). The medic took a closer look at me and said, "Oh, so you're that guy. I've heard about you."

I have only one pair of civilian glasses with me in theatre, and no hard case (one of those last-second packing oversights). I also have army-issued ballistic eyewear, and a pair of Oakleys that I bought prior to deployment. A tiny pair of plastic nerd glasses that the army has issued me fit into either of those two pieces of eyewear. The problem with the issued ballistics is that they push the glasses inwards and give me severe and nausea-inducing tunnel vision. The problem with the Oakleys is that they are verboten. Due to a series of direct orders, I decide to conduct this patrol using my ballistic eyewear, bringing my civilian glasses as a backup. This basically means that I will be partially blind for long parts of the patrol.

After repacking my chest rig, I take a look at my uniform, the standard Canadian desert-pattern camouflage shirt and pants. When I was first issued them, forever ago in Shilo, I thought that they were the coolest-looking uniform in the world. Four months into my tour, they still look pretty badass.

There are subtle differences between the uniforms of someone coming from KAF and someone residing outside of it. No one in the company wears a red flag; instead, we all have green ones with a low infrared signature. In KAF, everyone wears a reflective patch similar to what cyclists wear to be seen at night—but our goal is *not* to be seen at night. We never wear field caps, and try our hardest to avoid wearing outer (combat) shirts whenever possible. I've found that you can tell basically everything about soldiers by the way they wear their uniform. Red flag and field cap instantly raise the WOG alarm. Boots that are not bloused (pants rolled down to below the top of the boot) and shirt sleeves rolled halfway up mean a fighting soldier, usually one far from the searching eye of a sergeant-major.

In Canada you can tell almost everything about a soldier by his or her beret. The cap badge indicates the wearer's trade; the way that the beret is formed indicates whether or not they give a shit about their job and how far down their forehead it rests indicates how cool they think they are. I've found that it takes about ten seconds to judge a fellow soldier by looking at his or her uniform; I've also found that these judgments are seldom wrong.

My uniform shirt has two pockets sewn on the arms at an angle. Some of us paid to have this done in Shilo. The idea is that this will allow us to access things from our shirt while we are wearing a Kevlar vest (which covers the pockets we normally use). However, the vest limits my motion so much that these pockets are basically obsolete; I have to ask people beside me to open them. In them I carry a tin can filled with cigarettes, my digital camera, and my headlamp. The last time I was in KAF, I had a patch made for me and the other members of my home unit; it reads "746 det Afghanistan"; *det* stands for "detachment," which is usually a three-person team of signallers who are "detached" from their unit to augment another one. I had these patches made up and sent to the other members of 746 Communication Squadron. I keep mine covered up, as all morale-lifting patches have been banned by the powers that be. It remains there as a reminder of home and better times. Finally, I add my gloves, a tan pair that I bought at the American PX in KAF. They are thin, durable, and tight fitting, allowing the maximum amount of feel. There are holes in the fabric on my trigger finger, right middle finger, and thumb. I hold the bulk of the weight of my weapon with these fingers, so the fabric wears out there first. My fingers poke out of the holes.

I try everything on while wearing shorts and sandals, and make sure that the weight feels stable. I can't imagine how I'm going to make it through this patrol; the weight is crushing into my chest, and for a few seconds I have a hard time breathing. I take everything off, work on the straps, and take out a few things that I don't absolutely need (one package of nuts and a few Gatorades). I never actually weighed all my kit, but others did. A conservative estimate is between 45 and 70 kilos. This is going to suck.

The day has whiled itself away as I packed my kit. By the time I stow my pack beside my bunk, lay out my uniform the way I want it, and put my weapon back in the rack, it's almost dinner time. Our room is a long, concrete-walled space with a communal table, a fridge near the door, and a TV and Xbox at the far end. It is lined with wide bunks, each of which holds a twin mattress. We are fortunate to have a tiny bit of personal space. Most people have created a masturbatorium out of their bunk by hanging extra sheets as curtains. Many have escaped into their own private sanctuary to sleep or watch movies on their laptops. A few are playing video games on the communal TV, and the sound of automatic weapons emanates from it. *Rainbow Six: Vegas* and *Tiger Woods PGA Tour 09* are the current favourites.

A subdued tension permeates the room, and I notice that people are being dicks to each other more than they otherwise would. I'm still not fully integrated into the infantry culture, but I'm accepted as a nerd who knows how to run radios. People try to get a rise out of me by saying that Kirk was a better captain than Picard (which he obviously was not). Sometimes I'm called "Doc Brown" after the doctor in *Back to the Future,* due to my unkempt dirty hair, zany statements about radios, and preoccupation with flux capacitors. I like these guys, but I don't feel that I'm one of them. I'm quieter than I naturally am, and I watch more than I speak. Smith, a short Filipino-Canadian soldier covered in tattoos, picks on me like a high school bully. It's never in earnest, but he's just one of those guys who needs to constantly prove his dominance. He spends part of the day trying to scare me with a rubber snake. I think it's all pretty childish, and I try to ignore him and carry on, but his antics alienate me a little from the group.

After four months in-country, I still don't know exactly how I fit in. Later I come to realize that that's just the way the infantry acts.

Everyone gets a little nervy before patrol, and some people decide to pick on others to defuse their anxiety. It's important to infanteers that they know their comrades are going to stand up for themselves in a real fight, so they constantly test each other. On the outside their actions appears childish, but in reality they are as pragmatic as anything else they do.

In October, when we were finally rotated out of Afghanistan, the army sent us for three days of "decompression" at a five-star resort in Cyprus. I was sent with the bulk of the headquarters personnel, as the military tries to keep sections together on decompression to allow soldiers to work through some of the things that happened on tour together. I still didn't feel that I was a fully integrated member of our motley crew when we arrived, but one night of debauchery was enough to change that.

After not having tasted alcohol since the end of our previous leave, most of us didn't last long. That first night I sat at the swim-up bar at the luxurious Azia Resort (every now and again the army is very good to us) and bullshitted along with everyone else about everything that had happened over the last seven months. We drank, fought, laughed, and cried together, and I finally felt like one of the boys. It was then that I began to understand why the infantry act the way they do. The things that we'd seen had left all of us vulnerable, and we needed to build up some armour around our hearts. The only people who could understand how that armour worked were our fellow soldiers. Behind the high school bullshit that permeated our lives were simply people hardened by what they'd seen, people who hid their emotions so well that they had begun to stop feeling.

One of the highlights of our stay was the reviews we garnered for the Azia Resort on *tripadvisor.com*. One review stated, "300 plus Canadian soldiers arrived fresh from Afghanistan and they wanted to drink as much as possible and fornicate in the hotel. We were unable to use the swimming pool as the soldiers were drinking and smoking in there."

Back in Sperwan Ghar, I finish eating dinner. It's about 1600, and we are set to depart at 2000. I go to the Internet trailer and check my e-mail: nothing. I'd already checked the day before, but it was still disappointing to see an empty inbox. I reread old e-mails and compose a few new ones. I feel the need to explain to Darcy the dangerous situation I'm going into, so I write the following lines:

> *My Dear,*
>
> *I will be away for a few days (don't tell the Taliban). You most likely won't hear from me for some time. I'm nervous because it's very very hot and there is quite a bit of fighting going on. Oh well, it will be a good story to tell when I get home.*
>
> *Things are looking up here though. I really do enjoy the challenge that this place is. I know the next little while is going to suck a lot, but I'm ok with that because it's going to challenge me and force me to do things that I wouldn't have thought I could do.*
>
> *If anything bad happens to me when I'm gone just remember that I love you more than absolutely anything and that you are the dearest girl to me in the entire world. I don't think anything untoward is going to happen to me though, and I don't want to worry you. I expect to sweat my balls off and then come back safe and sound. That's the plan anyway. I love you lots. Keep being my angel ok.*
>
> *Ryan*

There are very strict rules about what we can tell those at home on the Internet. We are not allowed to talk about troop movements, and as we are troops, we aren't allowed to talk about our own movements. I probably bent these rules a bit in my e-mail, but it is very difficult to prepare yourself mentally for "going out" without sharing anything with the people you love.

My half-hour on the Internet is intensely frustrating. In the haste to get us working terminals, someone had installed the trial version of the operating system we are using to connect. Every five minutes the screen goes black and a helpful reminder pops up saying, "Thank you for using Userful DiscoverStation Trial Version, your screen will restore in 10—9—8—7—6—5—4—3—2—1." Three of the four computers have screens smashed by frustrated soldiers. Up till now I couldn't believe that someone would intentionally punch the screen; today I have to physically hold myself back from doing it. I send an e-mail to my mom and my sister, and leave the trailer with five minutes left on my session. I wander back to my room.

A poker game is spooling up as I walk in, and Murphy is pulling out the large cookie tin that holds our chips. The chips are cheap plastic ones and their colour has no meaning in our games. Each person gets 50 chips—whoever has them all at the end wins. Four people sit around the table, and we play fast. We all want to get some sleep in before the patrol. In the end, it's me and Murphy. He bets it all on a stupid hand; I call and win the game. He throws down his cards and says, "Fuck, Flavelle, sometimes I just want to fucking kill you." No one likes to lose $20 to a signaller.

I leave and take a quick shower. Then I shave and drink a bottle of water. I walk back to my room in my favourite ripped shorts and sandals that have seen 14 countries and are well past their prime. I feel excited and nervous. I smoke and chat with Murphy about how he stores his CamelBak, and his ACOG sight (which he purchased with his own money). Finally, I climb the ladder to my top bunk, lay my head on my pillow, and will sleep to come. It refuses. Instead, I think about the patrol. I think about what fighting will actually be like, and how I will do. I think about home and my girlfriend. I wonder what she's doing. I think about *The Shield,* a TV show I've become addicted to. I think about society. Finally, my brain decides that it's time to shut down and I drift off to sleep. In only three hours we step off on patrol.

CHAPTER 2
SPERWAN GHAR TO ZANGABAD
14–15 JULY 2008

Not least of the qualities of good fighting men is their ability to endure. Bravery, military knowledge and expert marksmanship—these things have their place in the making of a soldier, but they are as nothing if the man cannot endure the unendurable.
—FARLEY MOWAT, *The Regiment*

THE PRINCESS PATRICIA'S CANADIAN LIGHT INFANTRY have a proud regimental tradition unequalled in Canada. They fought with distinction in both world wars, and won the Presidential Unit Citation during the Battle of Kapyong in Korea in 1951 (the only Canadian unit ever to achieve this honour). The Second and Third Battalion PPCLI have also won Commander-in-Chief Unit Commendations (awarded by the governor general), Canada's highest unit honour. These were won by the Second Battalion (which I am attached to) at the Battle of Medak Pocket in Bosnia in 1993, and by the Third Battalion during Operation Apollo, the deployment to Afghanistan in 2003. Although these honours are bestowed on the battalion, who wear them in perpetuity on their DEUs (dress uniforms), only those present at the time have the privilege to wear the awards on the front of their uniforms, right below the name tag. I know two soldiers who wore two separate Commander-in-Chief Unit Commendations. These soldiers saw the worst that the world could throw at them and came out the other side. Now they sleep, eat, and bitch in my room. This is a culture that is proud of its fighting tradition, and that ensures that it is carried on today—a world away from the 746 Communication

Squadron, my beloved reserve unit that turns out about 30 soldiers on Wednesday nights.

It is important to understand the regimental organization of the infantry in Canada and in Afghanistan. There are three regular force infantry regiments; the Princess Patricia's Canadian Light Infantry (PPCLI), the Royal Canadian Regiment (RCR), and the Royal 22nd Régiment, called the "Van Doos" (after *vingt-deuxième*, or "twenty-second"). Each of these regiments is subdivided into three battalions commanded by a lieutenant-colonel, who wears three bars on his epaulette. For example, the First and Third Battalion PPCLI (or I and III PPCLI) are stationed in Edmonton, Alberta, and the Second Battalion (II PPCLI) is stationed in Shilo, Manitoba. Each battalion is subdivided into five companies, commanded by a major (two and a half bars). These companies are lettered (and named) as opposed to numbered; within II PPCLI the rifle companies are named Alpha, Bravo, and Charlie, and they are the fighting elements of the battalion. Each rifle company is divided up into three platoons, commanded by a captain (two bars) or a lieutenant (one and a half bars)—also, it is pronounced *lef*tenant not *loo*tenant. If you argue that there is no *f* in *lieutenant,* I would respond that there is no *r* in *colonel.* These platoons are numbered starting with 1 in Alpha Company. Bravo Company contains 4, 5, and 6 Platoon; Charlie Company contains 7, 8, and 9 Platoon. Platoons are subdivided into sections, the smallest organizational body of troops in the Canadian infantry. Sections are commanded by a sergeant or a master corporal.

The fighting soldiers of a tour in Afghanistan (a rotation, or ROTO) are subdivided into three major elements: the battle group, which is centred on an infantry battalion but also contains a tank squadron; an engineer squadron; and an artillery battery. They are commanded by an organization known as Task Force South or TF(S), and are supported by the National Support Element (NSE). The battle group is headquartered in KAF. The battle group also controls a number of forward operating bases (FOBs) and patrol bases (PBs).

Near the bottom of this organizational structure, you find me. I provide signals support to Bravo Company II PPCLI as a reservist "augmentee." Our company operates out of Patrol Base Sperwan Ghar (PBSG), and is also in charge of three combat outposts (COPs). Bravo Company comprises three infantry platoons from II PPCLI—4, 5, and 6 platoon—as well as one platoon from III PPCLI (based out of Edmonton). The platoon from III PPCLI doesn't have a number, as it can't be called 7 Platoon (which already exists in Charlie Company). We designate it *24*, its call sign; Bravo Company, call sign 2, commands 21, 22, 23, and 24. The OC (officer commanding; i.e., the person who commands the company) is referred to as *29er*, which is spoken as "two niner," never "two nine." Although these details may be hard to wrap one's head around at first, they comprise the administrative and organizational structure that we live within and give rise to the communal language that we all learn to speak. In fact, as the tour progresses, Bravo Company becomes more important to me than anything in the world.

On my first day working with my home unit in Calgary, right after I finished basic training, we got a 40-minute briefing on the new radio system that was being fielded. I literally had no idea what was said during the briefing; I didn't even know what it was about. I spent at least the first 15 minutes thinking that references to TCCCS (the new radio system, pronounced "Tics") were about insects, and that the briefing was about how to deal with them in the field.

I wake up itchy. Tiny black flies that we call *no-see-ums* at home proliferate in Afghanistan. You can't feel their bite, but they leave a mark similar to that of a mosquito. I find my legs covered in bites when I wake up at 1930, and I scratch until they bleed. I can hear everyone else in the room putting on their uniforms. I'm still bleary-eyed, having slept for only about three hours.

I hate waking up in the military. I'm a night owl, and I prefer to sleep well past the beginning of the day. On basic training, we were reduced to about four to five hours of sleep a night for two months, and the morning kicked off every day at 0500. I was 17 and had never spent more then a month away from my own bed. By week six, if someone had offered me release papers and told me that if I signed them I could go back to sleep, I would gladly have said yes. After eight years in the military, I still haven't quite gotten the hang of instant wakefulness so common to the career soldier. I'd been jacked up for sleeping in on more than one occasion. The worst part was always the speech that followed: "If I'd done that back when I started my career, I'd have been charged and put on extras," they would inevitably tell me.

We're supposed to be a kinder, gentler army today, and the number of times I've heard a story start with "Things were harder back then" enrages me. Here are the simple facts: the war my army and my generation are involved in fighting is a real, live hot war. Yours was not. I'm tired of hearing about how drunk you were back when you were peacekeeping in Cyprus as a corporal. Cyprus is where we go to take a vacation from our real war. I don't mean to imply that there aren't remnants of the old generation who have taken what they learned and adapted it to the modern operational environment, but I've noticed that they are the exception and not the rule. At a certain point, despite the army's best efforts, people stop trying to learn. Usually this is because they think they've mastered the job.

I was at a friend's wedding recently, and I met a few other guys in the military from my generation. Our conversations followed a familiar pattern:

"Oh, you're a medic/signaller/infanteer/engineer eh? What unit are you with?"

"Weren't you guys over on TF 3–06?"

"Yeah."

"You guys did a lot of fighting . . ."

"I remember being in this one firefight . . ."

At the same wedding, I had conversations with various individuals who have been in since "Christ was a corporal." They had a different pattern:

"Do you know (insert other old codger's name here)*?"*

"Yeah."

"I remember one time on exercise we got so drunk together that we could barely even stand, and then we didn't even get charged."

Kinder, gentler army indeed.

The major problem with the "back in Cyprus" crowd is that many are in leadership positions. In stressful situations, soldiers instantly and intuitively fall back on their training. This rule doesn't only apply to battle, or even patrolling. Living in a war zone is a pretty stressful thing to do. Those whose lives have been devoted to prompt, unthinking obedience to the chain of command, and to maintaining proper dress and deportment tend to make those things priorities even in war zones.

For example, after having lived, worked, and patrolled with the same group of people for the first half of my tour, we addressed each other by our first names. When Sergeant-Major Cavanagh caught wind of this infraction, he instantly brought the hammer down. Under no circumstances were we allowed to refer to those in leadership positions by their first names. If we were caught, we faced a charge. I can't think of a more ridiculous military rule to enforce. This isn't basic training; we all understand how the chain of command works. The bottom line is that when one of our junior leaders told us to do something, we did it. If we didn't, we would hear about it instantly and loudly. It doesn't matter whether I say "Yes, master corporal" or "Sure thing, Liz." Bonds of friendship had begun to develop, and rank no longer seemed like an impediment to knowing a fellow human being. But the army has different ideas.

The most horrific and morale-shattering e-mail I've ever read was sent by a high-up Canadian non-commissioned member (NCM). It started with the same bullshit that we constantly tried to ignore if no one was looking: red flags must be worn on KAF, boots must be bloused at all times, beards are not acceptable under any circumstances (the way to get around the ban on beards is to talk to a medic and get a chit saying you can't shave due to a medical concern). This e-mail informed us that if we weren't healthy enough to shave, we weren't healthy enough to be in Afghanistan. I'd read a number of e-mails similar to this one, promulgated by folks who appeared to have more rank than brains, sitting in an office far away from where things actually happened. No big deal. As I continued to read, however, I noticed one sentence that infuriated me. It stated, "I've noticed that over the course of this deployment, those who maintain a high standard of dress and deportment are more often singled out for honours and awards than those who do not." Basically, this person was implying that those who follow the minutiae of army dress are better soldiers and somehow braver than their unshaven counterparts. Everyone in our company routinely tried their hardest to breach the dress standard as far as possible, yet our company had committed some of the most noteworthy and bravest actions I can think of, often refusing to have their names submitted for awards. They felt that they were doing their jobs, just like everyone else in the company, and deserved no special recognition. The KAF WOG out for a day trip on a resupply run who fires his weapon at the enemy is far more likely to be better dressed. He's also far more likely to have his name put up for a medal than any of us. I felt that our honour was being impugned because we bent the rules regarding dress. Sometimes I hate the army.

My earlier nervousness is a distant memory as I pull on my pants. I've already laid out a fresh pair of underwear and socks, helping to streamline dressing into a two-minute procedure. I finish putting on my shirt and walk outside to our picnic table, possibly my favourite place in Afghanistan. I grab a bottle of water, light a cigarette, and watch people filter out of the room. We don't have to be ready to go for another 10 minutes, so I watch my section start to move around me. I butt out my smoke into a spent artillery shell and put on my fighting kit.

I have determined a specific order to this process that works best. First I put on my flak vest, strap it up and shake around to make sure that the Velcro still works (sand wreaks havoc on Velcro, and I've had to sew new strips on three times over the course of the tour). Next I throw on my chest rig and ask a friend to help me with the straps on the back. Then I put on my weapon, as my sling has a clip that can be unattached, and I've found the best way to carry my weapon is with the sling underneath my pack; I can still fight with it clipped up, but can unclip it if I need to pass my weapon off to somebody, or adjust something. Over top of my sling I put my pack, which feels heavier every time I try to put it on. Finally, I grab my helmet and walk over to the assembly area. It is 1950, twilight.

I think about what we are going to do, and about whether or not I actually want to do it. The glamour associated with patrolling has lost a lot of its lustre, and walking the fields of Afghanistan has become a relatively commonplace, yet all too dangerous, pastime. I know that we're in for a rough go, and I figure that I might as well come along for the ride. In the long run, it's a better story than sitting in a command post. I think about what I would do if I were given the choice; I'd probably still go. If anything were to happen to any of my friends on this patrol, and I'm not there to help, I don't know what I would do.

However, I don't have a choice. In Calgary, I made exactly one decision that got me to where I am today, and that was volunteering to go overseas Everything else was decided by others, all of whom are getting paid more than I am.

Earlier in the tour I was in KAF with the rest of headquarters. We had been forced to leave an operation while it was still ongoing, to escort the OC to a "war council." I was screwing around with some radios in the back of our LAV and I got the speaker to work. What I heard floored me. "0, this is 2. 9 liner, over." 0 is the command call sign. The CP in Sperwan Ghar's call sign was 2. "9 liner" is the short form for a medical evacuation request. People gathered around our LAV as we heard the details come across. An IED strike had taken out one of 5 Platoon's LAVs, and we were requesting a medevac for an injured person. As soon as the OC and sergeant-major returned to the LAV, we floored it back to Sperwan Ghar, where we were told to wait for further orders while the OC sorted out the situation on the ground. We sat and watched a pirated copy of *EuroTrip* while we waited to be told what was going on. No one so much as loosened their boots. About an hour later, the sergeant-major walked into our room. "Kit up, we're going to link up with 5 Platoon in Talukan," he said.

This order seemed blatantly ridiculous. The road that we were to travel was infested with IEDs. Moreover, no one had had eyes on it for the last four hours since the IED strike that took out one of 5 Platoon's LAVs. We were sure that the Taliban would have planted more IEDs to prevent exactly what we were planning to do. Too bad. We were going.

At that moment I realized just what an important thing choice is. Not the choice between shopping at Walmart or shopping at

Superstore, but the ability to choose whether to participate in things that directly affect your safety. I had given up that right. I was going to get into the back of that LAV, stand air sentry, cross my fingers and toes, and hold on. That was my only choice.

The cold, hard reality of military life is that no one makes any effort to treat you as an individual. You are a soldier; that is all. It is refreshing to be reminded that no matter what our third-grade teachers taught us, we are not all unique and delicate flowers; we are people who together form a community. Communities function best when their constituent parts don't hold too closely to ideas of their own intrinsic value. In the military we are painfully aware that each one of us is merely a cog in a much larger machine. The machine breaks down if we don't do our best to perform that role. Hauling a radio so that an officer doesn't have to, or pushing buttons on an obstinate piece of kit, may not seem like immensely important roles, and they aren't; but they are cogs that keep the wheels turning toward success. The military doesn't view us as unique, and it doesn't need to. Subsuming yourself into a larger and more important entity carries with it an immense feeling of freedom. Not the freedom to decide, but the freedom to no longer have to.

When we arrived in Talukan after a charmed ride down the IED-infested road between it and Sper, we found out that Terry Street had been killed. Terry was a good man. I remember that he would come into my office in Shilo in an attempt to avoid work. He was young, quirky, and funny. I'm glad that I got the opportunity to know him before an IED ended his short life. He was one of those guys who was the centre of attention and the leader of the crowd. He was well liked within his platoon and outside it as well. That was the only night I couldn't sleep in the entire tour.

I take off my pack and drop it in a heap beside me. I sit and lean back to back with Chris on the sharp rocks that surround our camp. Until basic training I'd never known how effective a seat two people can make. I can't think of a better symbol for camaraderie than two soldiers sitting down and leaning against each other so both can be comfortable. My bayonet digs into my thighs as I sit. I smoke and pass my tin around. The inevitable has arrived, and there is absolutely no going back. I take out my night vision goggles and attach them to my helmet. Each one of us will walk outside that gate into the maw of Panjway in just a few short minutes. Why be uncomfortable when you don't have to be?

I'm not nervous as I sit, waiting. Instead, I think about how I've been allowed into the circle of infantry. I tell jokes and pass smokes around and feel happy to be among them. My overriding concern is not the upcoming patrol, but the fact that I appear to be included in the group. The infantry form a circle reminiscent of those formed by the gorillas in the movie *Instinct,* in which Anthony Hopkins plays a scientist who, after studying a pack of wild gorillas, slowly becomes one. A line flashes through my mind: "Suddenly, just like that, it happened. I was no longer outside the group. For the first time, I was among them." This might sound a tad melodramatic, but it's how I feel. I am proud to be inside the circle, and for a few moments that is all that matters.

This pleasant and peaceful interlude doesn't last long. Before I finish my smoke, the lead elements are on their feet and pushing toward the front gate. We are behind both 4 and 9 Platoon in the order of march, so I still have time to finish my cigarette. Finally, I see people around me standing up. I throw my bag over my shoulder, lean over, and do up the waist strap and the chest strap. I start walking. The weight feels unbalanced, and I swing from side to side as I walk, to get a feel for my pack. I unclip my handset and inform call sign 2 that we are departing. It is about 2000, and the last remnants of twilight are diminishing. We can hear the call to prayer echo from the mosques near Sperwan Ghar. I cock my weapon, loading a live round into the chamber, and place it on safe.

The first time I was issued live rounds in theatre was the first time I'd been given bullets without someone standing behind me making sure I didn't do anything unsafe. It was an immensely powerful feeling. In Canada, the military is extremely cautious about how it gives out ammunition, accounting for it carefully, and making soldiers give a "statutory declaration" before leaving a range. The declaration is "I have no live rounds, empty casings, or pyrotechnics in my possession, sir." But on our first day in Afghanistan, a large box filled with loose 5.56mm rounds was put in front of us. There were full metal jacket, tracers, and armour-piercing bullets mixed together in a jumble, left over from the previous tour. We could take as many as we wanted. I filled up my magazines most of the way with about 25 rounds each (one shouldn't fill them all the way, as the first few rounds are liable to jam). About a month later, as we left the wire on my first combat operation, I had the unique and slightly terrifying feeling of loading a live round into the chamber of my weapon. Although I had done this a few times in training, now the round was loaded for the express purpose of engaging the enemy. It was strange to feel the metamorphosis of a rifle, which I had grown accustomed to carrying since I joined in 2001, from a lifeless burden into the killing machine that it was designed to be. After four months in-country, the novelty had worn off, and I accepted the live round in my chamber without much thought— just another day at the office.

Getting outside of the front gate is a bit of an ordeal. We have to walk around the mountain top and down a steep hill. Every few metres we stop as the platoons ahead of us work out their spacing and try to get the proper pace established. It feels like waiting in line at a grocery store; walk 10 metres, stop, wait, wonder why you are stopped, start, walk 20 metres, stop, repeat. Finally, we pass the front gate. We've gone about 400 metres and my shoulders begin to express how unhappy they are with the amount of weight that I'm carrying. We walk silently even before we get outside the gate. It's not that the patrol is noiseless; I can hear the muffled rustling of people's kit, the quiet beeping of my radio, and a few whispered interchanges in front of or behind me. It's not even that we walk in a particularly stealthy way; we just do our best not to make any noise that could give away our position. We are all trying to put on our "game face," which is an important skill to have when patrolling in Afghanistan. The game face is more a mental than a physical change; it's a mindset that a good soldier adopts when outside the wire. We are supposed to act like hunters, observing everything as silently as we can. We need to be mentally prepared for anything this country can throw at us, so we act the part. If you pretend long enough, eventually your game face becomes who you are. The silence makes me feel alone as we walk outside the gate. The world closes in as I try to focus on my surroundings and maintain "noise discipline." It's not that the Taliban won't see us coming—they probably have sentries posted in one of the nearby mud buildings—but silence is just a good habit to get into. A long line of soldiers, many of whom can't shut up for more than five minutes when they are in Sper, stretches silently and almost surreally toward the horizon.

We are walking down the main route outside of Sperwan Ghar. This route has been IEDed a few times, so we try to avoid stopping on any culverts, or pulling too far off onto the shoulder. We reach the main culvert, where we have previously discovered a number of IEDs. I take a knee on the rocks and look out at the landscape. There is still enough light that I am once again struck by the beauty of our surroundings. We can see children wandering in a field, and farmers going about their daily business. The green fields surrounded by brown mud walls give way to the openness of the late evening sky and the riverbed beyond them. I feel comfortable kneeling on one knee with my weapon resting on my thigh. After about five minutes in this position however, I begin to wobble as the weight of my pack makes it difficult to balance. It feels like I'm trying to stand on one leg, and my knee and thigh begin to ache. I look around at the infantry; they seem to be having no problem. I sigh and wonder how long it will take the lead soldiers to confirm that there isn't an IED placed underneath the culvert.

Earlier on the tour, I was sitting in the CP, whiling away the long hours of a radio shift with a copy of Patrick O'Brian's *Master and Commander* and a cup of coffee when I got a call from one of our observation points (OPs) stating that a "fucking jingle truck" had broken down on the road leading to Sper.

"Are they doing anything suspicious?" I asked.

"I don't know, it's a truck broken down by the culvert."

There wasn't much I could do. "Okay, observe it and let me know if anything interesting happens." I hung up the phone. "Hey, Sergeant, there's a truck broken down on the road," was all I thought to pass on to the duty officer.

Three hours later, when I was sitting on the picnic table, smoking, drinking water, and trying to get up the nerve to go for a run, I heard a dull explosion in the distance. It was an IED. The "broken-down" truck was covering some Taliban who were digging in an explosive at the culvert. It had blown up a vehicle coming down the road to Sper. Luckily no one was killed. It just so happened that a reporter for *Legion Magazine* was in the vehicle behind it, and a vivid description of the IED strike later appeared in that magazine, the IED that I had missed. I was pulled into the command post and grilled for about a half hour: "What exactly did you hear? Why didn't you enter it into the log? People could have been killed. Your job is to pass information, and you didn't."

I didn't know what to say. I blamed myself for that IED for a long time. In the end, I realized, it was a fucking truck broken down on the road. What was I supposed to do? Call out the fighter jets?

As I think about this, an ANA Ford Ranger comes flying down the road doing "mach chicken" (very, very fast). There are three Afghan soldiers in the back, one hanging onto a .50 cal machine gun, and the other two looking bored as they go over the ruts and bumps on the gravel road. They pass right over the culvert that is being searched. I see the soldiers in front of me shrug, stand up, and carry on. We begin our shuffling procession again.

I can't believe how slowly we are walking, and people begin to close up naturally. This is bad; it is of the utmost importance that we maintain spacing of between five and ten metres when we walk. That way, if one person steps on an IED, it doesn't take out the person in front or behind him. Also, if we get lit up, a cluster of soldiers provides a convenient target, and it's a lot harder to sort ourselves out after the rounds begin to fly.

We stop again and I find myself standing right behind the OC, so close that I could almost touch him. Major Lane stands even closer to Chris, who turns around and points at me, "Fuck, Flavelle, watch your fucking spacing."

I feel like an idiot and resolve to make a more conscious effort as the patrol progresses. The OC does not. Chris later tells me that he wasn't actually yelling at me, but hinting at Major Lane. His pleas fell on deaf ears, and Chris had to endure the OC's close presence for most of the patrol.

If I could use only two words to describe Corporal Christopher Nead, they would be *powerful* and *precise*. Chris is short and stocky, with blond hair that spikes everywhere when he lets it grow (he once said, "War is hell—on your hair"). He is occasionally referred to by his friends as a "troll doll." He bought every addition that one can buy for his personal weapon (a C8 carbine), and when we deployed he had a brand-new ACOG sight (immensely superior to the one we were issued), a rail-mount system to better secure additions like a laser sight or flashlight onto the barrel, and a dual magazine holder. I once held his weapon and was amazed at its weight (C8s are generally much lighter than C7s like the one I carried). Chris works out often and seems to bristle with power. He is a qualified Canadian sniper.

Canadian snipers are among the best in the world. The very word *sniper* carries with it an aura of hardcore. Whereas the Communication Reserve is about as far down the credibility totem pole one can get, snipers are the celebrities of the military community. Everyone looks up to them, talks about them, and to a certain extent wishes they could be one of them. Almost everyone knows that a Canadian sniper, Corporal Rob Furlong, once held the record for longest confirmed kill (2,430 metres, or 1.5 miles). At my unit in Calgary, I would have had about as much chance of interacting with a sniper as I would with Peter Mansbridge or Jarome Iginla. Chris Nead lives up to the reputation of Canadian snipers as being highly disciplined: he even managed to quit smoking while on his sniper course. He is also jolly, slightly vindictive, and an immensely interesting person to know.

While in Recce Platoon, an entirely separate entity formed by the battalion's snipers and reconnaissance soldiers, he had a "disagreement" with the master sniper, and had been put back into B Company with us. We met on a live-fire night range. Neither of us had a partner, so we were paired to run through the "night pairs" range, which involves using your night vision goggles (NVGs) and laser sight to hit pop-up targets at varying ranges. I didn't do particularly well, it being only the third time I had ever worn NVGs and my second time on a live pairs range. However, Chris was amazing. As soon as I would see the indistinct shape of a target pop up, Chris's laser would be on it and it would be down. Afterwards the sergeant-major, who was acting as safety staff, said "Corporal Nead, excellent job like always." He then looked at me and said condescendingly, "Flavelle, stick to the radios." It was advice I tried to take as often as possible. Six months later, as we walked out into Panjway, I took my every cue from Chris. More than anyone, he was the person I tried to emulate.

We turn off the main road, which is covered in gravel, and onto a hard-packed mud road leading west. We are getting farther and farther away from safety with each step. We enter the first village that we have to pass through; it has four different names depending on who you ask. This was a problem that we encountered in almost every village we entered; this part of Panjway is like an endless village, and locals identify with different geographical landmarks depending on where they live. So two locals living at opposite ends of the "block" might associate with a different tribe or mosque and call their village a different name. Although they all reside in the same group of buildings, no one seems to be able to agree on a name. The village is a conglomeration of mud huts and sea containers; it is entirely unremarkable.

The first time I passed through it, there had been a bustling market selling rotten bananas, random car parts, and cigarettes for two bucks a carton, and that was the white-guy price (Pine Lights, made in Afghanistan; you get what you pay for). It was a Friday, the Muslim holy day, and the mosques had unleashed a torrent of people. I was surprised at how friendly and welcoming the villagers were. The kids crowded around, and the men seemed intensely interested in asking questions. Our terp (interpreter) was soon overrun with requests to engage in conversation, and one little boy even felt my rifle and looked through the sight. It was a very positive experience.

Two months later, in a village about four kilometres away, a child who was about 12 was used as a suicide bomber against our company. The man who remotely detonated the suicide vest exploited the fact that we didn't, at that time, search children. Looking back on the amorphous mass of people that had crowded around us that day gives me shivers. We were in far more danger than I understood at the time.

The interesting thing about Afghanistan is that the Taliban follow a fairly strict fighting schedule. During the harvest (when we arrived in February), they were content to watch us and smoke the newly harvested hash. By the time I got back from leave, the game had changed. I miss those simpler times when I felt I could trust Afghans. We have an expression that is supposed to govern our interactions with the locals: "Be polite, be courteous, be prepared to kill everyone that you see." When I arrived I thought this expression callous; old men detonating 12-year-old boys from across a field have a way of changing your perspective.

We are walking through a ghost town. There is no curfew in effect, but the average Afghan has come to realize that it's safer to stay behind closed doors at night. We hear the nocturnal activities of villagers, lighting fires and talking in hushed tones. The streets are deserted. We follow a wadi through the village. Wadis are irrigation ditches, and they vary greatly in width and depth; they are ubiquitous throughout the "green belt" of Panjway, siphoning water away from the Arghandab River. We stop, and I notice Chris covering a door to a compound. It is a large, metal, two-sided door, and he stands to the side, facing it with his weapon pointed toward the ground. He is ready to aim and fire at any threat that might come through the door. We walk a few more metres and stop again. Now I'm standing right beside the door and I realize that it is my responsibility to cover it. I stand at the edge of the door, and turn my body toward it, planting both feet firmly on the ground. I point my weapon at the ground, but brace my right hand on the pistol grip. I hope the door stays closed.

I hear a faint rustling on the other side, and suddenly the door opens violently. I feel each hair on my neck stand up and I raise my weapon, take off the safety, and flash my Maglite. This movement takes less than a second. I need to decide instantly if the man who is now illuminated is a threat.

"*Wadraga!* Stop! " I yell.

The man in my sights is old. He wears baby-blue man jammies (I'm not even sure what else to call them; they look like pyjamas) and a white turban. He has a look of utter terror on his face. Baby-blue is a good thing; different tribes wear different colours, almost like a uniform. Blue clothing is usually worn by a tribe that seems relatively friendly to us. Baby-blue, white, and brown are good; black is bad. The terrified look on his face and the fact that he recoiled from me instantly are also good signs. Luckily our terp, Peter, is standing right behind me. He says a few words in Pashto, and the man quickly closes the door. I can hear the metal bolt slam shut.

"What did he say?" I ask.

"He say he is going for ablutions for prayers. I tell him, Go back inside and stay for the rest of night."

I haven't encountered a Taliban suicide bomber; I've encountered an old man who didn't hear us moving through his village and picked a poor time to walk out his front door. The Maglite attached to my weapon is the brightest flashlight I have ever seen. When he opened the door, it must have looked like the afterlife was waiting for him.

I turn off my Maglite and take my finger off the trigger. I am surprised at how close I was to killing this man. In that brief, terrifying second I felt reassured by the unaccustomed feeling of hard metal on my forefinger. From my first day in the army, I have been trained never to put my finger on the trigger unless I intend to clear or fire the weapon. Overseas, I carry my weapon almost everywhere; it is never farther than 10 metres away from me. In Sperwan Ghar, I often go whole weeks without putting my finger on the trigger. For the most part it is a weighty burden; but in one second it metamorphosed into the weapon that it was designed to be. I feel powerful, and nervous. I am glad we are moving on.

I feel bad for that man and the few more grey hairs I've given him. I also feel better about how I might respond in a stressful situation. I had been 100 percent prepared to pull the trigger if he had been armed. I walk with my head held a little higher.

The adrenalin surge engendered by my little encounter stays with me as I continue to walk. I feel attuned to the night; I feel that I can do anything. We stop beside the wadi and sit down while our lead call sign figures out the best route. From across the wadi I hear a sound that makes me bring my weapon up again.

"*Allahu Akbar! Allahu Akbar!*"

Men are yelling "God is great!" from the other side of the wadi. I flip down my NVG and turn it on. I see a few guys lying prostrate on the ground. *It's on now*, I think. I watch them further; nothing happens. I don't see any weapons.

"Peter, what the fuck is going on?"

"They're praying; it's that time of day."

Christ! That's two separate groups of people I've almost lit up in the span of 15 minutes. My hands shake; I've got to get better control of my nerves.

Afghanistan is an eerie place at night. It is pitch dark and perfectly silent now; the only sound comes from the flowing wadi. We try to avoid using our NVG, as it is better to preserve good night vision. The patrol is beginning to take on a quixotic quality.

We are on our feet and walking again, faster now as the patrol hits its stride. We stick to the road until we are outside the village, and I struggle to keep up. The weight on my back is more noticeable now, and sweat begins to drip from under my helmet. We have left the hard pack and are following the path of the wadi as it winds around grape fields. We bash our way into these fields and the countryside passes in a blur. We stop every few hundred metres to observe the area and to allow those in front to figure out what route to take.

Every time we stop, I have to make a decision: should I stand, take a knee, or sit down? Standing allows me to start moving instantly, but it's not the best tactical posture as it makes me an obvious target. Taking a knee is the best tactical stance, but it quickly becomes immensely uncomfortable despite my knee pad. Sitting is the most comfortable, but it is hard to get back up and, more importantly, when sitting I cover more surface area that hasn't been touched by those in front of me, increasing my chances of setting off an IED. Every time we stop, I wait, look around, and try to get a feel for the situation. After a few seconds, I think about taking a knee; often I sit. I don't know if somebody who has never patrolled can understand how much satisfaction there is in sitting down. Getting the weight off my shoulders and leaning back is the most comfortable state I can imagine in comparison with standing.

Our fast pace continues unabated until the OC stops suddenly. He is staring at the ground. He flips down his NVG and scans the area. He turns on his blue flashlight and leans over.

"I think this is an IED command wire," he says.

He asks me to come take a look, and I walk up beside him and scan the area with my NVG. I don't see anything on the ground.

We push back and provide a 10-metre cordon around the area. The OC uses my radio to call the engineers, and soon we see the grunting face of Warrant Officer (WO) Terry Wolaniuk coming up with another engineer. I take a closer look at the engineer with the WO and realize that it's Allan, the signaller from my home unit in Calgary. Allan was one of my roommates in university and we are close friends. Now we have been drawn together on a desolate dirt road in Panjway. I smile and whisper a greeting. He smiles back. There is no time for pleasantries, however, as he has to help the WO defuse this potential IED. WO Wolaniuk walks close to the command wire, leans over, and flashes his Maglite.

"It's a fucking twig."

On patrol, we walk in a very rigid order, known as the *order of march*. My position is right behind the OC, who walks behind Chris. I walk in front of the terp, Peter, who is in front of the forward observation officer (FOO) party (I figure it's just more fun if you call it a party). Our terp never really gets the concept of the order of march and keeps trying to pass me. I, however, stay rigidly in position behind the officer commanding for the remainder of the patrol.

Focusing on the man in front of me takes up more of my time than anything else on patrol. *How far ahead is he? Where is he looking? Shit, I'm too close, too far away. It's dark, where the fuck did he go? I can't even see him.* Concerns of this nature constantly plague my mind.

The man in front of me is Major Mike Lane, the officer commanding of B Company. He looks about the same as any other Canadian officer. I've learned to tell the difference between an officer and an enlisted man, even out of uniform. He has short black hair, and a Homer Simpson five o'clock shadow that is never fully grown or fully shaved. He is shorter than the average soldier, a trait that has earned him the endearment "Lord Farquaad," after the character in *Shrek*. When we met, I thought him distant and aloof, but otherwise an average infantry officer. He chewed tobacco non-stop, and the first distinct memory I have of him is with a wad of dip in his lip.

We were in Shilo at the time on an "air mobile" exercise. The plan was to practise getting dropped into an operational environment, and then getting picked up. We were to use Black Hawk helicopters brought in from the United States (with American pilots), to simulate the reality on the ground (Canada did not, at that time, have helicopters in Afghanistan). Of course, this being the Canadian military, the helicopters broke down before they even took off. We waited around for four hours after the scheduled H hour (military term for start time, it stands for "Hour hour"). Finally, we rode into the field in MLVWs–Medium Logistic Vehicle Wheeled, usually shortened to ML—standard, reliable transport trucks built in the 1960s, but still going strong. Most of us believed this was inevitable and few soldiers had actually planned on riding a chopper. We were told that a part needed to fix the chopper was being emergency FedExed and would arrive that night. We carried on with the first part of the patrol and moved into a laager. *Laager* (we pronounce it "leaguer") is the army word for defensive circle, in this case a ring of soldiers looking outwards. After a sleepy radio shift, I settled down to a cold Manitoba night and slept in the fetal position on the ground. As dawn approached, it was my turn on the radio again. I watched as the OC gave orders to his assembled platoon commanders.

"Orders—General Situation—We are going to be getting the choppers at about 0730 this morning. We will be mounting up and departing to this grid, Objective Molson." As he gave his orders to a group of keen young officers kneeling in front of him, pen and paper in hand, I watched Major Lane spit tobacco into a 500ml water bottle. I remember thinking that I had never seen an officer chew, let alone spit into a water bottle during orders. I soon realized that this was just one of many infantry foibles I had never encountered before. At that moment, I received a message on the radio:

"2, this is 0—be advised, there will be no helicopters today, all movement will be conducted via Mike Lima [MLVW]. I say again, there will be no helicopters today."

No explanation, no detail, and no reason were given as to why we wouldn't be receiving the choppers. Instead, all we got was the voice of God coming over the radio and spoiling our plans.

"2, roger, out."

As usual, I was to be the harbinger of bad news. I asked Ryan LaFontaine, my fellow signaller, to watch the radio and walked over to the OC with a hangdog expression.

"Sir, I just got a message from 0. There will be no choppers today."

Major Lane stopped mid-spit and looked at me as if I had two heads. "Are you fucking serious?"

"Yes, sir, sorry, I just got the message."

That was my first personal contact with Major Lane. He would later become the guy in front of me on most patrols. I had no idea, at the time, of the role he would come to play in my life overseas.

We push on to the Arghandab riverbed, and walk along it. We descend a steep slope and move quickly along the silty terrain of the mostly dried up river. A few times we have to cross the river itself, and I get my boots wet. As we walk, we get a welcome message on the radio: "29er, this is Haji. Be advised we have eyes on your lead elements at this time."

The guys at the Haji outpost can see us; we are almost done the first leg of our patrol.

I feel stronger as we inch ever closer to COP Haji. The first leg hasn't turned out to be so bad. In about 15 minutes, we can all see the HESCO Bastions and razor wire on the horizon. In 30 minutes, we climb a very steep slope and walk the rest of the way into the COP. We are greeted with cases of cool water.

"Twenty minutes, troops," says the sergeant-major.

I sit beside our section commander, Jeff Brazeau, take off my helmet, and grab a bottle of water. I ask Jeff to take out my tin of smokes from my shirt pocket; I light one and relax. Fatigue is beginning to set in, and I'm covered in sweat. I relish the immense comfort of sitting, smoking, and not having my helmet on. I hear a few guys talk around me, mostly about the OC's IED.

"It was a fucking twig!"

"Seriously man? You're fucking me."

"Nope, actually a twig."

I smile and continue to relax in silence. There's still another leg left tonight; we need to push three kilometres farther as the crow flies, to Zangabad.

The first time I saw what later became COP Haji was on a long patrol to clear IEDs from Route Fosters, a dirt road that ran all the way to Mushan. Our job was to provide left-flank security for the patrol, and we walked back and forth in the hot sun while we waited for the engineers to perform their dangerous tasks. At that time Haji was still a police substation (PSS), manned by Afghan police instead of Afghan army. The only Canadians there were a group of POMLT operators (Police Operational Mentor and Liaison Teams, pronounced "pomlette"). When we pulled into location, the PSS had serious radio problems that needed to be solved. After everybody else adjourned to the carrier to eat a ration and sleep, I found myself neck-deep in wiring problems, antennas, and programming failures. It took me almost two hours to sort them out. When I walked back to our carrier, everyone had finished dinner and was relaxing on the Afghan sand. Master Corporal Lizette LeBlanc, our section commander who was on leave during this patrol, threw me an American ration. No sooner was I halfway into my jalapeno and cheese pouch when a sergeant from 5 Platoon came up to us.

"I need your fucking signaller," he said in a thick Newfoundland accent.

I sighed, got up, grabbed my helmet and weapon, and went over to his carrier, where I encountered a few problems that I had never seen before. The computer system and user interface that we use for our tactical radio system had been designed in the late 1980s. That radio system doesn't enjoy heat. The basic user interface into the vehicle's computer is a small box called a command indicator (CI), which is covered in buttons and has two lines of green text. The CIs in the LAV that I was working on were throwing letters and numbers at me that I'd never seen before. "IBIT FAIL" and "RC FAIL," the army's version of the infamous "PC LOAD LETTER" message from the movie *Office Space*, flashed intermittently on the screen. I had to dump everything in the radio system, reset the computer, reload the radios, and climb all through the LAV checking antenna cables— a time-consuming and exhausting procedure. Finally, after about 30 minutes of effort, I heard the reassuring beep of three working radios. As I was conducting my final checks, someone came up to the back of the LAV behind me. "Who's that?" he asked the sergeant.

"Oh, him? He's just some fucking sig op."

I had spent the day patrolling with the infantry, I'd kept up, dodged IEDs, and helped cover the advance of a battalion's worth of vehicles on foot. I then skipped my well-deserved supper and fixed an epic radio failure, something that the infantry had already tried and failed to do. But in the end I was "just some fucking sig op." As retired General Roméo Dallaire's father told him when he enlisted, a soldier "should never expect to be thanked."

Haji is a tiny enclosure of no more than 50 square metres. It is surrounded with razor wire and HESCO Bastions. These are three-metre-long steel-mesh cylinders with a diameter of five metres, filled with dirt by bulldozers or, in a pinch, soldiers. What they lack in aesthetics, they make up for in their ability to stop bullets, RPGs, and recoilless rifle rounds. We sit outside of the camp itself, inside the wire.

I finish my bottle of water and ask, "Hey, Chris, what did you do with your water bottle?" I don't want to leave trash lying around, especially after the Haji guys were courteous enough to give us some of their own cool water.

"I just threw it over the wire where those ANA guys are sitting."

That's kind of a dick move, I think, making the ANA clean up our garbage. "Are you sure, dude?"

"Yeah, that's what I did."

I sigh and throw my water bottle over the wire.

"Flavelle! What the fuck are you doing? Do you want the ANA to clean up your garbage for you?!" Chris yells this loud enough that everyone can hear him.

"Fuck you, bud."

Sometimes Chris can be a bastard.

"Kit up!" The word runs through the group as people yell it out. As soon as a few people stand up, we all realize that we should be doing the same. I call this automatic response "sheep senses," and they are honed from basic training on.

I once again throw my pack over my shoulder, lean over and do up my waist and chest straps. I grab my helmet and put it on as I walk.

Gooshe. My bliskit pads, which are soaked in sweat, make a disgusting sound as I push my helmet back onto my head. They have cooled off in the night air, and I can feel my own cold, recycled sweat making rivulets through the dust that covers my face. I shudder.

We stand around and wait for the patrol to get on the move. Soon we are once again walking into the dark night of Panjway.

We descend the steep hill that borders Haji to the north. My boots are wet and I have a hard time seeing the ground, as my glasses have begun to fog up. I miss my footing at the bottom of the hill, and perform an "ass over teakettle" manoeuvre. I finish with a combat roll and am back on my feet before anybody knows the difference. The OC turns around and shoots me a look, but I'm off and walking again. This is the first of many falls to come.

We walk along the edge of the riverbed. To our north the Taliban are probably all in bed, sleeping a drug-induced sleep and dreaming about their IEDs and RPGs finding their targets. We continuously scan the north of the riverbed for spotters or ambushes. There is no sign of life. It doesn't feel like the night for it anyway. Although we have a vast body of objective evidence indicating how dangerous this area is, the cool, quiet midnight carries with it no threat. We walk across the surface of the riverbed as if in a dream. A thin sliver of moonlight illuminates the lunar surface that we tread on, in complete silence, utterly removed from the situation around us. I listen to my own breathing and the quiet beep of my radio, which I've turned down to a barely audible level. Every few hundred metres we stop and send in a locstat, the position of our leading and rear elements. I watch the north of the riverbed through my NVG. The world is translated into a green and black television screen that is slightly out of focus. I don't see any people, but the north side of the river is almost 600 metres away. There could be someone hiding in any one of the mud huts.

When I took my high school Physics 30 diploma exam (one of the standardized tests that all Alberta students must take in order to graduate), one question was how night vision goggles work. I knew the answer, and would like to share it with you. NVGs don't create light; they merely amplify the light that is already there by means of a two-sided screen inside the NVG. One side of the screen receives the photons (wave/particles of light) that reflect off the ground from ambient light sources such as the stars or the moon. The other side pumps more photons (provided a working AA battery is inserted) toward the eye than entered the goggles. So, in short, all that NVGs do is amplify the number of photons in the environment. In a pitch-black room (with absolutely no ambient light), nothing would be visible.

The eye naturally focuses on whatever range you are looking at, but NVGs do not. To focus them one has to adjust a dial, similar to binoculars. When I look through my NVGs, each wavelength/ photon of light enters into its aperture, becomes amplified, is outputted toward my eye, goes through my fogged-up ballistic eyewear, is bent by the plastic glasses that rest inside, and is finally received by my eye and interpreted by my brain. This all happens at approximately the speed of light. The whole process is the culmination of at least 200 years of scientific endeavour, from the creation of glasses, through the moulding of plastic, to the science behind functioning NVGs. But an understanding of the means by which NVGs operate does not make them any less frustrating. A physicist who gets run over by a bus can intellectually appreciate the forces at play, but that doesn't help him look both ways.

The biggest problem with NVGs is that they eliminate depth perception, which is the product of the difference in time that it takes each separate eye to receive light. With artificially amplified light, both eyes receive it at the same time and therefore can't tell how far away the light is coming from. This is why the army has switched from night vision goggles (two eyepieces) to night vision monocles (one eyepiece). They are lighter and allow users to maintain depth perception with the other eye.

Like everything else in the military, the use of NVGs improves with practice. As a signals reservist, I'd never used them before my pre-deployment training in Shilo.

As I scan the north bank of the riverbed, searching for Taliban, our pace is again increasing. I walk faster, and feel sweat once more pour down from my helmet. I feel very warm, though the air is cool, and I wonder how I will feel in the heat of the day. Walks like this are what the infantry call *humping*. I don't know why; it feels more like walking very quickly with way too much equipment strapped to my body than humping.

We breach out of the riverbed and back into the fields and villages that comprise our area of operations (AO). We have been out from Haji for almost two hours, and I'm getting tired. We are only a kilometre away from COP Zangabad, but in between lies a mishmash of poppy, grape, and marijuana fields, all of which are surrounded by mud walls between one and three metres high.

We used to walk along the major roads to get to the COPs, but eight days prior to our departure Private Colin Wilmot had been killed by an IED on a similar dismounted patrol between Zangabad and Haji. That patrol had avoided the roads, but had skirted a goat path beside a wadi. Wilmot was second last in the order of march; he was the patrol's medic. A good friend of mine was on that patrol. He said that he had stuffed his pockets with Gatorade and Otis Spunkmeyer muffins, as they had run out of junk food in Zangabad. When he got back after helping carry Wilmot's body over a kilometre and a half, the muffins were covered in his friend's blood. Private Wilmot was our company's fourth casualty. Over a year later, I still wear a black "death" bracelet marked "Pte Colin Wilmot C/S 24—KIA July 6 2008 Afghanistan." It was given to me by my friend right before he left to go back to Canada.

Now we avoid anything that even approximates a goat path.

As we climb out of the riverbed, I see a group of destroyed mud huts. They look like archaeological ruins of a Stone Age dwelling. Only one wall remains standing, and its windows look out to the north. Whether it was us, the Taliban, the Russians, or time that destroyed these buildings I will never know. They imbue the landscape with an even eerier quality. We walk up the hill and soon find ourselves crossing a road and jumping a wall into a grape field.

Weariness begins to encroach. I have all but given up taking a knee. Our stops become longer as those in front of us try to find the safest possible route. This is IED territory, and we know it. Almost all of our casualties have been taken in a three-kilometre radius of where we are standing right now. Every step is becoming a chore, but the priority is to watch where I'm going and step only where someone else has. The days of marked minefields and probing the earth slowly with bayonets are over; we have no choice but to walk through an area that we know to be mined.

Walking in a grape field in France is an enjoyable way to spend a warm summer afternoon. It evokes romantic images of pressed linen shirts and new love. Walking through a grape field in Afghanistan is a somewhat different experience. The grapes are planted in mud furrows whose walls reach to about chest level (see photo on page 215). The rows are spaced evenly to accommodate the average Afghan man working in them. Canadian soldiers are, for the most part, wider than the average Afghan, especially when kitted out like storm troopers. The vines catch on our packs and make an exceptional amount of noise as we trudge and bounce our way through the narrow rows. Grape fields also make perfect Taliban fighting positions. The mud is thick enough to stop most bullets, and simply by ducking, an enemy fighter can escape through the length of the field, and out the other side unobserved.

The ground is wet with irrigation at this time of year, and my boots become very slippery when wet. I basically skate through the last 20 metres of the grape field before having to climb the wall on the other side. My boots refuse to give me traction as I attempt to jump onto the top of the 1.5-metre wall, and I have to use all my strength to pull myself on top of it. Now my kit and I, together weighing over 135 kilos, are balancing on the top of the wall that is only about 30 centimetres wide. I'm greeted by a nearly three-metre drop on the other side. I try to figure out a way to lower myself down the wall, but after much scuffling and swearing I finally just pass my weapon off to the person waiting below and jump, or rather fall like a sack of potatoes. The tactically quiet portion of the patrol appears to be over, and we sound like a herd of bulls tiptoeing through a china shop.

After an eternity we hear the welcome news over the radio: "29er, this is Zangabad, we have eyes on the lead elements of your patrol now, over." It's only a matter of time until we reach the COP. The last stretch is the most dangerous, as a number of IEDs have been found on all of the routes leading the rest of the way. We sit and wait. My eyes stay closed longer and longer as I blink, struggling to stay awake. Finally, I pinch myself, pull out my water, and pour some on my face. I'm down to the last bottle in my chest rig, and I can feel the volume of sweat pouring down my face increasing. A rivulet dodges my nose and enters my mouth. I lick my lips and taste my own salty sweat, flavoured with the dirt that cakes my face. It tastes warm and zesty. (Once, after I returned to Canada, I went for a long autumn run. When my sweat dripped into my mouth I gagged and had to stop.)

Another message comes in: "29er this is 21A. Um . . . That wadi appears to be impassable. It looks like we are going to have to pull back and try a different route, over."

Fuck sakes. I don't blame the guys leading our patrol, they have the hardest job today, and they are taking the biggest risks of any of us. I'm not angry so much as slightly defeated. We are told to pull off the track so that 4 Platoon can walk on a known safe route, and after about 15 minutes we see the lead elements of the patrol snaking back on us. They are followed by everybody behind them in a long line, so each of us is treated to the sight of every single person on patrol as they pass us or we pass them. I catch quick glimpses of 80-odd soldiers in various states of alertness, watchfulness, and unhappiness. Some have taken a knee and are watching our surroundings like hawks; others lie all the way back on their kit with a look of abject defeat. After we pull back onto the main route, we bash through a few more grape fields. Finally, we find a spot where the wadi is shallow enough to be crossed, and we make it to the other side. In a few minutes we see COP Zangabad on the horizon. It is about 0300 by this point and we have been patrolling for seven hours. The end of the first day is finally in sight.

We walk slowly the rest of the way into the COP. As we arrive, we cease to be an organized patrol and become a restive mob of soldiers, most of whom just want to sleep. Call sign 24 is currently in charge of Zangabad, and they have set up piecemeal "tents"— shelters ramshackled together from cam poles and groundsheets (thin plastic tarps)—but these are little more than shelters from the blazing Afghan sun. They have been set up outside of the COP itself, inside the razor wire. Although bigger than Haji, Zangabad cannot contain an extra 80 soldiers, and most will have to sleep outside the protection of the HESCO Bastions. I take off my helmet, gloves, and pack and sit down. I light a smoke and glory in not having to walk anymore. I don't know where I am supposed to sleep, so I leave the remainder of my kit on. As soon as the sergeant-major, who is behind us in the order of march, arrives he begins issuing orders. I haven't even finished my smoke when we are told to move inside Zangabad, where we will receive a briefing. I grumble about this unforeseen end to my comfort, and listen to others bitch in a similar vein. I carry my pack while we shuffle inside Zangabad, and my right arm is tired by the time we sit back down around the mortar pit inside the COP. Warrant Officer Davies waits for us all to sit down. He is a soft-spoken man with the traditional brown moustache of a lifer. He proceeds to outline the situation we find ourselves in.

"All right, boys, here's the deal. There isn't enough room for all of ya inside the COP, so you'll be sleeping outside under the groundsheets that we set up today. Water can be taken out of the big pile over there." He motions to a mountain of boxes, each of which contains 12 bottles of water. "Don't take our cold water, we don't have enough to go around." There is a massive freezer that long ago admitted defeat just outside the CP. It's filled with bottles of water, but none of them are cold. Some of them are cool, and cool is a precious resource.

"We've been getting mortared every day for the last two weeks, so there's a good chance that it's going to happen again tomorrow. You guys are going to need to dig trenches in the morning. Everyone can leave by platoon. Have a good sleep." As an afterthought he adds, "Oh, 29er Tac and the engineers, you guys can stay inside the camp, we've set up accommodations for you right over there." He motions to another set of groundsheets. Underneath them lie cots—sweet, blissful, beautiful cots that will keep us up off the sand for the night. The other soldiers, those that aren't in 29er Tac, instantly start bitching: "It fucking figures that those guys get to stay in the camp. Fucking brown-nosing 24."

People move to their assigned sleeping areas in an orderly fashion. I'm sitting far away from where we are sleeping, and by the time I get there, all the cots are taken. Oh well, at least I get to sleep inside the HESCO Bastions, which greatly reduces my risk of catching a mortar. I drop my pack and helmet on the sand, and stand up to take off my chest rig. Just two simple clicks and it comes off, falling into the sand beside my pack. Finally, I remove my body armour and feel the relief that only someone who instantly loses 15 kilos can know. My shirt is soaked in sweat and the breeze cools me down. It is the coldest point of the night and I begin to feel a chill. I take off my shirt and revel in lightness of body and soul.

My sleeping gear is attached to my pack by two Bungee cords, and I unclip them and put them in my pocket. I lay out my egg-cartonesque sleeping pad and put my ranger blanket on top of it. I smoke another cigarette and watch everyone else lie down. I double-check my kit in my brain, an important habit that I've picked up over the years. I have a checklist in my mind so that I don't lose anything important. Starting at the feet I run through it: boot bands, check; wallet, don't need it; Gerber multitool, check; rank and flag, check; gloves . . . gloves. *Fuck, I left my gloves outside.* I grab my weapon and wander outside with my headlamp on. I crawl over people who are already asleep and find the cam pole that I sat beside when we first arrived. People are still complaining about the unfairness of the sleeping arrangements.

"Fucking 29er Tac, I wish I was with those lazy fucks."

"Yeah, they never even patrol, man, and when they do they get all the Gucci gos."

I track down my gloves, put them in my pocket, and walk back into Zangabad. I sit back down in the sand and try to process what I've been through today. I feel immensely worn out, but not tired. A lot of emotions are swirling around inside me. Working with the infantry has, in many ways, reduced me to an almost monosyllabic existence. I've hardly said a word since the patrol began. I feel the need to express myself on another, less pragmatic plane. I pull out my journal and, illuminated by the red glow of my headlamp, I write the following lines:

> *Walking the moonlight surface of the moon.*
> *Dust turned to mud,*
> *Turned to walls turned to falls.*
>
> *Shoulder to aching shoulder, side by side;*
> *We walk and sweat and hate and hurt.*
>
> *Pawing for that last bottle of unpretentious water.*
> *And the sweet release of technological awareness.*
>
> *We find only green relief, blurry and unsubstantial;*
> *Ghostly light illuminating ghostly life.*
> *Revealing endless moonscape piled high,*
> *Grapes, opium, hash and surprising onions.*
> *Graves and grave walls of mud and garbage.*
>
> *Until the magic of razor wire on the horizon;*
> *Then sweet smoke and water and dirt.*
> *Turned from hateful pain to sweetest comfort.*
> *Ensconced in the ranger blanket release and numb.*

I turn off my headlamp and put it back into the arm pocket of my combat shirt. I then ball up my sweat-soaked shirt and put it at the top of my sleeping pad. I'm asleep before I even finish getting into my ranger blanket.

CHAPTER 3
COP ZANGABAD TO SP MUSHAN
15–16 JULY 2008

What none of the editorial writers ever mentioned was that the noble common man (the soldier) was obscene as an old goat, and his obscenity was what saved him. The sanity of said common democratic man was in his humor, his humor was in his obscenity. And his philosophy as well—a reductive philosophy which looked to restore the hard edge of proportion to the overblown values overhanging each small military existence.

—NORMAN MAILER, *The Armies of the Night*

I AM EJECTED FROM A PERFECT, BLISSFUL SLEEP on the sand by the sound of a distant explosion.

"Stand to!" I hear the sergeant-major yell. Are we under mortar attack? Somehow I thought that it would be more frightening.

I pull my glasses out of my boot and try to see what is going on. I'm greeted by a surprising silence. The peace that reigned during my sleep appears to have returned. *Stand to* is the military term for "wake the fuck up and man a defensive position." I'm amazed to see almost no movement, and for a few moments I think that I might be dreaming. People sit up and look around, and some of the call sign 24 guys poke their heads out of the command post.

"That was just some fucking IED maker blowing himself up. Go back to bed," someone from the CP says. The sergeant-major looks sheepish.

I guess that a distant explosion like that is a fairly common occurrence in the COPs, business as usual. Making IEDs is a very difficult and dangerous procedure. The result is that a great number of would-be jihadists blow themselves up. Unfortunately, this means that the ones who don't kill themselves are very good at what they do. That's the way evolution works.

The morning is still cool and comfortable. I lie back down and am instantly asleep once again. I'm sure that either the sun or enemy action will get me up when I need to be. Intellectually, I find the ease with which I go back to sleep surprising, but physically I'm exhausted. It's about 0700, and I'm perfectly happy to grab what sleep I can.

The sun wakes me up at about 1030. By this point it has been unbearably hot for about two hours. I wake up underneath my ranger blanket soaked in sweat. I'm dehydrated, and I have the dirty feeling in the back of my throat that I get when I don't brush my teeth. I come to slowly and, grudgingly and finally accepting defeat at the hands of the sun, throw my ranger blanket off and sit up. The explosion earlier this morning has taken on a completely impersonal quality, as if I had flipped the TV to some interesting channel, watched for a few seconds, and then shut the TV off.

I remain sitting for a minute or two; I don't quite feel up to facing the day. I look around, and most people are lounging in the shade, talking and relaxing. Almost nobody is wearing pants, as underwear is considerably more comfortable. I left Winnipeg in February when it was – 40° and by this point of the tour it is about 80 degrees hotter. Those who are wearing pants have them rolled up to the knee to fashion "combat shorts." The British are issued shorts and vests that you can soak in water and then freeze to wear under your flack vest. But we are told to cover every exposed piece of skin with kevlar, and are not allowed to roll up our sleeves. Open cases of water litter the shaded areas that have been set up for us. I get out of my sleeping bag, pull on the socks that I wore yesterday and my boots, and saunter over to one of these cases. Warm water flows into my mouth and I try to drink an entire bottle. We will be on the go again tonight, and I need to drink as much as I possibly can. I go back to my kit, pull out my cigarettes, and smoke one in the heat of the day. So far I haven't said a word to a soul, and I feel disconnected from my surroundings. I don't really have a spot to call my own. Zangabad is 24's territory, and there isn't very much room left in the shade. Finally, I pull my kit in between two cots and sit down. There is nothing to lean against except a wall of boxes containing water bottles, so I lean against them and finish my smoke. I pull out my toiletry kit and walk over to the Zangabad "bathroom," a black bag filled with water situated over a basin. Beside it is a table with soap and hand sanitizer, and a mirror hanging from the HESCO Bastion.

Once I finish brushing my teeth, I employ the "urinal," an empty bleach canister that has the top cut off, with a tube attached to it that runs outside the wire. I drink another bottle of water and walk back to our sleeping area. Here I find the topic of conversation has turned to my performance on the patrol yesterday.

"Flavelle, how many times did you fall last night?"

"I don't know, like three or four."

"It was more like fifteen," says Chris laughing.

My balance or lack there of, has become a subject of much hilarity for the rest of the section. I'm just lucky I haven't hurt myself like so many others have. Captain Jonathan Snyder died falling into a *kariz,* an open, unmarked well. I had seen dozens of kariz, and the thought of falling 20 metres into one is absolutely terrifying. Like so much else, however, I need to push that thought into the back of my mind. Mitigating risk is one thing, but if you allow yourself to become obsessed with the risks you are taking, you will become completely ineffectual. The best soldiers learn from the most dangerous aspects of the job, and learn to control their fear.

On an earlier patrol, we were following a tiny goat trail framed by a tall mud wall and a wadi, which was about two metres below the trail. I forgot how bulky my bag was, and when I turned I felt the weight of my pack push me forward, off the ledge. I had once seen an old Afghan man poop into a wadi, and now I was soaked in the water of one. I gained both credibility and a reputation on that patrol when, after being pulled out, I said quietly, "I think I got a little in my mouth."

On that same patrol, my wet boots, which had taken on the properties of skates on a sheet of ice, deposited me into a flooded opium field. I felt one of the poppies break open as I fell like a sack of hammers. Luckily, I didn't feel any physiological response from this encounter with Afghan narcotics.

The discussion of my balance issues continues.

"Whatever, man, it was dark and my glasses had fogged up," I respond.

"My glasses fogged up," Smitty imitates with a sneer. "Flavelle, you are such a fucking nerd."

I am a nerd, and I'm proud of it. I like *Star Trek, Star Wars, Battlestar Galactica,* and the *Teenage Mutant Ninja Turtles.* One must summon the nerd muse (Donatello?) to become a great signals operator—our job is to talk to sick radios and we must speak their language. In Calgary I surround myself with nerds. Unfortunately, I am the only person in headquarters to feel this way. If the army were your high school, the infantry would be the jocks; signallers would be the AV club.

I get up and walk over to the Zangabad rest and relaxation area. Handmade wooden benches surround a large wooden spool, pressed into service as a table. It is covered in magazines, water bottles, rations, and cigarettes; above is camouflage netting that protects against the sun. My friend Kevin Lowe is sitting at the table eating a ration. I pull one out of the box and join him.

Kevin and I have been friends since I first started training with the PPCLI. He is a short, blond private with tattoos of a poppy under his ear and his wife's initials on his hand. We became smoking buddies in Shilo, and my fellow signaller and I would help him steal food from the mess by giving him our meal cards (reservists are given free food, whereas the regular force has to pay for it). The rest of headquarters shuns him for his eccentricities, but I feel he is a kindred spirit. Once we got to Afghanistan, we spent a lot of time together at the gym, and our blocks of leave coincided. He was transferred to 24 after one of their soldiers was wounded. He is sitting at one of the wooden tables, making fun of a guy with a hairy back, who taunts in return, "Hey, Lowe, you look like a fag."

"Shut your face, Ewok."

I smile as I sit down beside him, and open my ration; clam chowder. This is the first time I've tried one of the new '08 rations, and I'm happily surprised. The best part is the carrot muffin shaped like a chocolate bar.

A lot of people swear by the American MREs (meals ready to eat), but I still like the Canadian IMPs (individual meal packets). I think it's because I haven't been force-fed rations for months on end, like all of the reg force. There is a fundamental difference in the diets of Canadians and Americans, and I like to think that fast food hasn't completely taken over our society. American rations contain such delights as ribwiches and hamburgers. Each ration comes with a tiny bottle of Tabasco sauce, and some come with an immensely fatty package of spicy jalapeno and cheese spread. I find the American rations give me heartburn. I prefer the simple, almost dehydrated bread and peanut butter of the Canadian rations. That being said, after any more than three days on any rations, I begin to think wistfully about real food.

Kevin and I smoke and eat our IMPs. The scene reminds me of an army version of a Quentin Tarantino diner, where people sit and smoke in between bites while calmly discussing the best way to kill people. We talk about patrolling, firefights, and what it has been like in the COP. I find out that Kev was on the patrol when Private Wilmot was killed. I ask him about what it's like to be in a large-scale firefight. We talk about Sperwan Ghar, the delicious yogurt that we are missing, his wife and kid, and my girlfriend. I try one of his Chinese Lucky88s cigarettes. It tastes disgusting, but I power through it. Kevin suggests a game of chess, so we break out a small travel board and set it up. We played often when Kevin was in Sperwan Ghar, and I have to grudgingly admit that he is a better player. He plays an intensely conservative game and waits for me to inevitably make a mistake. The only way that I can win is by playing a game of attrition, getting rid of as many pieces as I can, and by an uncommon stroke of brilliance finishing on top. We play about 15 games and I win only one. While we play, we talk in an unspecific way about getting mortared and shooting at people.

"You guys have been taking a lot of fire lately, hey?"

"Yeah, you know it's fucking loud," he says.

"Yeah." But I don't know.

"I was in the tower and we were getting lit up, and some beeb stood up with an AK. I shot him three times."

"Sweet." I can't think of anything else to say.

"Yeah. I didn't feel a thing." Kevin moves his knight into an attack position, and I miss the piece covering it on my counterattack. My queen is lost. Now it's only a matter of time.

In most movies I've seen about the wars in Afghanistan and Iraq, *hajji* is used as a derogatory slur for the locals. In Islamic countries, *hajji* is an honorific granted to those who have made the journey to

Mecca to partake in the hajj. I don't know how it came to be used in the same way as *gook* was after Korea. I also don't know why we choose to use the term *beeb* in the same way. We never refer to the locals as *hajji* (unless we happen to be talking about someone who is actually named Hajji); instead, we call them beebs, which perhaps stems from a shortened form of Habib, a common Arab name. I don't think anybody knows for sure.

Two years after the events in this book, I was riding my bike in Calgary. I was crossing the street to the grocery store on a green light, and a young woman with her hair covered, who was talking on her cell phone and driving an SUV, very nearly ran me over as she turned right into the intersection. I whacked her car with my palm and when I saw that she was on a cellphone, yelled, "You fucking beeb!"

That was the first time I'd called someone a beeb since I returned from Afghanistan, and I was surprised that my reaction had led to voicing a racist epithet. She did almost kill me, but I should have been mad that she was talking on her cellphone and not paying attention to the road; instead, I focused on her racial background. A latent, seldom expressed, smouldering racism that grew within me as the tour progressed is still a part of who I am, which is a difficult thing for me to come to grips with.

I try to get a grip on my frustration over losing yet another game of chess. If you show weakness around the infantry, you will hear about it. I refuse to accept defeat, and keep playing game after game while we split a pack of Lucky88s. Kevin steals me a package of Crystal Light and we drink water and play chess for about two hours. Eventually another friend, Private Nick Turner, comes up and engages us in conversation as we play.

Nick is a thin infanteer covered in tattoos, who exudes fitness, and is the only private I've ever met who's done not only a jump course (parachute) but also a sniper course. Both are immensely difficult to get on, and immensely difficult to pass. Nick is 24's platoon signaller, so we have worked together closely throughout the deployment. A heavy smoker whose disenchantment with military life in general is palpable, he badly wants to get out and become a police officer when he gets back to Edmonton. He embodies the violent professionalism that I've come to associate with the infantry.

Within each platoon, one infanteer is assigned the role of signaller, responsible for all the radios within the platoon. He or she usually carries the heavy radio on patrol, unless the platoon commander wants to do it himself. Platoon signaller is the most dreaded job in any infantry platoon, because it means long hours of fixing temperamental radios, instead of playing with weapons and kit or relaxing. As the company signaller, I work directly with platoon signallers, instructing them how to account for all their radio stores, and teaching them the tricks of the trade. By the end of our tour, I would confidently put any of the platoon signallers at the same level with any soldier in my unit. Although they learn the signaller's skill set grudgingly, the fact of the matter is that the army needs to communicate with itself. It just takes some longer than others to accept this reality and learn the basics of how to fix a radio.

My king falls again, and Kevin has to go on tower shift. He shows me his new living space, a cot on top of plywood in a room framed by HESCO Bastions, boxes of water and tarps. It lacks air conditioning. The air is stifling, and the smell of human bodies in tight proximity closes in on me. On the cots, soldiers are lying down, willing sleep to come. Some listen to iPods, some play video games on portable screens. Kevin's space consists of a cot, with his rucksack slowly exploding out into the environs. Packages of M&Ms and empty water bottles litter the area under his cot, and pieces of kit hang off the walls. A crate serves as an end table, and power cords zigzag at random over the plywood floor. Kevin pulls on a pair of pants (a formality necessitated by the unaccustomed presence of a sergeant-major in Zangabad), his body armour and his helmet. He leaves to watch for Taliban on one of the guard towers.

I go back to my patch of shade, lie down, and try to nap. It's about 1400 and the heat is almost unbearable. My radio needs maintenance, so I change the batteries, double-check the frequencies, and conduct a radio check. The day has been very quiet, and none of us really knows why. I head over to the CP to see if they are having any radio problems I can help with. Luckily, Nick keeps everything in good order; there isn't much to do. I double-check a few cables and make sure the antennas are seated properly. Their satellite Internet terminal, used solely for morale purposes, hasn't worked in almost a month. I climb up onto the HESCO Bastion, clean the dust off the radiating element, and recheck the signal strength. I can't find any problems. I go back inside the CP, and check the connections. I reboot the computer and try again: success. I tell the duty operator that he now has working civilian Internet and I see joy in his eyes.

I don't know what I did to fix the problem, but throughout the tour technology has just succumbed to my will. It's a good feeling. I've spent about an hour screwing around, and I go back to my sleeping pad and try again to take a nap. Mostly I smoke, think, and listen to the conversation ebb and flow around me. People are discussing the merits of various motorcycles, the tricks they've pulled on dirt bikes, and the parties they've had back in Canada. I don't really have much to add, so I lie down and nap intermittently.

We all try to sleep as much as we can, because sleep is nature's fast-forward button. By the end of the tour, some of us sleep for up to 12 hours a day if there's no patrolling, effectively cutting in half the time that we have to remain in theatre. On patrol, we don't expect any more than three hours a night, often less. Sleep becomes a commodity, much like food and water. Once I trained myself to stay awake under any circumstances, I found that I craved sleep more wistfully than I craved anything else.

Last light. I wake up in the fading orange twilight of the day. We will be stepping off soon. I feel exhausted and almost sick. My nap did little more than speed me to this point. I repack my kit and double-check it. I sit on the sandbags that encircle the mortar pit, pull out a package of nuts, and eat a few. There is still time to get in one more bottle of piss-warm water, so I smoke and drink and think about the patrol.

As I wait to step off, I pull up my soiled knee pad. It rests over my right knee, and has to be adjusted as I walk. I wear only one to remind myself to take up a proper firing position with my right knee down, so that I can rest my elbow on my left knee. The pad was sent to me from home by my reserve unit, along with a few porn mags, a copy of Charles Dickens's *Great Expectations,* and a signed unit photo. The porn mags were in an envelope marked "tax info," and for a few seconds I thought it actually did contain paperwork. I recognized hardly anyone in the unit photo, and for the first time I felt like an old guy.

My shoulders ache as I put my pack on. I sit again and wait for the patrol to step off. There is a bet on how many times I'm going to fall tonight, and Chris asks me what I think. "Not once, man, no more falls from here all the way back to Sper."

Tonight is darker than yesterday. We start moving. As we clear the outer cordon, I stop to make sure that the man behind me is moving. When I turn back I trip on the coils of razor wire that are spread out in front of the entrance to the COP. I fall on my face, and my pants get tangled in the razor wire. I can hear stifled laughter as about 10 hands help me up and brush me off. So much for "all the way back to Sper." I begin to feel increasingly disenchanted with this patrol. The beginning of this leg is the most dangerous, and we dodge the routes we believe to be IEDed by jumping walls and bashing through grape fields. I'm sweating heavily before 20 minutes are up. I can't see the ground in front of me and am walking primarily by feel. The ground is covered in roots and similar impediments, and I silently curse the dark, the country, my eyesight, the infantry, and the situation in general. My whole body begins to ache under the strain of my pack, and my legs feel tired.

When I stepped off on this patrol, I was in the greatest shape of my life, but constant patrolling puts an incredible strain on even the fittest bodies. I had been working out at least once and usually twice a day. (Army workout routines are usually tailored to increasing combat ability, as opposed to bulking up, although I have witnessed exceptions to this rule.) After I finished my shift I would run around the hill of Sperwan Ghar, at first just in shorts, but working up to running with all of my body armour and fighting kit on. Eventually I could run up and down the kilometre of incline to the observation point at the top of the hill with all of my heavy kit strapped to my body, including a radio. Now, after a mere 24 hours of patrolling, my body is in pain.

Not even the fittest soldier in the world would say that patrolling in Afghanistan is easy, and some of the older, seasoned combat vets eat anti-inflammatories like candy. The strain of walking, running and fighting under the press of kit is exceptionally demanding. Most fighting troops lose considerable weight overseas (I lost over 15 kilos). Although some are better at patrolling than others, we all feel the strain. The trick is not to let anyone see how much it hurts. To be ostracized from the group is the secret fear of all combat soldiers. In the end, all you can truly rely on is the group, and you can't allow others to see you as weak. If they do, there are thousands of overt and covert means they will use to shun you, removing your only support structure. So we grit our teeth against the pain and pretend that it doesn't hurt. This is how we all keep putting one foot in front of the other.

We reach a shallow wadi separating two grape fields, and have to jump. I watch those in front of me, and listen to the *crump* as they hit the ground on the other side. Some make their footing, some don't. I can't see the ground on the other side, no matter how closely I look. I pull down my NVG and scan the ground. This doesn't help, as I can't distinguish what green line and what black line constitutes the ground. I push my NVG back up, and realize that I just lost a good part of my night vision. Now the wadi looks like a black maw waiting to swallow me whole. I take a few steps back and attempt a running jump into the darkness. Both feet miss the landing, and I slam my face into the hardened mud on the other side. An explosion of stars flash in front of my eyes; a lot of weight just carried my face into the ground. The mud has been compressed by Afghan farmers over the centuries and it feels like concrete. My nose begins to bleed. Luckily, instead of being sucked into the innards of the earth, I find myself standing about shin level in water. It would have been easier to just step down and walk through the wadi.

I pull my weight awkwardly up to the other side. The OC has continued walking, and I don't know what direction he went in. My glasses have almost completely fogged over, and they are now covered in dirt. I take them off and try to find a clean piece of shirt to wipe them on. I flip my NVG down, but I don't see any of the IR (infrared) lights on the helmets of those in front of me. Panic begins to set in. I know that I will find the remainder of the patrol, but I'm afraid of what will be said if I have to come on the radio. "29er, this is 29er pronto. I need you to stop as I have lost eyes-on, over." I'd never hear the end of it. Captain Michelson, the artillery forward observation officer (FOO) comes up behind me, and points me in the right direction. He looks at me and sees the state that I'm in.

"You all right, Flavelle?"

"I'm just great, sir, thanks for the help."

Part of me wants to sit on the ground and cry; most of me is determined never to give up. I stand up and ignore the pain, and push as hard as I can to catch up to the patrol. As I walk I clean my glasses on a sock that I brought specifically for this purpose. When I put them back on I feel better. By the time we sit down I am happy and confident. Strength can well out of one's soul just as easily as pain and sorrow.

The motto of my reserve unit, 746 Communication Squadron, is "Determined." The greatest compliment I received from the infantry was from my friend Master Corporal Lizette LeBlanc: "Flavelle, you might not be good at everything, but you never give up." Liz knows a few things about determination; she is the first-ever female regular force infantry master corporal in the history of the CF (after the tour she was promoted to sergeant). She is an Olympic-level athlete, and has taken part in some of the worst fighting on Task Force 1–06. She earned the respect of the soldiers around her, and I am happy to know her. When she called me *determined*, it made me feel like I was. The army experience is made up of many encounters that destroy your morale, and a few that lift it. Good soldiers need to understand and acknowledge their mistakes and capitalize on their strengths.

We walk along a stretch of road framed on either side by walnut trees. We have entered an unnamed village, and the walking is much easier now. I feel calm, confident, and strong. The basics of patrolling are returning to my actions: keep your spacing, cover doors, take a knee. I walk along a flat road with my head upright despite the pain—and fall on my face. I had completely missed seeing an old crater in the middle of the road. This crater was probably caused by an IED, and I feel a chill down my spine.

Fuck this, I think, and take off my double-layered ballistic eyewear, replacing them with my regular, reliable glasses. Instantly the night seems to grow brighter and clearer. I can see the world around me once again. The only problem is that if an explosion occurs, my eyes will have no protection. I force that concern out of my mind, I have to be able to see where I am going.

We have exited the village into dried-out opium fields that stretch out flat as far as the eye can see. A faint sliver of moonlight has emerged from the earth's shadow, and the grey dust looks white in this faint glow. A long orderly row of soldiers stretches out along the ground in front of me and behind me. I can see the silhouette of each man rising above the dust, walking with upheld head and pride despite the exhaustion and pain. The soldiers in front of me walk erect, scanning as they go and exuding confidence and professionalism. In my experience, that look is unique to the infantry; it is the look of someone who is doing a difficult job and doing it well. Strong legs protrude out of masses of kit as we walk across the field, and I feel as if the shades of Canadian soldiers from battlefields past are walking with us, and are embodied in us. For the first time, I feel part of the long, proud Canadian military tradition that is so often forgotten, misunderstood, or just marginalized.

Soon enough this strange and peaceful interlude is completed, and we breach once more into a pungent marijuana field. We walk through the tall plants, and I think about how easy it would be to take some. On the other hand, what the fuck do I want Afghan weed for? I have developed sufficient distrust for this country to dissuade me from any desire to consume their crops. Moreover, how would I even smoke it? I don't know of any instance of a soldier smoking weed in Afghanistan (we weren't even allowed to smoke cigarettes in front of the locals). I can't say definitively that it didn't happen, but I can say that I saw absolutely no evidence of it. I did, however, once see a terp get blazed while we were on patrol.

We were sitting beside our LAV in Mushan at the time, preparing to start the move back to Sperwan Ghar. It was the first day of Ramadan, the Muslim holy month, when believers fast from sun-up to sundown, abstaining from food, drink, and smokes. The sun had just finished coming up, and I was drinking water and stowing kit. My nostrils perceived the telltale aroma of Afghan weed that brought back memories of my downstairs roommates at university.

"What the fuck, Lucky? You can't smoke, it's Ramadan."

"It's okay to smoke; if I see God I say, 'I smoke' and he say, 'It's okay.'"

Whatever, I thought. Soon enough we were mounted up and I was standing in the air sentry hatch, with Chris behind me. After about three hours of scanning the Afghan landscape, I popped my head down to grab a bottle of water. Passed out on the bench seat was Lucky, the terp. Beside him was a pile of empty bags that used to contain all of our cookies and chips. He was snoring with a pile of crumbs on his chest.

Before deploying, I'd heard of the drug fields of Afghanistan. We were told that the major crops of the country were opium, marijuana, and grapes (in that order). In my mind, I imagined that I would come across a few opium fields every now and again. In reality, the drug fields are everywhere. *Ubiquitous* is almost too weak an adjective to describe them. South of the Arghandab River, it's almost impossible to walk 100 metres in any direction without hitting an opium or marijuana field. The marijuana reaches two metres tall, higher than the turret of a LAV, and grows like a weed: a few untended seeds blew into our camp and began to germinate (we destroyed them). My tour spanned the entire growing season. When we arrived, there was nothing but flat desolate mud fields.

About a month into the tour, green shoots were evident throughout these fields. By two months, brilliant pink, white, and red poppies had disseminated colour onto the landscape. By the time I returned from leave, these flowers had turned into opium-filled bulbs; a month later, these heavy bulbs were bowing their heads. There cannot be a more apt symbol for the Canadian commitment to Afghanistan than these poppies: they morphed from our national symbol of remembrance into a cruel, mind-altering, life-destroying narcotic that funds our enemies and damages our society. All my clever ideas about how to deal with drug cultivation in Afghanistan (we should buy their crops and turn them into painkillers; we should just pay the farmers and burn the crops, etc.) paled in comparison to the pure volume of narcotics that we encountered.

We continue our forward motion toward Talukan. The ground begins to break up as we walk through fields that seem to have fallen into disuse. We reach a wadi that is particularly hard to cross. The packed mud on either side makes it very easy to trip. I slow down and walk carefully to the edge of the wadi. I've learned from my experiences earlier in the evening, and I cautiously take a step down before jumping to the other side. Success. I turn around to make sure that Captain Michelson makes it over safely. He is a middle-aged officer who exudes quiet professionalism and is a testament to his generation. I'm amazed that he has kept up as well as he has. He falls heavily, trips, and badly rolls his ankle. I rush back to help him up. He stands up awkwardly and limps through the next few steps. I ask him if he needs a doc, but he says that he can make it. He's a tough old guy.

We carry on with the patrol, and soon breach back into the riverbed. The patrol stops, as it so often does, and I take the opportunity to sit and relax. I hear over the radio that one of the engineers has been injured; apparently he has rolled his ankle. I feel nothing but scorn for this unknown engineer. We all have to wait for the doc to patch him up and he will slow down the patrol until we reach Talukan, which is still over a kilometre and a half away. We wait. After about 20 minutes I see our doc, Master Corporal Jonathan Mertens, walking with a pack on his front and a pack on his back. Behind him shuffles the injured engineer, in obvious pain. I take a closer look and realize that it's Allan, my fellow signaller and close friend. He looks pale white in the moonlight, and I feel bad for my earlier derision. Allan must have hurt himself pretty badly to need medical attention. We continue toward Talukan at a slower pace. It is midnight, and we have been on the go for about six hours. As we breach out of the riverbed, I hear the roar of a motorcycle coming up behind us. A lone fighting-age male (FAM) is crossing the riverbed from the south to the north. We stop and search him, but don't find anything. It's pretty obvious that he is a Taliban informer. Why else would he be crossing the riverbed toward a Taliban-controlled village in the middle of the night? His answers follow the familiar pattern of every Afghan we question:

"Where are you going?"

"To my cousin's."

"Why?"

"To help him farm."

"Have you seen any fighters in the area?"

"No."

"Have you been in the area for long?"

"About a month."

"What about the firefight last week? Did you see that?"

"Oh, yes, some guy from Pakistan came and then he left."

Some guy from Pakistan, that's all we ever hear about. If I had a dollar for every time I heard about some guy from Pakistan who appeared out of thin air, only to disappear as soon as he attacked us, I'd come home a considerably richer man.

We know he's Taliban, he knows that we know he's Taliban, and there is absolutely nothing we can do. He isn't wearing a uniform or carrying any weapons, so there is no way that we can plausibly detain him.

We are soon in sight of COP Talukan. It's always a great feeling to be in sight of the COP because you think that if they can see you, then they can see anything that might threaten you. This logic is erroneous, but it's still nice to feel safe after a mentally exhausting period of waiting for the world to explode around and under you.

Our progress is greatly slowed by our injured, and we don't arrive at the COP until well after midnight. I sit down beside Captain Michelson and ask how he's doing.

"Oh, fine, just fine," he says through gritted teeth.

"Sir, you had better take some painkillers, we've still got a long way to go."

"No, no, I've never felt better."

I know what its like to lie about how much pain you're in, and I drop my pack and go find the doc inside Talukan. I ask him to take a look at the FOO and see if he can make it. I then sit down and ask Allan how he's doing. He is lying with his boot off in obvious pain. His ankle is noticeably swollen.

"It's not broken," he smiles. "I'll be good to go by the time you guys get back." I hope he will be. I ask him how it happened, and he tells me that he'd tripped while crossing one of the innumerable wadis between Zangabad and Talukan.

"When I landed I felt a *pop* and, oh man, you should have heard me swear. 'Jesus H. fucking faggot Christ!' is what I said. I terrified a terp with blasphemy he didn't understand about a religion he doesn't believe in. He thought I must have hit an IED."

Allan laughs. I'm glad he still retains his sense of humour.

Obscenity and the military fit together perfectly. I have met a lot of combat NCMs who don't smoke, and even some who don't drink, but finding someone who doesn't swear is a bit of a challenge. Obscenity is a tool harnessed by the lowest ranks of the military. When a group of soldiers sits together and tells stories there are no words that are off limits. Outsiders are forced either to accept what is being said or disengage from the group. Thus vulgarity has the power to strengthen the bonds within a group and, at the same time, exclude outsiders. Once you have decided to engage at this lowest possible linguistic level, you are forced to accept many other norms inherent to the group. War is not, after all, an environment known for its refinement.

There is a certain joy in abandoning all restraint on language. Being in a group where you are free to use the worst swearing in the English language, swearing that I hesitate even to type, has a powerful attraction. In an environment where we are greatly limited in the choices that we can make, having the ability to laugh at language that would make our mothers reach for a bar of soap gives us back some of our freedom.

WO Abrahams, the 6 Platoon warrant officer, sees me and gives me a bottle of cool water. We smoke together while we wait for the OC to finish talking to the platoon commander. We talk amicably about life in Talukan, rumours that it will be torn down, and some of the firefights 6 Platoon has been in. The cool water is blissful, as Talukan has the only working refrigerator between Sperwan Ghar and the province of Helmand. I try to savour every drop, but before I can finish we are moving back outside. I throw my pack on again and sit. The doc has just finished working on Captain Michelson, and he gives him some painkillers to get him the rest of the way to Mushan. It is 0100 and we are once again on the move.

We walk down a broad, straight road that leads due west from the COP. The west tower has good visibility on this road, so we confidently walk down the middle of it. It feels good to dominate a road free from the fear of IEDs for a change. We make excellent time, and push south into the unclaimed desert below us. Nomadic herders inhabit the area. They are called Kuchis, and they set up semi-permanent camps, staying for a few months before moving on.

When we first arrived in-country, a group of soldiers who had been in Talukan for two months preceding our arrival had to walk back to Sperwan Ghar, because the helicopter they were relying on had failed to show up. They went on a patrol to buy camels from the Kuchis, but arrived during the animals' mating season and had no luck. Instead, they bought donkeys from the local market, strapped their kit to the sides of these beasts, and led them the 10 kilometres back to Sperwan Ghar. I have a picture of a group of smiling Canadian infanteers standing in front of a donkey with three barrack boxes strapped to its side—just when you might think our modern technological army had made beasts of burden obsolete. On the other hand, maybe our modern technological army has simply replaced beasts of burden with us, its soldiers.

As we patrol through the desert slowly, not a living soul can be seen. We are making extremely good time, the moon is brightening, and the evening is growing colder. We stop every few hundred metres, and I think of the beauty of this moonlit landscape. It feels devoid of human presence, completely surreal. Everything around us is silent, and the long file of soldiers in front of and behind me doesn't make a sound. Now that my eyes have become fully adjusted to the dim light, the landscape appears as a long line of blue-grey sand joined to a mass of blue-grey buildings that seem just out of reach. My radio continues to beep, and I continue to watch where I step. The sweat drips down from underneath my body armour and I feel cool and wet. My head feels itchy; the sweat-soaked pads lining my helmet have been rubbing my forehead for over six hours. My shoulders still ache, but more and more I'm beginning to push that discomfort out of my mind. I scan the area and keep my head up; I avoid falling, and strength wells up inside me. I think that only those who have suffered and succeeded as we have can know this feeling of strength.

Technology provides a calm, pervasive din that breaks the spell of silence around me; I can hear the beep of my radio as messages are transferred, the squawk of our interpreter's radio that he uses to scan for Taliban messages, and the squeak of my kit as I shift my weight.

We reach a grape field about 600 metres short of Strongpoint (SP) Mushan. It is about 0300, and I look forward to a restful sleep inside its walls. I hear the OC try to raise them on the radio: "Mushan, this is 29er. Do you have eyes on? We are approaching your location from the SE, over." No response. "Mushan, Mushan, this is 29er, 29er, radio check, radio check, over." I close the distance between me and the OC and pass him my handset. He speaks into my more powerful radio and tries again. Frustration begins to enter his voice.

"Mushan, Mushan, this is 29er, 29er, radio check, radio check, over."

I extend my antenna, and try it myself, all to no avail. We call Zangabad and see if they have communications with Mushan: "Zangabad, this is 29er, do you have comms with Mushan?"

"Zangabad, wait. Mushan, this is Zangabad, radio check over ... Zangabad nothing heard, out. 29er, this is Zangabad, I do not have comms with Mushan."

"Sir, if we can reach Zangabad we should be able to reach Mushan. Either their radio is busted or someone is asleep," I say. I switch frequencies and try again. I pull out every trick in the book, but I cannot reach them. From our location, we can see the ANA strongpoint, a dark shape in the distance. It feels strange that we can see it, but not talk to it. I begin to imagine that the SP has been taken over by the Taliban, and that we are walking into a trap. This is utterly ridiculous, and I force my overactive imagination to stop.

The OC calls in the Operational Mentor and Liaison Team (OMLT, pronounced "omelette") commander, and the 4 Platoon commander. He sits down and explains the situation. He asks the OMLT officer if he can send a group of ANA soldiers forward to walk into the camp. He in turn asks his ANA commander if he would be willing to do this. The ANA commander responds that he is afraid that if they walk up to the ANA-manned tower in Mushan unannounced, they will be shot at by their own men. The ANA are notoriously trigger-happy, and no one wants to take that chance. We decide to fire a para-flare, a portable flare that descends slowly on a parachute, to see if that will wake up the guy on shift. No dice. We call Sperwan Ghar and ask them to fire a 155mm illumination round from one of the M777 artillery pieces stationed there. The fire mission is approved and within a few minutes we hear the uncanny sound of an artillery shell flying over our heads. *Whiz, pop, boom!* The area is lit up like daylight—surely that will wake someone up. We try Mushan on the radio again, nothing. This is a ridiculous situation; an entire patrol of over 80 men is sidelined by someone asleep on shift 600 metres away.

It is 0330, and we are all getting tired. The OC decides that if we can't get into Mushan, we will stay in the grape field in front of it. We will push out security and wait for dawn, before moving the rest of the way into the SP. We are rearranged into platoons and begin to filter into the thin rows of the grape fields. I can't help but think about the snakes and spiders that must live here, and the fact that I won't be able to see them at night. This is another mostly irrational concern that must be pushed out of my head. For the first time tonight, I feel genuinely unsafe and uncomfortable.

Setting up security takes another half-hour, and by 0400 we are ready to "go to ground," such as it is. I don't even take my pack off; I just sit in the lush field and wait for our orders to be confirmed. No one is happy with the situation, and I've been in the military long enough to know not to get comfortable until you are sure that you can. I think about smoking a cigarette, but decide against it. It feels like every cell in my body is screaming for tobacco, but there is too much bad energy around me to risk it. Out of nowhere, I hear on my radio, "29er, this is Mushan, radio check, over." The voice sounds bleary, like when you wake someone up with the phone.

We swallow our pride and anger, and move out of the grape field. We walk the remaining 600 metres down a long, broad stretch of road. I'm soaked with sweat and exhausted. We walk slowly, and I have to force myself not to cradle my weapon against my chest.

It is more comfortable to carry the C7 by crossing your arms over it, but this is frowned upon, as you wouldn't be able to use it instantly if needed. One of the unspoken rules of the infantry is that, on patrol, you must be prepared to fight with only a moment's notice. Although this may not be, strictly speaking, completely necessary, those who are not ready to fight are ridiculed behind their backs. In the end it's all about the LCF ("look cool factor"). The correct way to carry one's weapon is with the pistol grip grasped by the bottom three fingers and the front hand guards or fighting grip held by the other hand. I find that my right wrist begins to ache after long periods of holding my weapon this way, but there is only one way to get better at doing something. By this point of the tour carrying a weapon has become completely unconscious, and I usually carry it as prescribed, or with the right hand alone on the pistol grip, or by holding it at its centre of gravity, which is just in front of the magazine housing. I can also let go of my weapon and it will hang off my sling beside me.

We are in Mushan by 0430, and I am sitting at the entrance with my helmet off, smoking a cigarette. I feel exhausted and angry. It's as if the strength and pride that I'd gained on the patrol was stolen from me in that grape field, and for the first time I wish that I had never come on this patrol. I drink another bottle of water and try not to feel sorry for myself. The sergeant-major returns from his coordination meeting and takes the warrant officers with him. Soon enough we are moving to our assigned sleeping areas.

Mushan smells smoky. It has been mortared on and off for the last month. One of these mortars caused a fire that very nearly burned the camp down. Six ANA soldiers were killed in that attack. The ground is covered in black char, and there are considerably fewer tents than there were the last time I was here. We are given one of the few remaining modular tents set up prior to our arrival. The tent encloses the spot where the mortar that started the fire landed, a large crater surrounded by blackened earth. We are told that we are to sleep right on top of the crater. We find a few large pieces of plywood to place over top and lay out our bedding. I feel strangely safer sleeping here, the idea being that mortars are like lightning: they never land in the same place twice. I doubt that this is accurate, but I've found that my mind will make whatever logical leaps are necessary for me to feel safe. It's as if I refuse to accept the reality of being in a dangerous situation.

So far on the tour, I've been remarkably lucky. The only dangerous situations that I've been in were a relatively minor firefight and an IED exploding 20 metres in front of me. Most of the company hasn't been as lucky, and we've already lost four soldiers and incurred a number of wounded. Photos of Sergeant Jason Boyes, Private Terry Street, Captain Richard Leary, and Private Colin Wilmot hang outside our CP in Sperwan Ghar, and I see them every day before I go on shift. We all carry those faces with us on patrol, and we try to make sure that their sacrifice was not made in vain.

The sky is beginning to turn blue as the sun prepares for its appearance. I am exhausted, and I take off my kit and get into my ranger blanket. My mind is still very active, and I have a hard time getting to sleep. One of the ANA soldiers at the guard tower greets the sun with his morning call to prayer; the foreign language sounds like it is being shouted in my ear.

"We get it! Allah is fucking Akbar! Shut the fuck up!" I yell. I hear a few chuckles as the soldier finishes his morning ritual. I lie back down and fall asleep.

CHAPTER 4
SP MUSHAN
16 JULY 2008

There ain't no such thing as a free lunch.
—Robert A. Heinlein, *The Moon Is a Harsh Mistress*

ALL OF THE FOOD THAT THE ARMY PROVIDES IS FREE, and it is pretty good. Since I joined in 2001, there has been a recognizable effort to improve the quality of rations and messes (*mess* is the army word for "cafeteria," as well as "bar"). When Darcy visits me while I am taking an army course, I even feel comfortable taking her into the mess for a meal; most feel like upscale cafeterias. Regrettably, the improvements in the quality of food seem to coincide with the project to all but eliminate alcohol from official army life. In the 1980s and '90s, it was expected that flats of beer would be brought on every exercise, so that each soldier could enjoy two beers a day. Now, almost every exercise I've been on has been "officially" dry, and there are huge penalties levied against those bringing so much as a flask into the field.

For the most part I've always been impressed by army cooks (with the exception of a few bad apples). They have a difficult and often thankless job that has them waking up at 0430 and keeps them working until at least 1900. In the field, meals are provided on a rigid schedule that often halts training. Troops are served in order of rank, with the lowliest private eating first. This ritual was developed as an exercise in leadership, and to reinforce the idea that a leader must always take care of his or her soldiers first. Usually there is far more food than the troops can possibly consume, and often much of it is thrown out. Army feeding plans are based on the idea that a fighting soldier needs 1,200 calories per meal, but most soldiers aren't fighting or training to fight on a daily basis, even in the field. The result is usually far too many calories ingested compared with the amount of effort expended. For example, I spent almost every day of our exercise in Wainwright sitting in the back of a LAV, listening to radios. Although this isn't always an easy task, I wasn't burning many calories, and I actually gained weight. I've always thought that it was strange that a fighting formation would be so obsessed with food that scarcely a meal is missed. On patrol, we earn every calorie that we intake, and when it comes right down to it, we pay for our meals in sweat.

For the second time in two days, sleep fights a losing battle against the sun. For the second time in three days, I wake up itchy. I slept in the shade, splayed out on the blackened sand, and when I awake tiny black pieces of charred earth are intermingled with the bites of sandflies. I have had happier mornings.

Sandflies are a big problem in Afghanistan. Thankfully, they do not infest your clothing or stay on you for any period of time. If you allow any exposed skin to touch the sand, however, you quickly find out about it. The bites feel like tiny pinpricks, and it seems like there are millions of them. These flies also carry a disease called *leishmaniasis,* which causes sores to break out all over your body and can be deadly. A friend of mine was infected by sandflies, and the symptoms didn't present themselves until after he returned to Canada. It took the docs some time to figure out what was wrong with him, and the Canadian Forces finally had to fly in medicine from Germany.

I was exhausted last night and basically collapsed into sleep; the result is that my arms and face are covered in tiny red spots. The pests don't attack anything that isn't touching the sand, and when I hide inside my ranger blanket I usually wake up bite-free. But when I sleep, I like to take up the maximum possible amount of room (much to my girlfriend's chagrin), so I often sprawl outside my blanket.

Even thinking about sleeping in the desert of Afghanistan still makes my skin crawl.

My spot is at the front corner of the mod tent, half on and half off a piece of plywood. A box of rations sits open beside me, so I help myself. Baked beans will be my breakfast. It is 1130, and I yawn in spite of the heat. I finish my ration and go and smoke by the medical station, which is kitty-corner to our tent. I drink a bottle of extremely hot water, which tastes of plastic. I smoke slowly, and try to strike up a conversation with the medic, who is hanging out nearby. I know that he's had a rough go of it, and he answers all my questions in a brusque manner, as if he wonders who the fuck I am. I give up and smoke another cigarette in silence, but neither the tobacco nor the water holds any joy. I feel hungover and hot.

My section is discussing the best way to cool down water in the heat. The most popular method involves soaking a sock, putting two water bottles into it, then hanging it up in the shade and letting the air cool the bottle as the moisture wicks out of the sock. It brings the water temperature down a few degrees and makes our lives a little bit better.

I work on sorting out my kit, which I dropped haphazardly last night. I pile everything together at the top of my sleeping pad. I go through my basic radio maintenance and change out the batteries. I go over to the CP wearing a T-shirt, underwear, boots, and my weapon. I get new batteries and go back to my kit.

We carry lithium batteries overseas. These are a precious commodity in Canada, and I had never even seen them before my pre-deployment training. The ones that we are usually issued are nickel-cadmium, and they can be recharged. The white lithium batteries have a considerably longer life (up to 48 consecutive hours), but you cannot recharge them. If you put them in the issued battery charger, an obscenely bulky and heavy abomination that makes you wonder what decade you are living in, they will explode. I once believed this to be another army myth, but it is completely accurate. I watched the venting plug explode into noxious, and probably poisonous, fumes when somebody accidentally put one into the battery charger. The batteries each weigh about one kilo. This may not seem like much, but I carry four, on top of my 14-kilo radio. The weight adds up quickly.

No single army reality is absurd, but when taken together they become tantamount to insanity. We are going to patrol in Afghanistan—*makes sense*; you will be carrying the radio—*makes sense*; you will also be carrying your weapon and 10 magazines of ammunition—*makes sense*; you will wear body armour, a helmet, and a chest rig—*makes sense*. It will be above 50 degrees during the day—*hold on!*—and you will not be allowed to roll up your sleeves—*really?* If you take your helmet off during the patrol you will be jacked up—*well, that just seems unnecessary*. If you wear any non-approved patch you will be jacked up—*I don't really see a reason for that* . . . ad infinitum. The army is a series of decisions, made with a soldier's best interests in mind, that quickly snowball out of control.

If you try to figure out the reason for one strange decision, you are usually confronted with an equally strange decision. For example, when enough people consistently flouted the ban on "non-issued" eyewear (sunglasses), the sergeant-major had to finally explain to us that the rule was in place in case we were injured—the army might refuse to pay us a pension if we were blinded while wearing Oakleys. This leads to the question, would the army actually deny us a pension if we went blind?

After I'm done my radio maintenance, I go back to the Mushan CP and ask if they have any radio problems I might help them with. The OC and the sergeant-major are in the CP, so I figure it would be prudent to wait outside. I track down a bottle of water, and sit on the homemade wooden chair outside the CP. I smoke another cigarette and, this time, enjoy it greatly. I look around at the transformed SP Mushan. Whereas every other base that I've been to has noticeably improved every time I arrived, Mushan is missing the majority of the tents that were present the last time I was here.

SP Mushan is one of the most depressing places I have ever seen. It is located about one kilometre outside the village of Mushan, which consists of about 100 buildings and no more than 200 people (most of whom left when the fighting season began). The strongpoint is a tiny pimple on the otherwise flat face of the desert it inhabits. It is surrounded by about one kilometre of dried-out opium fields separated from the village proper by the deep wadi that I have already described falling into. The architecture amounts to a square wall of HESCO Bastions. Around the HESCOs is razor wire, and the square is dotted by observation and firing positions. It is inhabited by a company of ANA soldiers, and the only Canadians permanently there are a three-to-five-person OMLT team, responsible for training and advising the ANA.

Inside the strongpoint is a well used for drinking water by the ANA. It is the only source of anything cool in the camp. Outside, a large painted plywood sign hangs: "Welcome to Mushan." In the place of the *o* in *to* is a mortar fin once attached to an enemy munition that landed inside the camp during the attack in which six ANA soldiers were killed or wounded. The ensuing fire almost ignited the stored ammunition, which would have caused an explosion and taken out the rest of the camp with it. One side of the strongpoint is framed by a makeshift shower (a bucket punctured with holes), and the bathroom (*shitter* is a more appropriate term). The other side houses the headquarters, the OMLT's RG-31 anti-mine vehicle, and a couple of 10-metre antennas set up by fellow signallers. Three shipping containers (sea cans) make up the strongpoint's stores, and two modular tents make up its rest area. It is in one of these tents, hastily erected before our arrival to afford us some small amount of shade, that the rest of HQ and I sleep.

The camp smells of dust and burnt garbage. A huge pit outside the camp houses its waste, and once a day a soldier with a can of diesel will set it on fire. As the majority of the garbage is rations, the smell reminds me of summer barbecue. It is insidiously pleasant. Some members of the OMLT will stay in camps like this for upwards of four months, a few for their entire tour. The week that I spent in Mushan over the course of the tour was more then enough for me.

We get the word that we are going to have food and water air-dropped in on our location. *Cool,* I think, *this will be different.*

The plan is to have a Canadian Hercules aircraft fly low and slow with the ramp down, and parachute out pallets full of rations and water. As we wait, people pull out digital cameras, a constant fixture of any patrol. I stand on top of a pile of sandbags and hear the drone of the engines from the southeast. I catch a glimpse of the Herc flying low, see it turn, and watch as pallet after parachuted pallet come flying out. The ANA have spooled up a patrol to recover them. Most land in the target area, the opium fields to our southeast. Some land in and amongst the compounds farther south. An ANA Ford Ranger painted desert tan flies out of the SP, heavily laden with Afghan soldiers. The ANA are able to recover about 80 percent of the pallets. We figure that having food and water drop randomly from the sky into an Afghan mud compound can't be bad for our image with the locals, so we leave the other 20 percent where they are, a gift from the Canadian air force. We also think that our random parachute drop will give the Taliban something to ponder before they decide to attack us with mortars. The stores that we recover are pretty mangled from their trip, and for the remainder of our time in Mushan we drink from crushed water bottles.

Someone finds a game of Risk, and a few of us sit down to play. Jeff Brazeau, Smitty, a master corporal from 4 Platoon, and I sit around a table and set up our armies. The 4 Platoon guy is a big farm boy from Saskatchewan; like me he is a reservist. He is intensely proud of his upper-class German heritage, and wears his blond hair long on the top and short on the sides, similar to a more famous Austrian corporal. I am forced into a bad position in Europe after the first turn, and my defeat is quick and inglorious. I watch the game from the sidelines and smoke cigarettes. The German shores up his position in North and South America, and uses it as a springboard for his conquest of the world. The game doesn't even take an hour to complete.

Every soldier in Afghanistan is granted one three-week vacation from the war. Home Leave Travel Assistance (HLTA) allows a soldier to fly out of Afghanistan to any location in the world, and subsidizes some of the travel expenses. Some of my buddies went to Australia, Bali, the Caribbean, or Thailand. I went to Europe with Darcy. We saw seven countries in 24 days (France, Belgium, the Netherlands, Luxembourg, Germany, Austria, and Switzerland). Each was a unique adventure, but probably the highlight of the trip was the couple of days that we spent in Dijon, France. We did a winery tour, walked the entire town, and were generally the youngest of the tourists wandering the streets. Dijon has the best food I have ever eaten. One night I asked the waiter what I should have (always ask a French waiter, they know more about their food and their restaurant than you ever could), and he suggested *Boeuf Bourguignon* with a bottle of strong red wine. It was one of the most delicious meals I've ever had.

Today, about a month after I watched tears well-up in my girl-friend's eyes at Charles de Gaulle Airport, I am sitting in Mushan looking for lunch. I go back to our tent and pull out a half-smashed new '08 ration. I look at the red bilingual label on the crushed package: "Lunch/*Diner*—Menu No. 3—Beef Bourguignon—*Boeuf Bourguignon*–'08."

Seriously? Beef Bourguignon? It's like the army went out of its way to ruin a happy memory by serving this to me in the hot Afghan sun in a half-destroyed package that was recently dropped out of a plane. I open the package and look inside at the brown goo that might once have been beef. It is possibly the most depressing encounter I have ever had with food, and I sit and consume my "meal" in silence.

It is about 1600 at this point, and the heat is beginning to let up slightly. As I eat, we are told what the plan is for the next day: We are going to advance into the village of Mushan behind a line of infantry and ANA. We will then cordon off a few compounds that we suspect contain insurgents and weapons caches. After the area is secure, the engineers and infantry will search these compounds. It's the same old plan and is similar to most of the patrols I've taken part in on the tour. The big difference is that now the fighting sea-son has begun. This will be my first daytime patrol during which the Taliban are expected to put up a fight. Almost every foray out of Mushan for the last month has gotten into contact with the enemy; we don't have any reason to suspect that tomorrow will be different. So far we have been remarkably lucky—no mortars have landed near us, and we haven't encountered any IEDs. The silence begins to take on an almost ominous feeling. I know that tomorrow will be different.

On our tour, we use four phrases to describe fighting the enemy: *TIC* (troops in contact) is the official way to describe such an encounter over the radio after the fact; *contact* is the word used over the radio to describe any enemy engagement (for example "2, this is 21, contact, wait out"); *gunfight* or *firefight* is the way that previous tours described any contact that lasted less than six hours; *gun battle* or *battle* is a gunfight that lasts over six hours (battles are extremely rare on our tour). Each word describes the same thing, but the context in which each is used varies greatly. For example, I wrote in my journal prior to departing Sperwan Ghar, "About to depart on fighting patrol to Mushan . . . I will probably be in my first TIC within the next six days." I mistakenly used *TIC* instead of *contact,* an error I learned to correct after I had actually experienced a contact.

I throw out the remainder of my ration and lie down. I need to get as much sleep as possible, so I try to nap in the diminishing but still sweltering heat. I meet with some success, and fade in and out of consciousness as conversations about the sexual prowess and misadventures of the infantry swirl and fade around me. Sleeping across from me are the two snipers who are attached to our patrol. Their C14 sniper rifle is set up on its bipod facing me. I've never been hugely into weapons, but it would take a pretty committed hippie to think that this rifle isn't cool. It is a bolt-action weapon with a five- round magazine. The barrel has spiralling grooves, and on the muzzle is a cylindrical titanium suppressor. At the end of the suppressor, a maple leaf is etched around the muzzle. I find it a unique expression of Canadian identity that a .50 cal round, fired by an extremely well-trained Canadian, must pass through the centre of a maple leaf en route to its target. The rifle is painted camouflage tan, and it looks like something out of every 12-year-old boy's fantasy. One of my regrets from the tour is that I never got an opportunity to fire this weapon.

On Remembrance Day 2008 my mom asked me to speak to a class at her former school (she was a newly retired grade 2/3 teacher). I worried over what I would say to a group of kids about what I'd experienced. In the end I gave a speech on how hot it was, what the kids' lives were like in Afghanistan, and what we did there. It wasn't exactly a dissertation, but my audience was receptive. Afterwards there was a question and answer period. Most of the questions were mundane, and I did my best to answer them truthfully and politically. One kid, however, asked me a series of very specific questions.

"*Did you have a C7?*"
"*Uh, yep, the C7A2 assault rifle.*"
"*Did it fire the 5.56 ammunition?*"
"*Yes.*"
"*Did you carry fragmentation grenades?*"
"*Uh . . . yeah.*"
"*Did you ride on a Black Hawk helicopter?*"
"*As a matter of fact, I did.*"
"*Did it have a chain gun?*"
"*It had a 50 cal—where are you learning all this stuff?*"
"*Video games.*"

The halcyon days of Super Mario Brothers appear to have passed.

I wake up at about 2000 and head for the bathroom. As I pass the sergeant-major, he sits up from a relaxed position on top of his sleeping pad and pulls me aside.

"Flavelle!" he says, "we're leaving at five tomorrow morning."

"Yes, sergeant-major," I reply.

"Those OMLT guys are coming with us, there, and someone's gotta watch the radio tonight."

"Roger that, sergeant-major. Do I have to do the entire shift? Am I coming on the patrol?" I try not to hope that I will stay behind.

"Fuck, Flavelle, you're coming on this patrol, and I don't care who you have to muckle onto to help you out tonight, but sort it out. I thought you used to be a master corporal in the reserves?"

Chief Warrant Officer Cavanagh (the sergeant-major) is a regular force infanteer through and through. I believe that he takes distinct pleasure in reminding me that, although I was once a master corporal (the lowest leadership position in the army) in the reserves, I am now a lowly sigs corporal, which basically amounts to nothing.

"Understood, sergeant-major. So all the platoon sigs?"

"Yeah, get that Lagonia guy, and what's his name?"

"Cunningham?"

"Yeah, and muckle onto those chimos too there, they should help out as well." *Chimo* is the nickname for a Canadian combat engineer. I've asked a lot of people what it stands for, but never got a straight answer; the general consensus is that it's the Inuktitut word for "hello," "goodbye," and "cheers."

"Roger that, sergeant-major."

Now I have the task of telling people that they cannot sleep the whole night through before a brutal patrol, when we know that the Taliban are out. *Fuck.* I wander into the open area where 4 Platoon is sleeping, nod to a few acquaintances, and ask around to find the platoon signaller.

"Hey, you seen Lagonia?"

"Yeah, man, he's sleeping near the officer, somewhere over there, by the shitters."

He points me in the general direction, and I totter off toward the Mushan latrine, a plywood door closing onto a plywood bench with a toilet seat attached, surrounded by porn mags. You open a plastic toilet bag (we carried a few so as not to deplete the COP's stock), hook it onto the nails provided, and recline to read a two-year-old copy of *Hustler* with unaccustomed avidity. When finished, you unhook the bag, seal it and throw it into the garbage outside (which is burned every few days). By following the general direction of people pointing, I find Lagonia underneath an issued groundsheet on top of his sleeping bag, listening to an iPod and trying to doze in the hot Afghan evening.

"Hey, Lagonia, you gotta pull a radio shift tonight, that's coming from the sergeant-major, I put you on from 10 to 12." (Although writing in military time has been beaten into me over the years, I usually don't use military time when I speak.)

"Seriously? Fuck you, man."

"Sorry, dude, I gave myself 12 to 2."

I wander around the camp and tell two other platoon signallers that they will have to forgo sleep tonight to listen to a radio. It is 2100 at this point, and I return to my sleeping pad. I'm not tired, but it is dark and quiet, and I can hear snoring along with muffled conversation. I lie down but I can't sleep. I think about tomorrow, and what combat will be like. I think about home and how far away it feels. I think about the ethereal quality of morale, and how the human mind copes with stress. I think.

CHAPTER 5
MUSHAN
17 JULY 2008

Everyone wants to go to war—until they are at war; then they want to go to McDonald's.
—MASTER CORPORAL JARRAD LAIRD, 746 COMMUNICATION
   SQUADRON

UNLIMITED LIABILITY. For soldiers, this phrase has a unique connotation. It means that, at some time in the uncertain future, we may need to lay down our lives in defence of our country. Specifically, it means that we may not only be asked, but also in certain circumstances forced to die in its service. This concept is entirely unique in the public service; not even police officers can be lawfully ordered to their deaths. Unlimited liability means that, technically, we can be ordered to charge a machine gun, or defend a location to the last bullet, even with the certain knowledge that the action will result in some or all of our deaths. To a teenager intent only on avoiding a job flipping burgers, the spectre of the Huns invading seemed very far off indeed when I joined up in June 2001.

As with so much else on my tour, I discovered that an intellectual appreciation of a concept has little relation to its physical manifestation. Once I chose to deploy to a war zone with the infantry, unlimited liability became a cold hard fact. The nuances of this state began to make themselves felt. I was never ordered to defend a location to the last bullet; I was, however, ordered to drive down a known IEDed route in the middle of the night. I was also ordered to stand up and face a machine gun, and stay put during a mortar barrage. Looking back, I'm proud to say that I belong to the only legal organization that requires unlimited liability, but initially I didn't realize how very real that prospect was.

I am sitting on a pile of sandbags with a satellite phone in one hand and my digital camera in the other. I am calling my girlfriend and my parents in Calgary, thanks to the miracle of modern technology and the misuse of Canadian army resources. I've memorized the international dialling code, and punch in the 15 numbers patiently. I have to make sure that the antenna is pointing in the right direction. The connection is full of static and I feel apprehensive as I hear the phone ring. *What if they don't answer? What if they do?*

My dad picks up the phone on the other side of the world, and I talk to him about what the weather is doing; I ask about my mom's garden and the early success of the raspberry bushes. I talk about his new iPhone, the barbecue, and the fence he is planning to build. I studiously avoid talking about where I am, what is happening around me, or any part of my life other than what I've had for dinner. The military has gone to great lengths to ensure that I am afraid to describe my surroundings. We received countless briefings in Canada and KAF about what we can and cannot say. As a radio operator, I understand the kind of equipment one would need to intercept a satellite telephone call, and I don't believe that the Taliban in Mushan have that capability. But I also don't want to describe the danger I'm in at the present moment. I feel that my parents would only worry about me more if they knew where I was. I also don't think that they can ever understand the situation I am facing. They don't have any context with which to understand my experiences, and I don't feel like giving it to them. It's easier to just pretend that everything is okay, and talk about the weather.

I feel differently when talking to Darcy—as if she is supposed to share the hardship and the fear. I just feel that she understands me more than my parents do, and that she won't flip out if I tell her that I'm scared. I picture her smiling face when I close my eyes. When I hear her voice I remember being in Europe, holding her hand, falling asleep with her on a train. She is my link to life outside Afghanistan. We can talk about the future and the past; when we do, it feels real, exciting, tangible. My dad passes the phone to her. "Hey, sweetie, how are you?" I can tell from her voice that she is smiling.

"I'm doing great, my dear. It's sunny outside, and your dad is making hamburgers on the grill. I've been studying in the sun all day." She is staying with my parents while she attends summer classes for her psychology degree at the University of Calgary. She tells me about her problems with classes, papers, and commuting on the C Train—I remember a time when those were my problems. It doesn't seem real that people could be concerned about such things. Finally, she asks how I am doing.

"I'm kind of scared tonight, Darcy."

"Why, sweetheart?"

"Well, it's very, very hot outside and I have to leave in a few hours to go on a fighting patrol. I don't know what's going to happen."

"I love you, no matter what."

I don't know if she understands what I mean, and I don't think she knows what to say. Maybe I shouldn't have said anything. But hearing her words reminds me that there are things other than Mushan, rations, and fighting patrols. I miss her terribly. I wonder if it was the right decision to come to Afghanistan. But I don't know how to say what I feel. We are living in different worlds. As I hear her talk, I can picture her blue eyes and long hair. I remember the world that I left, and feel like it is waiting for me at the other end of the patrol.

The conversation continues. I talk a little bit about my day, about playing Risk, about the radio shift, and about missing her. It makes me feel better; it makes me feel like everything is going to be okay. After about 30 minutes, I hang up the sat phone and sit in the silent night, listening to those around me snore.

They say that there are no atheists in foxholes. I am certainly not a spiritual person, more of an armchair agnostic. Although I doubt that there is a God, I would rather stay out of the argument altogether. However, when I find myself inside the modern equivalent of a foxhole, my lofty intellectualism quickly erodes. Despite my convictions, I find myself becoming steadily less agnostic as the tour progresses. I don't claim to know the answers to the big questions, but I lift up my eyes and beg anything that wants to listen to spare my family suffering. I am so afraid of what tomorrow might hold that I need the comfort of something more powerful than I am.

I look up at the stars and hope that there is a God, and that I will be protected from this place of bullets, razor wire, and death. Finally, I pray a silent prayer that I will be okay, and that if not, my family will understand and will know that I love them. It is 0200, and I only have three and a half hours before the patrol is set to begin.

I take a deep breath of the cool, refreshing Afghan air, sigh, and totter off to my beloved ranger blanket.

Waking up in an army camp conjures images of bugles, horses, and trumpets. In my experience, reveille, despite its pretentious name, is simply a series of people softly shoving and poking their neighbours awake. This noise is followed by the sounds of people waking up around you, shaking off their sleeping bags, and putting on their kit. For a few seconds I try to hide in my ranger blanket, but there is nothing I can do. The morning has arrived. By the time I finish picking my helmet out of the sand, pulling out my smokes, and sitting down to await the patrol, orange light is beginning to show on the horizon. I sit and watch it grow, and smoke my second cigarette of the day.

The frantic activity around me has subsided into groups of people sitting around, looking large in their body armour, smoking, talking, or dozing. As the sound of an ANA soldier greeting the sun with his morning prayers echoes through the camp, the word is passed: Kit up, get on your feet. So we stand up and shuffle into position, feeling once again the weight of our packs. I look at Chris's goggles and wonder how he gets them to stay in place so well. I smoke another half of a cigarette, and after an interminable time the man in front of me starts to walk.

We are taking our first steps into the bright Afghan sun. My stomach is twisting itself up into knots. Frankly, I'm nervous. For the last three days, the Taliban haven't made their presence known, but we can feel them watching us from every grape hut and compound we pass. I know deep down that today is going to be the day. We plan to search most of the compounds in the village; we plan to hit the enemy where it hurts and seize his weapons before he can escape. We know that we won't be allowed to do this without a fight.

We cross about a kilometre and a half of flat mud fields before reaching the outskirts of the village. They are completely level, and broken into a grid by tiny mud walls that allow them to be flooded. The last time we walked through these fields, they were filled with poppies drooping low with the weight of seed pods containing unrefined opium. As the harvest began, the fields were filled with young Fighting Age Males (FAMs). (Soldiers refer to them as Fighting Age Guys.) Their eyes had burned holes into our skulls as we patrolled past them. It would be these men who would take up arms against us after the harvest was complete. About a month later, we are walking through the same fields, now devoid of any sign of life, and only an ominous silence greets us.

This silence does not last long; the ANA, cheerfully running, marching, and chattering their way into position, infect the landscape with life. They leave a trail of ration garbage almost everywhere they go, and when you follow them you merely need to look for the empty packages of Power Banana Chips and Honey Nut Cheerios.

We stop along a mud wall that comes up to chest level, and I look out onto the landscape. Nothing really seems different. I can see children and goats wandering around, and the village appears to have the same listlessness we encounter almost everywhere we go. Seeing women and children is usually a good sign, as they tend to flee before the Taliban fire on us. Nothing seems out of the ordinary, so I sit down to get the weight off my shoulders and drink a bit of water. I ask Chris if he would like to get a picture together. He agrees, and I ask Peter, our terp, to take it. I have the picture to this day. You can see Chris telling Peter to turn the camera on its side. In the background stand Major Lane and CWO Cavanagh. Whenever I see this picture, I think of Chris, Peter, and that cool morning.

Peter is a gangly teenager who looks as if he has outgrown his combats. He has an adolescent's downy moustache but acts like an adult in everything he does. I have learned that he is from a good family in Kandahar Province, and that he is a proud Pashtun—he wears a haughty expression whenever he talks. He's told me that his parents have a two-car garage, hard to imagine in the mud-walled hicksville of southern KP. Once some Taliban got onto a bus he was travelling on and tried to kill everyone working for the International Security Assistance Force. Peter had his ISAF papers on him, but they didn't search him. In Afghanistan, kids grow up more quickly than they do in the West, and Peter is looking forward to getting married on his next leave.

Peter has a remarkably effeminate way of smoking a cigarette, and he is one of the few terps who doesn't rely on sycophancy. He never covers his face to hide his identity when we are on patrol, and I think he really believes in what we are doing. He interpreted for the last rotation of Canadians, the Van Doos, and he picked up some uniquely Canadian slang. His speech is liberally sprinkled with Québécois curse words, and we finally have to forbid the blasphemy *tabarnak* in our LAV. The sergeant-major once chewed him out for not wearing a helmet, and when we walk into the village proper he sullenly wears a large green Kevlar helmet over his cheap imported baseball cap. I think he always resented the sergeant-major for speaking down to a Pashtun of his imagined stature, and he was transferred a few weeks after this patrol. He once asked for my e-mail address, but I did not give it to him. He may very well have been selling information to the Taliban, and I couldn't take the chance.

I am a generally friendly person, and I like to meet new people and develop new relationships. But in Peter's case, I can't bring myself to fully trust him. It's not that he isn't a nice person; I enjoy talking to him about Afghan culture, his family, and his childhood. But he is Pashtun, and I've heard too many horror stories of anonymous e-mails sent to family members at home, or to Pakistani hackers. Maybe some of these are apocryphal, but it doesn't matter. I don't trust any Afghan I meet, and to be fair, none of them have earned that trust. I felt bad saying no to Peter, and I could see in his eyes that he was insulted, but it was too great a risk.

As we walk into the village of Mushan, I think again about the neatly laid out dirt roads, and the engineering feat that was required to build three-storey houses (not unlike Osama bin Laden's compound in Pakistan) out of nothing but mud and garbage. We walk slowly as the heat begins to increase and stop often for water breaks, or to allow searches to be conducted, or to wait for people to get into the proper position. A line of Canadian soldiers forms itself to cover as much of Mushan as possible. We search for weapons, IEDs and bomb makers. My early-morning jitters begin to leach out of me as the Afghan sun pours in. The patrol stops being exciting or dangerous, and becomes for the most part monotonous.

I concentrate on my water consumption and the person in front of me. I talk briefly to the artillery observer behind me, and smoke cigarettes slowly despite the fact that they've already lost their appeal. We move a few slow kilometres and jump wadis and ditches. I focus on every footstep I take and try to ensure that I'm walking where someone else has. We continue with our almost lackadaisical pace until we reach a narrow road with a chest-level mud wall on our left and a wadi on our right. In the distance, I hear what I'd been expecting to hear ever since the patrol started.

Incoming gunfire sounds a lot more high-pitched than you would expect and a lot louder. Often, you don't hear it as much as you feel its concussion in your ears. It has become pretty common-place to hear weapons in the distance; we hear them at night at our patrol base, and I've heard a few distant firefights on earlier patrols. But this is different. It is closer and more immediate. The sound is coming from about 300 metres away, a mid-range that I am not used to. We hear only a few machine gun bursts, but they stop us in our tracks. A pause follows—just long enough for me to think that I've imagined the whole thing. Then the torrent breaks, and we hear one of the Canadian or ANA platoons start to return fire. They are much closer to us; in fact, I can see a friend in 4 Platoon sprint up into position. Immediately, my radio squawks to life and the contact report begins coming over the air: "29er, this is 21, contact, wait out."

As we wait for 4 Platoon to get more information on exactly what's going on I sit down. I don't really know what to do. The reality of the situation is just beginning to dawn on me. This is not another exercise to wait out, in the certain knowledge that there isn't any danger; this is a real live firefight, my first sustained close contact with the enemy. After training for seven years, this is the first time that it all really matters. The first time I have an opportunity to strike back at an invisible enemy that has taken its toll on our company with IEDs buried in the road. The first time I am in a situation where my decisions could become a matter of life and death.

The world seems to close in around me, and I have trouble thinking clearly. I'm not terrified, like I thought I would be; I'm more confused. My training has taught me to take cover and try to get to a good firing position. I kneel below the wall, listening to the fire erupt around me. It sounds like the percussion section of an orchestra; I can hear the staccato drum roll of Taliban machine guns and the response of individual pings of lone rifles, and the bass booms of M203 grenades. I hear on the radio that 4 Platoon and the ANA are both in contact along an approximately one-kilometre line. The fighting elements begin feeding back information: grids of enemy contact, locations of friendly call signs, estimated strength of enemy positions, and so on. The snipers climb onto a roof in an attempt to find a good firing position. It all happens the way it would in Wainwright or Shilo, *but this time it's for real.*

I crouch behind a wall for only a few seconds before I see the OC get up and start walking quickly forward. He wants to further "define the battle space," and it's my job to follow him. As I stand up, two or three RPGs sail over the wall to our left in quick succession. They were aimed too high and explode in the abandoned field behind us. I'm not sure exactly how close they are, but I hear the scream as they pass, and see leaves on the tree behind me blow back and forth. I get the idea fixed in my brain that the Taliban are using my antenna, which sticks up almost half a metre above my head, as an aiming marker. They may very well be, as my antenna is probably the only thing visible to the enemy some 200 metres away. The

OC needs my radio, and I can see the sergeant-major running up and down the wall, trying to figure out who fired at us, and whether they are still firing. I harbour a strong desire not to stand up and show my antenna again, so I crawl over to where the OC is sitting, cursing his smaller radio and my inability to fix it (it is working properly; we are simply out of range). I sit down beside the OC and, like a pop-up window in my brain, the words, "I've made a series of poor life decisions to get to this point. If I had made better decisions I wouldn't be here getting shot at" flash in front of my mind's eye.

I try to decide if what I'm doing is prudent or cowardly. The firefight continues to rage around me. My responsibility shrinks to a small portion of field across the wadi that I cover in case the Taliban try to flank us, and my radio, which provides the OC with the ability to talk to command. Through the fog, I see Chris brush some thorns off a dip in the wall we are hiding behind, and thrust out his C8 while bullets continue to fly over the wall. I'm struck by how cautiously and professionally he pushes his weapon toward the sound of gunfire, and it dawns on me that I should probably do the same. Before this moment, I had expected combat to be reactive, to merely do what I had been trained to do. Although this is, to a certain extent, the way I am responding, I've never had to focus my will onto an action like I did at this moment. The rational part of my brain screams out to stay down and wait for it all to go away, but my training demands that I take up a firing position. I remain lost in a decision loop until I see Chris carefully but confidently push his head over the wall. I rally my will and stand up awkwardly.

The first thing I see is two soldiers from our weapons detachment (the guys who carried the C6 machine guns) trying to climb onto the roof of a small grape hut to our left. It's a simple enough task in most situations, but the combination of a machine gun weighing 18 kilos, 15 kilos of ammunition, and about 45 kilos worth of personal kit (body armour, pistol, helmet, water, etc.) makes the process considerably more difficult. I look out into the field from which we received the RPG fire. By this point, a line of Canadian soldiers has spread out into firing positions. Section commanders are running around ensuring that everything is covered. The OC frantically takes notes on his map and passes information back to our higher call signs. In the field in front of me, I see flashes of brown combat uniforms, 4 Platoon advancing toward the enemy. For the briefest moment, I also think I see a turbaned head skulk out of sight from one of the mud compounds on the other end of the field. To this day I'm not sure if that head belonged to the Taliban, a civilian, or my imagination.

Looking back from today, the firefight takes on a cinematic quality. It doesn't seem like I was actually there. I had a feeling of utter detachment that I couldn't and can't quite define. For the most part I was numb, responding more than deciding how to act. It was as if I was an intensely interested observer going through the motions of being a soldier without actually being there. There was so much adrenalin going through my body it's not surprising I felt strange.

The weapons fire begins to die down, as the Taliban flee before the advancing Canadians. It looks like a simple "shoot and scoot," the normal Taliban response when we probe close to something they want to protect. Their usual plan is to fire long enough to pin down the Canadians while they rush whatever they don't want us to find out of the area. Most of the time, we usually have a pretty good idea of what the Taliban are hiding, but as they are unfettered by body armour and by the fear of IEDs, they usually escape on some winding path that we can't easily follow.

The threat now becomes booby traps in the compounds that the enemy have abandoned, and we call up the engineers to assist us in clearing them. After watching for a few minutes I decide that it would be prudent to hydrate while I have the opportunity, so I sit back down and drink half a bottle of water.

Hydration: the army has a term for everything, even drinking water. I taught a two-month basic training in the summer of 2006 and the consumption of water quickly became our universal palliative. No matter what a recruit's problems were—too tired, sore feet, bored, marital difficulties—our response was the same: "Get some water into ya." In Afghanistan, hydration was imperative. At one point, while trying to lose weight for my leave, I was working out two to three times a day, and drinking upwards of six litres of water. I would be up twice a night, frantically pulling on my sandals and trying not to run into anything in a mad dash for the porta-potty, but I never felt so healthy.

On patrol, hydration is especially vital. In the heat of the day it could easily reach over 50 degrees Celsius, and sweat poured from my body. Usually when we finished a daytime patrol my uniform looked like I had been swimming in it; the sweat would drip all the way down past my knees and elbows. A friend of mine with a hairy back sweat more than I could have thought possible, and I know that he gave serious consideration to shaving everything.

The problem was that our body armour was impermeable, so our sweat did not evaporate. On top of that, my radio, which was probably the best personal radio available in the world, had one flaw—it overheated. It would reach temperatures of 60 to 70 degrees, and carrying it was like having a hot plate shoved into my flak vest. It was an absolute necessity to carry, at a minimum, six litres of water, and in Mushan I was carrying nine. It's easy to forget how much water weighs. To give you an idea, when we stepped off from Mushan I had the equivalent of four and a half two-litre bottles of Coke on top of the rest of my kit. Many of us would find it difficult to carry this much Coke from the grocery store to the car. The water also had to be packed in a very specific manner. I had two 2.5-litre CamelBaks, as well as four 500-millilitre bottles in my pack, and four in my chest rig. Two of those could be easily accessed from the front zipper pocket (along with my smokes), and two were placed in a side pouch. All told I had easy access to 4.5 litres of water with another 4.5 in reserve.

We had also been issued water purification tablets so that we could drink the plentiful water flowing in the wadis or wells of the villages we passed through, as a last resort. But seeing the locals defecating in a wadi, I ruled this out as a viable option for myself. By this point, all of my Gatorade and Powerade packets were gone, and I was left to drink water that was the same temperature as coffee and tasted distinctly of its plastic container.

I finish gratefully sucking back a bottle. As our other call signs advanced, they were re-engaged, an indication that we might be approaching something very important or something that the Taliban were having a hard time moving. The insurgents had fled to a mosque in the centre of the village, and had kept up a running gunfight the whole way. As friendly call signs advance into compounds or past mud walls, I notice that the OC is having trouble establishing communications with them. Instantly the sergeant-major turns to me and shouts; "Fuck, Flavelle, get over to the OC and give him your fucking radio, what do you think we brought you for?"

Dismissing the crudeness of this comment, this *is* actually what I was brought for. It's not my immense soldiering skills or witty repartee that the infantry needs me for; I'm basically a walking Very High Frequency (VHF) cell phone.

I stand back up, more cognizant than I have ever been of how high my antenna sticks up over my radio, and walk over to the OC. The gunfire can still be heard, but it is taking place farther and farther away from us. The OC grabs my handset and immediately begins speaking into it. The sweat pours from under my helmet and down my back. As the OC talks into my radio I sink back down onto the ground and wonder just how much more of this I can handle. I lean back and my antenna touches my neck, giving me an electric shock (I am the shortest path from the radio to the ground). Salty sweat is an excellent conductor, and an antenna-shaped line is quickly burnt into my body. As I unleash a torrent of oaths, the OC looks at me and says mildly, "What the fuck, Flavelle? Why can't I reach Mushan?"

Once again I have the enjoyable task of explaining basic radio theory to the infantry. I prepare to launch into a "shortest path to the ground" discussion, but before I can speak we are up and on the move again. The sniper team attached to us has spotted a possible Taliban gunman 700 metres away. Before they can get authorization to fire, however, the snipers call back. Apparently after ducking down behind a wall, the man dropped his AK-47 and picked up a shovel. There is no way to be certain that he is an insurgent, so the snipers are not given the authority to fire. He could have been just a guy trying to water his crops, or he could have simply hidden his weapon when he saw ISAF forces.

The landscape of Afghanistan is like nothing else I've ever experienced. The long fields of brown and grey dust are spotted with squat mud grape huts and compounds. It all looks like something on Tatooine, and on one patrol I recognized Aunt Beru's house and could have sworn R2-D2 and C-3PO were somewhere inside. Over the course of millennia, the Afghans have shaped parts of the barrenness into something that approaches lush. With broad irrigation canals, and green crops of grapes, opium, marijuana, and wheat, some locales feel positively inviting. The centre of the village of Mushan, consisting of a mosque at the confluence of two wadis that frame the domed and multi-windowed building, is one such area. Most of the roads in the village lead to the mosque and the well outside it, creating a focal point where you would expect to find a bustling marketplace. But when we reached it there was no sign of life.

Mosques are ubiquitous throughout Afghanistan, and inside Panjway in particular. I once asked our old terp, Zia (who was replaced by Peter), how one could tell mosques apart from other compounds. "You see that doorway?" (He pointed to a circular indentation in the outside wall of the building from which the imam preached on Fridays.) I did a double-take; I had seen that same indentation on, it seemed, half the buildings I had passed that day. For the remainder of that patrol I'd asked Zia, "Is that a mosque?" Invariably he would reply in the affirmative. I counted 12 on a three-kilometre path. I have no idea how Afghan villagers could possibly require that many places to pray, especially as almost all the villages we passed through had no school, clinic, post office, or any other public service.

The mosque in Mushan is different from the simple mud buildings I am used to seeing. Painted white, it gleams in the noonday Afghan sun. Its windows are framed in blue, and it is riddled with bullet holes. After weeks without seeing any colour but brown, I find that the white seems very out of place, and strangely beautiful. When the enemy fled from 4 Platoon, they used the mosque as a firing position during their retreat. The Koran's injunction to "not fight them within the precincts of the holy mosque" (Surah 2:192) seemed to play no role in their decision to fire from the second floor. This didn't last long, however, and they soon fled, hastily taking potshots from nearby grape huts.

When we enter the centre of the village, it is already strongly held by Canadian soldiers, who are drinking water and forming a defensive ring. The OC finds the commander of 4 Platoon, and they sit down to begin discussing the situation. I see a couple of soldiers crowded around the well, pouring water into their helmets and putting them on, so I get in line. The water is cool and refreshing, and I feel it drain down underneath my flak vest. Searching out some shade, I sit down on a strange horizontal metal pole about 30 centimetres in diameter. (I think it may be an animal hitch for the mosque, but I'm not sure. I've never seen anything like it before in Afghanistan.) I light a cigarette and relax for the first time all day. As I pull out a bag of honey-flavoured almonds, I reflect that this patrol isn't turning out that badly after all. We are given five minutes to drink water in this oddly tranquil oasis, and some people even take off their helmets to revel in the shade, until a glower from the sergeant-major ends such ideas. At length, the OC comes to sit beside us. As he sits down, the weight from his backpack shifts him, and he falls awkwardly backwards, like Humpty Dumpty, almost rolling into the wadi. The sight of his boots flashing before us and the tiny squeal he makes as he hits the ground gets to all of us, and we start laughing. The more he struggles, the more ridiculous he looks, and our rattled nerves succumb completely to mirth. Somebody helps him up, and we finish our water bottles, zip up our kit, and prepare to move on. The respite was short and we are once again on our feet, preparing to lurch back the way we came and meet up with the ANA 600 metres to the south. The day patrol is far from over.

On the way, we pass the remainder of 4 Platoon, who have extended into a holding position to look out at the fields we know the enemy has fled into. I'm surprised at how many of the faces are familiar, and how many people I exchange a quick word, joke, or look with. It's now about 1300, and the sun begins to beat down with a new intensity. I've finished my last bottle of easily accessible water, and I am down to my 4.5 litres of reserve. My kit feels substantially lighter without the water, and my shoulders ache noticeably less. I have to wait until the next stop before I can pull off my pack to drink more. As I walk, laden down underneath my kit, the heat seems to be absorbed into my every pore. The sun becomes an iron that presses onto my helmet and body armour, warming my core temperature as I fight to keep lurching, one foot in front the other. I have to make a conscious effort to maintain the basics of patrolling: stay five to 10 metres back from the person in front of you, look over walls and around corners, cover doorways until the person behind you can cover them, keep your head up, above all else. By the time we link up with the OMLT commander, a pounding headache has begun to make itself known, and I feel as if I could fry eggs on my shoulders. We sit down, and I take off my backpack, escaping into pure bliss. As I root around for my spare water, heated to just below boiling point by proximity to my radio, I hear the familiar words of the sergeant-major: "Flavelle, what the fuck! The OC needs the fucking radio!"

I sigh internally, scramble to haul the weight of my pack once more onto my shoulders, and hurry to the OC's side. I sit, extend my antenna, and try to stomach the hot water I've just pulled out. Although I know that I may be entering the first stages of heat exhaustion, it has become a chore to swallow the plastic-flavoured water. At this point I would give almost anything for an ice-cold glass of Coke. The OC has decided to forgo the shade of the trees that grow beside the wadi, and instead is sitting in the harsh sunlight. There is nothing that I can do but sit and sweat, and wonder why he isn't going into the shade. I contemplate saying something, but this would constitute a breach of military etiquette, and I don't really feel up to being glared at by the sergeant-major again.

Heat exhaustion starts as a pounding headache, and then an uncomfortable feeling of warmth spreads throughout your body. Spots appear in front of your eyes and your ears ring. It gets harder and harder to put one foot in front of the other; eventually darkness obscures your vision, and you pass out. Heat exhaustion, like a myriad of other military maladies, is something that you hear about, and train to deal with, but that you never really expect to experience. This all changed in Afghanistan. For once, all the military's talk about the importance of pre-training, physical fitness, and hydration turned out to be legitimate.

When we arrived in February, the average high was about 35 degrees Celsius. Over the course of the next few months the temperature began to rise, and by July highs averaged around 42 degrees. Often, it would get even hotter, and the hottest day recorded on our tour was 59 degrees (we were all a little disappointed that it didn't reach 60, a nice round number).

In Mushan, the temperature is now fast approaching 50 degrees. Despite the pre-training and the focus on hydration, people begin to pass out on other patrols with increasing frequency. This could create a massive problem, as casualties may require a helicopter evac. Infanteers are accustomed to suffering in silence; the infantry piles derision onto soldiers who can't complete a patrol. Although extenuating circumstances are taken into account, for the most part those who succumb to heat exhaustion are shunned openly or derided privately. (If you have recently returned from leave, allowances are made for the amount of alcohol consumed and the resulting damage to your liver.) When my friend and fellow signaller collapsed on a particularly brutal patrol, he was, for all intents and purposes, forbidden from going out again. I quickly became known as "that signaller who didn't pass out," and I was forced into an awkward position between a friend and a group of people who simply no longer wanted him around. I don't think that any but the fittest are immune to heat exhaustion and, as is so often the case, I think the hostility of those who shunned him stemmed from their own insecurities.

On one patrol through the village of Zangabad, we were checking out a school to see if reports that the Taliban had taken it over were accurate. After walking all day, I promised myself a rest when we reached the school. The second-in-command (2iC), Captain Troy Leifso, who had taken over while the OC was on leave, had other plans. He wandered the grounds, cheerfully surveying the overturned desks and the children's strewn papers. My ears began to ring, and it took all my self-control to keep forcing one foot in front of the other. My vision was closing in, and just when I thought I couldn't take it any more, we sat down in the shade and I took my helmet off. I gluttonously swallowed a bottle of water and a granola bar before I began to feel up to patrolling again.

Sweating underneath the Mushan sun after covering some five kilometres in the heat of the day, I begin to feel the onset of the headache that will lead eventually to heat exhaustion unless I manage to cool myself down. I decide to just quietly stand up from my radio and leave it beside the OC while I walk over to Chris beside the wadi. We smoke a cigarette underneath the flowing branches of a mulberry tree, and I plan how to dash the 10 metres to my radio if the Taliban attack. It's 1430 and, despite my best efforts, I begin to wish that I had stayed back at Mushan, drinking warm water and sitting on radio shift.

A love of being badass lives inside every soldier, and there isn't anything more hardcore than patrolling through an Afghan village when the Taliban are out. A spot on these patrols is much sought after, and we all know that we can hold our heads as high as anyone else in the country (except the Special Forces, and possibly fighter pilots). Deep down, I am proud that I am here, and proud that I can make it and keep up. But there's still a tiny voice in the back of my head that wishes that I could have stayed in Mushan, or better yet Sperwan Ghar—or even better, Canada. When we are relaxing and at our ease after a patrol, this voice is a distant memory; but here with the sun beating into my brain and the future uncertain at best, the worm of fear grows stronger, to paraphrase Farley Mowat.

As if my silent prayer were being answered, I hear the OC begin to coordinate our movement out of the village and back to SP Mushan. The Taliban have fled, and all of our objectives have been cleared. While we were wandering around the village, the ANA and 4 Platoon, with help from the engineers, have cleared all of their objectives, the majority of the buildings in Mushan. Their search has yielded a number of components used to make the IEDs that hamper our progress every day, and although we hoped for more, we are satisfied with the small victories the day has brought. We have forced the Taliban to flee, and may have even killed or injured some of them (they drag their dead with them, making it impossible to be sure). Now, for the first time in that long uncertain day, the end is in sight. It's just a simple matter of waiting for the ANA and Canadian platoons to link up on either side of us, and push the two kilometres back to SP Mushan. Then it's cool well water, rations, and sleep for all of us.

I never expected that I could become positively gleeful over the thought of rations but, other than a few handfuls of almonds and a couple of granola bars, I haven't eaten all day. A fervent desire for rations is proof positive of the insidious power of the army to warp all that is good and just inside you. I guess I haven't been out long enough to truly hate rations from the depths of my soul like so many others.

When we first arrived in Sperwan Ghar by way of a flight on an American Black Hawk, I was amazed at the quantity and quality of food available. We arrived just before lunch, and the cooks (the hardest-working and most underrated group in the military) had put on soup and sandwiches for us; one of three meals that they would provide six days a week for the remainder of the tour. On top of that, there were boxes and boxes of cereal, granola bars, fruit, instant noodles, and Pop-Tarts. A friend of mine (who for propriety's sake will remain unnamed) walked into the mess tent with me. He took one look at the blueberry Pop-Tart that someone was eating and promptly ran out to vomit in the porta-potty (his actual words were something like "Is that a . . . *retch* . . . Pop-Tart . . . *retch?*"). On his previous tour, TF 1–06, he had been reduced to rations for so long that they had lost all appeal. After that, he would eat anything that wasn't a ration, and for days subsisted on a diet of Pop-Tarts. Obviously he hadn't given them a second thought the entire time he had been in Canada, but when he saw someone eating one overseas, the associations must have been too powerful. From that day forward, every time that we went head to head playing poker, I would take out a blueberry Pop-Tart and eat it in front of him to break his concentration (I'm not entirely sure if his ensuing threats to kick me "in the cock" were in earnest, but they may well have been).

As we wait for the elements to link up around us, I have an opportunity to sit and reflect on the day so far. All that we have been through is a simple shoot and scoot. This is the type of thing that other platoons in COPs or strongpoints encountered almost every day. However, it was my first sustained contact with the enemy and, more specifically, it was the first time I had ever personally been shot at. Part of me thinks the whole thing is kind of unfair. Why does some Afghan want to shoot at me? I've never done anything to him. In fact, I give Afghan children candy and toys every opportunity I get. Once, on an earlier patrol I had given my last ration to an obviously starving little girl. She had looked at me like it was manna from heaven, and had run away, gleefully and as fast as her emaciated legs could carry her. I was pissed at these people who went to the trouble to shoot at us when all we wanted to do was make sure that their children didn't starve. It was that moment when all the reasoning and intellectualizing I'd done about our role in Afghanistan left me. I wanted to help these people. *Fuck the Taliban.*

I continue to try to stomach water that has lost its appeal and think about the way I'd reacted to combat. It dawns on me that there are two types of soldiers: those who like getting into firefights and those who don't. The surge of adrenalin and the promise of action is a strong motivator for many. During the firefight I had felt it too, and after all the suffering I'd been through, all the training I had conducted, I was finally in a situation where everything mattered, a situation where everything was real. I guess that's why soldiers keep coming back to Afghanistan; once you've been in combat, everything else seems relatively uninteresting. However, the overwhelming emotion that I felt during that firefight was fear. Not a fear strong enough to prevent me from doing my duty—I still wanted to see what was going on, and fire my weapon and protect my friends. It was a different kind of fear, not paralyzing but intelligent, a voice that said very strongly: "You should not be here, and if you'd made better decisions you wouldn't be." I think that this was the hardest thing to stomach: that fundamentally, deep down, when I was in a tough situation, I wanted out. It takes a special type of person to want to be there and, as it turned out, I wasn't that type.

The arrival of 4 Platoon pulls me out of my reverie. I see Lagonia, the platoon sig, following right behind Lieutenant Chang, 4 Platoon's officer. They stop to talk to the OC, and I ask Lagonia how the day is going. He is a skinny infanteer. He smokes heavily, and always manages to keep that combative amicability that is unique to the infantry. He often hung out in my office in Shilo before we deployed, and I tried to get him out of as much work as I could.

"Hey, man, how was that?"

"That was sweet! I get to run around with the officer so I'm not tied to any one place, we lit those fuckers up, man. You do anything?"

"Are you kidding me? I fuckin' hung around the OC all day. The only thing I've been doing is wandering, man. I haven't seen a beeb since this morning."

I pull out my pack of cigarettes, a metal tin I bought in KAF that I keep wrapped tightly with an elastic band. We each smoke one and sit down in the hot Afghan sun while we wait for our officers to finish conversing.

I think that a signaller has a unique attachment to his officer. He is basically brought on a patrol for the sole purpose of ensuring that communications are maintained. This can involve simple "help desk" tasks, like fixing radios when they go down or keeping the programming up to date. More often, however, it involves being a pack animal for the officer's radio. A huge amount of responsibility falls on an officer commanding troops in the field, and an extra 14 kilos will only hinder the ability to move and think effectively. The role of the signaller, as it has been since before the Second World War, is to haul that extra 14 kilos and to make the radio available on the officer's request. Usually this burden feels like an unwarranted cross that we carry, sweating and grunting while trying to keep up to our unfettered superior. But it is a necessary task, if a deferential one. Our secondary responsibility as signallers is to take care of our officer, and protect him from the enemy. Major Lane chose to surround himself with people to fill this role, and Chris refers to himself privately as "the bodyguard" (or as "Kevin Costner"). Although this doesn't leave me much scope to fulfill my task as protector, I still feel the odd dichotomy of being a parent and a child at once. I'm sure that the same is felt by the platoon signallers, and I know that when Captain Leary died on an earlier patrol, no one took it harder then his sig. He was in KAF at the time, and skipped his leave departure date to fly back into the firefight and help avenge Captain Leary. I can't promise that I would have done the same for the OC.

At long last we are on our feet again, and heading back to the strongpoint. We walk faster now. The ANA are leading us, and they love to run in the hot Afghan sun. We pass through the village in a blur, and I see that life is returning to normal. Farmers are out in the fields, eyeing us suspiciously. Kids come up to us and beg for candy. I see a sheep running with a teenage shepherd in hot pursuit. I hunch my shoulders and try to keep up with Major Lane as mud walls, buildings, and fields pass me by. As we exit the village of Mushan, we stretch out into a long line, and I can see the lead elements almost a kilometre ahead of us. I start to breathe heavily as I try to keep up, and I can tell that the pace is taking a toll on those around me. Finally, we get within sight of SP Mushan, a square of HESCO Bastions dotted with observation posts. I can see in the distance the razor wire that signals an end to my suffering. It is only 1.5 kilometres away, but feels much farther. As soon as we cross that line, we can take our kit off, remove our body armour, and lounge in the hot sand, drinking hot water to our hearts' content.

SP Mushan is surrounded by open, dry fields, and the farther we walk, the farther it seems we have to go. The heat of the sun radiates off the ground. It is about 1430, the hottest part of the day, and the sun begins to suck out my strength along with my sweat. Every step becomes a trial, and my pack weighs more than it ever has. Even the short mud walls (no more than a metre high) that we have to jump become seemingly impassable. My throat dries out, but I lack the strength even to shift the weight of my weapon to grab the hose of my CamelBak. I force every ounce of my soul into keeping pace. The distance remaining seems to spread out as I lose my strength. Only about 700 metres remain and the end is in sight, but getting there feels like an impossible task. My headache returns, and with it nausea. Then I feel something I haven't felt all day, dryness. Instead of sweat dripping down from under my helmet, I feel absolutely nothing. I reach up to my head and feel my hair through the hole in the index finger of my glove. Nothing. I've stopped sweating. The rational part of my brain begins to panic. When the body stops sweating, it is the worst sign of dehydration there is. It means that the body is conserving what little water remains in the system and beginning to shut down—a sure sign that heat exhaustion will follow. Unfortunately, I don't have the power to properly hydrate at the moment, and the pace of those in front of me continues unabated. I have to either keep up or look weak.

I pause midstep, suck the remaining water out of my CamelBak, put my head down, and push to catch up. I force my feet to keep marching despite the darkness that begins to close in around me. I feel drunk and wobble when I stop. I force all the strength I have left into keeping up. After an eternity, we pass the razor wire of Mushan. I stop and lean over, breathing hard and trying to keep my balance. We have made it back inside the wire, the immediate danger has passed. I force myself to walk the remaining 100 metres through the camp to where we've laid out our sleeping bags. Finally, I drop my pack, pull off my helmet and flak vest, and collapse on a plastic lawn chair. I look down at my combat shirt; it's bone dry. I'm so tired I can't even feel elated. I don't even have the strength remaining to get my water.

After about 10 minutes, I feel strong enough to stand up. I stagger forward and watch the infantry take off their kit, drink water, make lewd gestures at each other, and similarly unwind. I see a few soldiers who are soaking wet, and hear them talking about the well in SP Mushan where the ANA are pouring cold water on people. I slowly make my way to the well, and am confronted with a line of sweaty Canadians waiting their turn. At the end of the line stands a grinning Asiatic ANA soldier pulling water up from the well.

Northern Afghanistan was settled by an Asiatic people visibly distinct from those of the Pashtun majority. This minority, known as the Hazara, were purportedly descendants of Genghis Khan. They suffered more than most under the rule of the Taliban, who persecuted them for their ethnic nationalism and Shia faith. The Hazara have supported the ISAF mission wholeheartedly since the beginning.

Standing in front of me is a living history lesson, stretching back to the times of the great Mongol empires, and he's willing to refresh me with cool water. When I reach the front of the line, he turns the metal handle on the well. Attached to a length of what looks like yellow surgical tubing is a gallon jug with the top cut off. I kneel down, and he pours the water over my head, soaking me completely. I feel like a completely different person after the water has washed over me.

After a few minutes my headache begins to return, and I decide it would be prudent to seek out our medic, Master Corporal Jonathan Mertens. I find him lounging on his sleeping bag wearing only pants and ballistic eyewear. He's engaged in a conversation with Jeff Brazeau about what constitutes a profession.

"Doc, fuck, man, a job is a profession."

"No way, man, working at McDonald's is not a profession."

"Yeah, well, what if you do it every day, or get promoted to be the manager, then is it a profession?"

I watch as this argument grows heated and a copy of Webster's Dictionary is tracked down. There is still no clear winner. After a few derogatory remarks about the weight and intelligence of those involved in the argument, I pull the doc aside.

"Doc, I stopped sweating on that patrol, that's bad news isn't it?"

"Yeah, man, did you pass out or throw up?"

"No, but I felt drunk and wobbly."

"Yeah, that's dehydration, you need to go and drink water until you piss clear, at least five litres."

"Thanks, Doc. Hey, do me a favour—don't tell anyone about this eh?"

"Of course, man."

My voice begins to fail. I don't know why it's so important, but I don't want anyone to find out how much I'm suffering. Some part of me needs to cover up the pain that I feel. Unlike most, I don't sit around and bullshit about how much the patrol sucks, or how my feet are doing. Instead, I go to my sleeping bag, sit down, and try to drink as much of the piss-warm water as I can handle. I smoke more cigarettes, and think about how they've lost their pleasant taste. Finally, I lie down in the sweltering heat and try to succumb to sleep. I roll my combat shirt into a ball and undo my pants. I don't feel up to taking off my boots, so I lie with them splayed out on the sand. I feel the bite of sandflies on any parts of exposed skin that touches the sand, so I finally curl myself into a ball to sweat, and allow darkness to overtake me.

I'm pulled out of the deep darkness by the welcome face of the sergeant-major.

"Flavelle, we're helping out those OMLT guys again tonight. Get another crew ready for radio shift there." *There* is his trademark word, and he manages to find a way to insert it into almost every sentence, along with the phrase *shit out;* orders groups with the sergeant-major can be a hilarious exercise. For example, a fairly common order sounds something like, "Flavelle, I don't care what you have to do to shit out a functional radio there, but make it happen." A friend of mine once kept a tally of these two phrases during an orders group. *There:* 64 times; *shit out:* 18 times.

I wipe the sleep out of my eyes and stand up. My feet feel like they are on pins and needles, as the circulation was cut off by my boots while I was asleep. I'm more thirsty and groggy than I have ever been. I look at my watch, 1630; about an hour's worth of sleep.

After I organize tonight's radio shift, I walk over to the command post and ask if they have any new problems with their radios. The CP is the only place in the camp with a fridge. It's a tiny bar fridge, and it doesn't do a particularly good job cooling the water below room temperature, but it's still the closest thing to cold water you can find. There is nowhere near enough to go around, however, and the OMLT guard it closely. I figure that if I can help them sort out a few radio problems, I can then beg a bottle of water or two from them. The OMLT officer gives me a few more radios that haven't been working properly and I begin to fix them. They have the same problems that I've encountered every day since I've been in-country, and I start the monotonous process of zeroizing and reloading them. One's antenna is snapped at the base, so I take the electrical tape I brought with me and rig up a quick emergency fix. All told the basic maintenance takes me no more then an hour, and when I'm done I ask the duty corporal if I can steal a bottle of water.

"Yeah, but don't tell anyone. That shit's just for us."

I gratefully go over to the celebrated fridge, steal a pack of Crystal Light, and go outside to smoke and enjoy water that, for the first time in days, is cooler than I am. I notice an old laptop that appears to no longer be used and ask the OMLT officer what it's for.

"That's for the TSK [tactical satellite kit]."

At some point on a previous rotation, someone had the bright idea of giving each base the ability to chat over a secure server, using a laptop plugged into a satellite dish that could enable a secure data transfer back to Sperwan Ghar or KAF. The officer tells me that it's been here since our rotation started, and that it's never even approached functioning properly, except to play Minesweeper and Solitaire. Finally a problem I can sink my teeth into.

At this point of the tour I wasn't familiar with this system, but the basics were easy enough to understand: power cable to computer, to antenna cable, to antenna, to satellite, to receiving TSK—a simple point-to-point system. I spend the next 30 minutes reading everything I can find relating to the system and trying to fix the laptop power cable with the help of my trusty electrical tape. I isolate the interface that the laptop uses to aim the antenna and set it to transmit. Nothing, zero signal strength. I follow the cable leading from the laptop to the antenna in its winding path through the headquarters; it takes me around various doors, people trying to sleep, and outside onto the roof (the roof is a pile of sandbags five thick on top of HESCO Bastions or plywood). There is no ladder available, so I scale the two metres to the top. When I get there I notice the excellent view I have of the village of Mushan, from where the SP receives small arms fire on a regular basis. I suddenly realize that I'm not wearing a helmet, body armour, or carrying a weapon. I feel like a sitting duck and get as close to the ground as I can while tracing the path of the cable.

At a few points, the roof threatens to collapse, and I have to spread my weight out as you would on thin ice. Finally, I find the antenna. It is a squat, square, panelled dish pointing toward the sky from underneath a camouflage net. I can hear it searching for a signal, and there is a digital readout indicating that it still has zero signal strength. I twist it and point it, all to no avail. I decide that the problem has to be a break somewhere in the shielded wire, and that I have to replace it. I spend the next hour running a new coaxial cable under, over, through, and around an HQ and a HESCO Bastion. By the time I finally get back to the antenna I'm sweaty and covered in dust. My combats have acquired a few more rips, and my hand is bleeding from my slipping and falling to the ground. I plug in the cable, confidently expecting the antenna to power up and the signal strength to immediately jump. Nothing. I let loose a torrent of profanity that can probably be heard in the village proper. It's so loud and, dare I say eloquent, that someone pokes his head onto the roof and says, "Hey, you okay up there?"

"Fuck this," I reply, and begin climbing off the roof. I sit and smoke. I had really thought that I would be able to make this system work. Then it dawns on me. I quickly butt out my smoke, climb back onto the roof, and look at the antenna. It's facing the ground, irradiating those sleeping below, as it has been since it was first installed improperly. One and a half rotations of Canadian soldiers have passed through, thinking that the stand was the radiating element of the antenna, and it has been shooting its signal into the HQ below since its inception. I push it upright and hear the reassuring ping of the antenna acquiring a signal. Now it's a simple matter of programming it to link up with the command post in Sper, and I will have successfully fixed this system.

By the time I finish establishing a secure link, the sun has begun to go down. I walk out of the CP feeling the beginnings of a blessedly cool Afghan evening. I feel like a conquering hero for defeating the obstinate technology. This feeling of supremacy over inanimate objects is the sole bright point of a sig op's career. Our radios are plagued with seemingly pathological foibles, but over the course of my career I have begun to pride myself on being able to tackle any radio problem, no matter how abstruse.

By four months into the tour, I've gained a reputation for being able to solve most technological problems. I don't mean to sound conceited; I just acquired the ability to talk to broken equipment, and figure out how to fix it. Unfortunately, the infantry have begun to believe that I can fix anything, even if I have never seen it before. My days are often taken up with requests to fix iPods, Xboxes, and other things that are well beyond my ability. Those things that I can't fix I pass to the LCIS tech (land communications and information systems technician) in Sper. He is truly the king of the nerds, and divides his time between playing pirated Game Boy Advance games on his laptop, and fixing anything technological thrown at him. For me, hearing the beep of a radio that I made work properly or the ping of an antenna finally pointing toward a satellite fills me with pride. It is that feeling that almost makes being a signaller worth it.

Shortly after I arrived in Sperwan Ghar, our printer broke down. A large Xerox colour printer is not something that one generally associates with a fighting infantry company, but like any other bureaucracy, the military has become reliant on fast, easy printing of computer files. I was told that it was my job to fix it, even though I had no idea how it worked. I took it apart as best as I could, used compressed air to clean out the ubiquitous Afghan dust, put it back together, and went through the settings. But I could not get the piece of plastic to give me paper. Finally, I copied the help number off the printed sticker on the side, and went to our satellite phone to call Xerox for help. I had to patch the call through a switchboard in Ottawa, and waited on hold as the 1–800 number dialled. I stood with a duty officer looking over my shoulder in the middle of a war zone listening to grainy elevator Muzak from a signal that had spanned two continents. Finally, I was able to speak to a human.

"Xerox Help Services, Chantal speaking, how can I help?"

"Umm . . . Hello, I have a model 200 Xerox printer that is no longer working. It gives me the following error message." I recite the error message.

"Okay, just one second. It appears that that error can't be fixed by you. What is your address? We will send a technician out to take a look at it."

"Uh . . . I don't think that that will be possible. I'm in Afghanistan." (What I should have said is, "My address is 1 Old Russian Compound, Sperwan Ghar, Kandahar.")

"I'm sorry, did you say Afghanistan?"

"Yes, ma'am. You are going to need to tell me how to fix this problem myself."

After listening to more Muzak, I eventually had to call in the LCIS tech, and together we fixed the problem.

Outside Mushan, I hear a din rise from the ANA portion of the camp. I wander over, and see an ANA soldier tying up the legs of a goat. Apparently, they want to celebrate our safe return to the strongpoint with a feast. Canadian soldiers crowd around as they decapitate the goat, recording its death with their digital cameras. I don't feel up to watching, so I go back to my sleeping bag and chat to a few of the infantry there.

"Man, that CP has got air conditioning."

"Really, like it's cold?"

"No, it's broken, but the fan works, and it's cooler than it is outside. The water is about room temperature." I see jealousy cloud the faces of my friends.

"You sigs always get the best fucking gos."

"Whatever, man, I fixed their TSK." A look of appreciation for my technical feat is noticeably absent from their faces, so I decide to just be quiet and lie down, and try to get some sleep.

In about an hour, it's announced that the ANA's feast is prepared, and that we can go get food if we choose. The doc points out the certainty of gastrointestinal problems that will result from eating the goat. We all remember a friend who got so sick from eating Afghan food that he nearly died (it had been sitting out for two days unrefrigerated before he ate it). I'm starved for real food, however, and I decide to give it a try. I line up behind a group of Canadian engineers. The Afghans believe that it is only hospitable to serve us first, as we are guests in their country. I get to the front and smile at the soldier who is dishing out stew onto a tin plate such as one might see in Canadian prisons.

"*Salam Alaikum*" (peace be upon you), I say, trying to show off what I have learned from talking to our terps. The soldier greets me with a smile, and dishes me out what I guess might be considered a delicacy—a nondescript tube that a short time ago was inside a goat. It could be an intestine, or part of the throat, or any manner of other tube one might find in an animal (my zoology is not sufficient to identify it). On top of this, my tray is heaped with potatoes, and a large piece of the flat naan bread that Afghans eat every day. I go back to our sleeping area and sit down. The smell of real food attracts others, and I share my plate with Murphy, who sits beside me.

"What the fuck is that?"

"I don't know, man, it's some kind of a tube."

I take a tentative bite and gag a little at the taste; this may have been a mistake. I decide to leave the tube on the side of the plate and work on devouring the tiny pieces of meat and soaking up the stew with my naan, which is absolutely delicious and completely fresh. I have my fill, lounge around and smoke with the infantry. I have another 12-to-2 radio shift tonight, and it's about 2130. I lie on my sleeping pad and listen to the conversation swell around me. The temperature has begun to fall, and it's about 25 degrees. I take off my boots and socks and quickly enter that comfortable state between sleeping and waking. The conversations take place farther and farther away from me, and reality finally fades out of existence. At long last, I can count on two and a half hours of uninterrupted, restful sleep.

CHAPTER 6
SP MUSHAN
18 JULY 2008

Damn you, Chimos!
—Captain Michelson

THE NIGHT IS COOL as I am shaken awake for radio shift. I spend a few seconds in my ranger blanket wondering where I am, and why I am supposed to wake up. My mind is unscrupulous in its attempts to allow me more sleep, and I almost allow my eyes to close once again. It is only with a forcible jerk that I throw my body into a sitting position. The night is perfectly still and dark; I can barely make out the huddled masses of the rest of the section sleeping around me. Occasionally, an isolated snore emanates from one of those forms. For me, the bleary-eyed monotony of another depressing army awakening has begun. I stumble as I put my boots on, and walk uncertainly through the unaccustomed dark toward the CP.

I find the OMLT operator reading a magazine behind the desk, and we exchange a nod. "Anything going on?" I ask.

"Nope."

He is snoring before I'm finished opening a four-month-old edition of *Nuts,* a British "lads' magazine" that shows nipples. I turn the pages slowly, but my brain doesn't seem willing to process even this soft-core pornography. I am more tired than I would have thought possible. I didn't realize the adrenalin rush of the patrol would drop off so far into exhaustion. Outside the CP I smoke cigarette after cigarette and try to think about the big questions, just to give my mind something to do, but I can't seem to marshal my thoughts. I wonder what love is, but end up thinking only about why I can't think about anything. With a sigh, I finish my fourth cigarette, stand up heavily, and go back into the CP. My throat aches and feels dry. The squalid taste of the cigarettes lingers in my mouth. I wish that I had a piece of gum.

"2, this is Mushan, radio check, over."

A few seconds pass before I hear the dozy voice of Ryan LaFontaine on the other end of the radio 14 kilometres away, as the crow flies, in the base that I've learned to think of as home. I am in danger of growing wistful.

"2, you are loud and clear, over." Ryan drawls out the word *loud*, thus questioning why I am breaking the silent serenity of a quiet night-time radio shift.

My answer comes in the professional quality that I try to inject into my words as I respond, "Mushan, loud and clear, out." I feel that if I can respond with perfect voice procedure, I will imply that I am just doing my job and trying to make sure that the radios are functional.

I feel a little bit guilty as soon as I finish my staccato *out.* I must sound pretty pretentious to the droopy-eyed listeners who are monitoring this frequency throughout Panjway. Moreover, Ryan is my friend, and it is rude to publicly call him out over the radio. There is such a thing as radio manners.

Although I envy Ryan his cushy seat back in Sperwan Ghar, I know that he is pulling 12-hour shifts. Your mind begins to go mushy after eight hours in an air-conditioned room, surrounded by a never-ending electronic drone, constantly keyed up to hear every word that comes out of three radio nets. Although I certainly feel that I am suffering, Ryan is suffering the mentally numbing purgatory of an endless CP shift.

Some dreary author I read in a half-remembered undergraduate philosophy class wrote that every relationship is a power relationship. With a rigid rank structure that doesn't allow for much dissension, the army seems to be the embodiment of this principle. Personally, I'm inclined to believe this statement. I have found that almost every interchange in life is usually a thinly veiled attempt to jockey for position with another person. Voice Procedure (VP), the formal way that we talk over a radio, is no different. The more rigidly the army tries to control the way that we speak, the more power we are able to communicate through our intonation.

I open up the TSK laptop and try to find interesting reports and returns on it. One of the habits that I've had to force myself out of overseas is snooping. The army works on a "need to know" basis, but the amount of access that I have to information that I *don't* need to know is staggering. A large part of me wants to contextualize what I am experiencing, and so looks for indications about what is going on around me. On the other hand, it could just be that I am constantly surrounded by information, and am by nature curious. It seems that every report I come into contact with overseas is classified, and I have to control my urge to learn things that don't apply to me.

I don't find anything interesting on the computer, as it hasn't worked for months. I open Spider Solitaire and begin the pointless procedure of trying to sort the cards into their respective piles. This is likely the only task this computer will be asked to perform now that I've fixed the power cable. I am quickly engrossed in this mindless activity, and play for the next two and a half hours. When I look at my watch it is 0200. I'm a half-hour late waking the next guy up for shift. Oh well, that will be a nice surprise when he finishes wiping the sleep out of his eyes. I find the 9 Platoon signaller, shake him, and go back to the CP. By 0230 I am back in my ranger blanket.

I wake up once again in the stifling heat of mid-morning Afghanistan. For the first time in three days, however, I feel rested. I stir and yawn inside my ranger blanket, and when I get up and pull a ration out of the box I feel good, ready to conquer the day. This will be fairly easy, as the day consists of little more than sitting around and hydrating. We will be on the go again tonight, but until then all I have to do is double-check my kit and nap. I feel like I've just woken up on a camping trip where I have nothing to do but make my own food and hang around with others all day.

As I smoke, I watch people going about their business. Most of my section lounges in the shade trying to escape the heat. A few people are engaged in attempts to cool water using the sock method, and a few are talking in a subdued way about women.

"I got to talking to that arty chick the other day. Apparently she and her boyfriend are having some problems."

"You would just love to swoop in there, eh?"

"Wouldn't you? All those chicks go to the gym together, and I was working out with them the other day. She's got a nice wiggle on her."

There are six women in Sperwan Ghar (depending on the number of medics who rotate through), but only three who are unmarried and dateable, all of whom are in the artillery. Discussing them has begun to consume hours of our time. At one point, we discuss the feasibility of getting the artillery to fire a mission right after they go into the shower. When a gun fires, all artillery personnel must report to their stations, and they would have to run out in their towels. As the signaller, I would have to radio in the call. It seems like a workable plan.

The artillery (arty) in Sper is superb. We have two M777 155mm howitzers in our patrol base, and their crews conduct themselves with poise and professionalism. By the end of our tour, it takes only five minutes from the moment that we hear a contact report over the radio to the time that their first round lands. The noise is incredible; in fact, it is less a noise than the feeling of a concussion against your body. The first time I heard it, I thought that we were being attacked, and that the world was coming to an end. Over the months, I've gotten used to the unannounced thunder, and it usually signals that something important is happening. Most of the time, I can avoid wincing when I hear the thud and boom of a 155mm round leaving the barrel at 827 metres per second. In the Internet trailers, the concussion doubles, due to the enclosed space. It shakes the doors open, usually while I am composing an important e-mail. I find it hard at these moments not to scream at the arty to shut up.

Near the end of the tour, we got a new LCIS tech. The day that he arrived, my glasses snapped when I fell asleep with them on. I asked him to solder them back together. He agreed, put them in a vise, and began the process of soldering. While he leaned forward to get a better look at what he was doing, the guns went off. He banged his head off a shelf and on the rebound very nearly hit his forehead with the soldering iron.

"What the fuck was that?" he asked with a look of alarm.

"It's just the arty, man, don't worry about it." I tried to say this with the air of a seasoned vet, and my tired, dirt-covered, bedraggled face reinforced this image. I felt smug and superior, but tried not to show it.

My weapon has not been cleaned since we left Sperwan Ghar, and it is covered by a thin layer of dirt. I blow on the hand guards, and see a cloud of dust appear. I sit down and pull out my cleaning kit (a rag, a paintbrush, a pull-through and some gun oil known as CLP). I unload my weapon (there is still a live round in the chamber at this point), and proceed to break it down. I find it satisfying to understand how things work, and I enjoy the process of taking apart a weapon.

Like most mechanical devices, rifles are fairly simple to understand when you analyze their component parts; the bolt is pushed into the stock of the weapon, either by manual force or by the explosion of a bullet. As it moves back into position, a round is fed up out of the magazine, and inserted into the breach. The spring on the hammer is released when the trigger is pulled, forcing the hammer to hit the firing pin (inside the bolt), which strikes the primer on the back of the bullet casing. The impact of the firing pin on the round causes combustion and a well-channelled explosion propels the bullet through the rifled grooves of the barrel and into or through whatever is on the other end—a simple, satisfying system. Unlike most other mechanical systems, however, our weapons are designed primarily to kill other human beings.

In the military context, a weapon has only two purposes: force and the threat of force. All of our training and efforts are little more than a complex system to get armed individuals to apply force at the right place at the right time. Military theorist Carl von Clausewitz said that "war is an extension of policy by another means." Soldiers are merely tools deployed to further a country's foreign or domestic policy—highly trained, highly motivated, and very well-armed tools.

I lay out the pieces of my weapon on an old T-shirt and sit cross-legged behind it. Out of long habit, I lay the pieces of the bolt out neatly and arrange them by size: firing pin–retaining pin, bolt cam pin, firing pin, bolt, bolt carrier. I wipe the dust off these pieces, and lube them up with some CLP. I put the bolt back together, and move on to wiping out the upper and lower receiver groups (the top and bottom of the rifle). I then clean the outside and pull-through the barrel. When I am done, I double-check the seating and function of my Maglite and my laser sight, and put the weapon back together. Lower receiver group slots into upper receiver group, front pin is pushed in, cocking handle is pushed halfway into the upper receiver group, then the bolt is inserted with a satisfying metallic *click* as it slots into place, followed by a satisfying *thunk* as the weapon is closed and the lower retaining pin is pushed back into place. Twenty minutes after I start working on my weapon, it is put back together, with considerably less dust. I cock it a few times and feel the newly lubricated bolt sliding smoothly back and forth. I pull the trigger, and replace the magazine in its housing. I feel a strange catharsis when I look at my newly cleaned weapon. I still haven't fired it in combat, but I have used it to apply moral force on a number of occasions. My weapon gives me a feeling of safety that is probably exaggerated. I feel better when it is clean.

Basic training is the formative experience in every soldier's life. No matter how many other courses you might do, from airborne to combat diver (the underwater knife-fighting course), basic is where you learn to think like a soldier. Polishing boots, marching up and down, and learning to make a bed perfectly do not on their own turn a person into a soldier. It is the constant, unending stress and discipline, endured for months, that fundamentally change the way a person thinks and acts. Recruits often rebel against this new, almost entirely alien mindset, and many quit. It is fascinating to see how people respond to prolonged stress, and every single soldier has a series of "back on basic" stories. As a soldier's career progresses, however, these stories are weeded out by a process of natural selection. The more experience you have, the less you need to fall back on your basic. But if other courses and experiences hone a soldier's skill set, on basic you become a soldier.

I did my basic in the summer of 2001, before the September 11 attacks. I was 17 when I arrived in dusty Dundurn, Saskatchewan, and I had never even put on a uniform. By the end of those two months of physical training, inspections, jackings, and what is affectionately termed *cock* (perhaps more appropriately defined as "remedial training"), I was a completely different person. Now, even though I'm a reservist, I don't really understand how civilians think. Just as soldiers are a closed book to the general population, the general population is a closed book to us. Like a tattoo, basic training is forever imprinted on a soldier's psyche; it can never be fully removed. After basic, you can never really know what it would be like to go through life without it.

It is not the instruction or the instructors that turn someone into a soldier. It is the times in between visits from them, when you are forced into a group dynamic that is wholly alien. It is those long minutes spent smoking with one eye out for an instructor coming to jack you up, and the other focusing on a story about how tight a buddy's first girlfriend was. It's the choice to give up choice, sitting where you have been told to sit for as long as you have been told to sit there. It is the shared feeling of the injustice of it all, that you have to stand at attention with your beret on in the hot sun while your instructors laugh and joke in the shade, that you have to spend hours making your bed only to see it ripped up in front of your face.

On basic training, the army tries to erase individual identity. It dresses everyone in the same clothing, makes you spend mind-numbing hours cleaning your boots/rooms/running shoes. It makes you stand at attention whenever you speak to someone of a higher rank, which is everybody (civilians are addressed as "sir" or "ma'am," but you don't see very many of them). It makes you stand at attention while you wait for your class on standing at attention. Combine this with a perpetual lack of sleep and constant physical training. Then do it all to a 17-year-old kid, still in high school, whose main goal is to see a naked girl who is not on the Internet.

The army tries its hardest to take away your individual identity, but it usually fails—because you begin to give it up freely. Thought processes begin to work along well-established and ancient lines. Soldiers care about food, sleep, booze, women, and smokes. These topics overwhelm almost every conversation, and even people with substantial education find themselves incapable of discussing anything else.

Did the army do this to you? Yes and no. The army tried its best with its rank, classes, and timings, but in the end, the individual is the one who chooses to care almost exclusively about booze, women and smokes. It is the individual who chooses to love the platoon while wanting to kick the teeth out of a few of it members. It is the long periods in between, when soldiers mentally prepare for what is to come, that changes their identity.

Every soldier looks at the same three things when passing another soldier: rank epaulette, cap badge, and beret. All the necessary information is passed in this way. Are they a lower rank or higher rank? Do I have to salute? What trade is the person I'm about to pass? Combat arms, logistics, signals? How is their beret formed? Do they care about their career, or are they apathetic? Every soldier has the same basic identity, but every soldier chooses for that to be the case. You must either change or fail to fit in. If you don't fit in, you are cut off from the support that is given by the group, the most important and durable aspect of military life. It's comforting to find such an unambiguous definition of who you are. It's all in the uniform.

My section commander on basic was a tall, lean LCIS tech from Regina, Master Corporal Jason Bromstad. He was the picture of an ideal signaller. Like me, he was a massive nerd. He was also immensely professional, relatively compassionate (which means

something different when discussing an instructor on basic training), and highly skilled. He had the longest, thinnest fingers I have
ever seen, and every day he would inspect our weapons, laid out
neatly on our beds, and find black carbon that we had unsuc-
cessfully tried to remove from some inaccessible nook. Every day
we would try harder to remove this carbon, and all to no avail. It
was one of the most frustrating experiences I have ever had, but it
taught me an important lesson: in the army, it is not always possible
to succeed (and remove every molecule of carbon), but that doesn't
change the fact that you must still try your hardest.

Overseas, we never had a weapons inspection, as we were trusted
to perform this most basic soldiering skill on our own. There was
also no real drive to remove every speck of carbon. Instead, we
cleaned our weapons to make them functional, and to prevent any
jams in the event that we found ourselves in a firefight. The realities
of combat led to pragmatism in everything that we did. The mun-
danity and stupidity of the endless quest for a spotless weapon was
replaced by the hard fact that we needed our weapons to function
perfectly in the event that we had to pull the trigger.

The day progresses at an almost lackadaisical pace. We will be on
the go again tonight, and I know that this will mean exhaustion,
aching shoulders, and danger. This reality seems distant while we sit
and while away another blistering day in Mushan. Our suffering has
become a reality that must be accepted, as you might be forced to
accept an odious relative at Christmas dinner. We don't really want
to be doing what we are doing, but it is necessary and important,
and there is no point complaining about it. We talk mostly of better
times, of leave, what Cyprus is going to be like, the qualities of our
wives and girlfriends, the men that they are cheating on us with. We
think about home longingly, but it doesn't seem like a real place.

Like when you try to picture what summer will be like in the middle of a cold winter's day, to us Canada is an impossible ideal that exists on some unreachable plain. I can't imagine being cold, or even what cold water tastes like.

I pull out my tin of Danish-made smokes, and have another Prince, the "brand of the House of Prince A/S." I still have no idea who Prince A/S is, or why he only is referred to by his initials, but the pack conjures up images of Danish royalty enjoying their well-deserved tobacco after a hard day of hunting. The reality of lung cancer and debilitating health doesn't enter the equation. I enjoy the smoke heartily, ashing onto the blackened sand of Mushan, and think about better times. When I speak, I can hear the gruff quality that the tobacco has given my vocal cords, and it makes me feel like a tougher man. It is 1300, and the temperature is 50 degrees in the shade.

After a while, I get up and start to wander around the camp. There are ANA everywhere, and they go about their daily business just as we do. To us, everything that they do looks strange. They sing Pashto and Farsi songs as they work, they hold hands with their friends as they walk, and they "jingle" (which means "to decorate or ornament") everything. Jingle trucks (so named for the noise their rattling baubles and chains make) are the standard means of transportation, and the Afghan propensity to decorate knows no bounds. One of the water trucks near our area has a giant mural on the back depicting a white woman with a sword and a tiger roaring beside her. In the background is a depiction of the truck itself, making its way up a mountain with a fighter jet presiding over the scene. The style appears to be an agglomeration of Persian, Chinese, and Indian styles full of pointy arches and Middle Eastern geometric designs.

Everything that can be jingled is jingled. One of the ANA-owned Ford Rangers in our camp has a massive bedazzled picture of Hamid

Karzai hanging off the rear-view mirror. The equivalent would be having a massive picture of Stephen Harper or the Queen hanging from one of our G-Wagons. I know of one ANA soldier who got into trouble for painting his AK-74 bright gold.

The ANA soldiers lounge around in their green combat pants and tan T-shirts. Their supply system is not as zealous as ours, and they need to make do with much less than we carry. Some even wear berets on patrol, and their personal kit is lighter than ours, little more than their weapon, flak vest, a few water bottles, and spare magazines carried in pouches and pockets. The benefit is that the Afghans can run faster and longer then we can, and we use them to catch Taliban who run away from us. One of the Afghans has a prosthetic leg, but he still manages to keep up on all of our patrols. Their uniforms look like castoff American fatigues, but the soldiers are always smiling, and willing to trade some naan bread for a smoke. Most exude kindness and bravery in all of their actions. But they have an unnerving habit of staring unabashedly at us when we pass them. Once when I was working out, an ANA soldier came into the gym and just stared at me for a half-hour. Although I'm willing to grant a certain amount of cultural leeway, that was still creepy.

Rumours abound about the Afghan proclivity for homosexual relationships, a phenomenon known to us as "man-love Thursdays." Religious and social conventions dictate that women must be hidden, that liquor is forbidden, and that homosexuality is a sin. The reality is considerably more sordid. Although I only once saw a woman without a veil, I did see homemade wine in large glass jars in one of the compounds that we searched.

Later in the tour, we were in Mushan on a routine resupply mission. We stayed the night so that the engineers could have two days to improve and repair the camp, and we had to do a shift of turret watch. The Canadian LAV is armed with a 25mm Bushmaster cannon, and the thermal imaging sights are fantastic. It was about

0200, and I was scanning the turret from side to side slowly, watching for enemy insurgents but seeing little more than cats and dogs. I scanned a little bit too far to the left on one of my sweeps, and saw two men with weapons walking around the razor wire that surrounds Mushan.

Holy fuck, Taliban, I said to myself. Although I'm not a qualified turret gunner, I understand how the weapon is fired and I prepared to take off the safety. Just as I put my finger on the trigger guard, I saw both men drop their weapons, and then their pants. Soon they were pleasuring each other in a trench that they thought was far from prying eyes. Whatever floats your boat, I guess.

A few Afghans stare at me, and smile as I wander around the camp. They seem friendly enough, but I'm afraid that their stares linger longer than is appropriate. I light another smoke, and go back to our sleeping area. As I sit down, we get the word. There is going to be a BIP (blow in place) of the IED components found yesterday. The engineers have been busy digging a pit outside the camp for the last few hours, and they have filled that pit with IED components and illumination carrier shells. When the artillery fires an illumination round, it burns white phosphorous in the air as it descends on a parachute. The carrier shell, the portion that actually carries the white phosphorous, can be scrounged and reused by the Taliban in their IEDs. We found a couple yesterday, and decided to BIP them along with the other components.

The engineers carry a lot of C-4 plastic explosive. Before departing on a patrol, they never really know how many things they are going to need to blow up. C-4 is fairly versatile, and can be used to blow in the doors of compounds or walls, or to create new openings; it can blow IEDs that are found on the patrol or BIP components in a safe location. Engineers always carry too much C-4, as they don't want to run out. Unsurprisingly, they are keen to use up as much of the dead weight as possible, as we are halfway through the patrol and they have not had the opportunity to blow anything up. Plus, why make a small explosion when you can make a big explosion? If it's worth doing, it's worth overdoing.

The engineers finish setting up the IED components for the BIP. They move back behind the HESCO Bastions and pass the word.

"Boys," we hear, "there is going to be a BIP." No big deal, we've seen enough explosions at this point that they don't really faze us. "Oh, and boys, you are going to want to put on helmets and get behind cover. This is going to be *big*." A collective sigh and grumbling can be heard as we find our helmets and flak vests, put them on, and sit behind a row of sandbags. I sit beside Murphy and talk to him about the "bullshit" safety regulations. We've all been through enough BIPs.

"Two minutes!" someone shouts. I light a cigarette. "One minute!" Good. Soon I can go back to doing nothing without my body armour on.

"30 seconds . . . 10 . . ."

Boom! The world shakes like I have never felt it shake before. One of the sandbag walls collapses, and the concussion takes the wind out of us for a few seconds. The BIP occurred five seconds before the engineers thought it would, but I guess these things are hard to judge perfectly. We smile and laugh at our own unforeseen fright, and as the dust settles we get back up. As I walk back to my kit, I see Captain Michelson, the FOO, noticeably shaken and staggering forward. He is being helped by two other soldiers. I look more closely at him, and I notice that blood is trickling down his face from the left side of his head. He is pale, and when he first sees me his mouth gapes once or twice as if he's trying to say words, but he is unable to. His eyes slowly focus, and he looks at me and says loudly, "Damn you, Chimos!" his fist shaking in the air.

During the BIP, a carrier shell flew over the HESCO Bastions, bounced off the top of two separate sea cans, and ricocheted straight into his head. He had been the one who ordered that carrier shell fired in the first place, two nights ago when we were waiting outside the SP. He was almost literally hoisted by his own petard. I'm terrified for the FOO, a tough old bastard through and through. He doesn't look particularly stable on his feet, and I try to help him walk over to the medic. There are already two people walking with him, however, and he doesn't want to be carried. He gets to the UMS (unit medical station), and lies on a cot. They apply a bandage to the wound, which is still dripping blood at a blessedly slow pace. I watch as the doc begins to work on him, and decide that I can probably be used best at the CP, passing on the messages. I walk quickly there, but when I arrive they have everything well in hand. The 9 liner (medevac request) is already being sent, and there is nothing I can do. Unfortunately, Mushan has gotten lots of practice with calling in 9 liners. I ask if there is anything that I can do, and I'm told to fuck off. Manners don't have much of a place during a casualty situation. I'm glad that I double-checked the radios last night, however.

I go back to my kit and sit down. I hear the story being retold for the benefit of those who weren't nearby. Someone finds the carrier shell and gives it to Captain Michelson. We find the ricochet marks on the sea cans, and feel like detectives for a few minutes. The shell had bounced off the steel frame of the first sea can, and punched a hole through the quarter-inch aluminum above it. It then came off at an angle, struck the frame of another sea can that Captain Michelson was sitting underneath and struck him in the head. He was lucky that the two impacts took so much momentum away from the shell. If it had been going any faster he would have been killed. I guess that he was also extremely unlucky that he was hit in the first place, but I'm a glass-half-full person.

———————————

Captain Michelson is a middle-aged officer who was originally a reservist NCM. I've found that officers who were once in the ranks generally filter to one extreme of competence or the other. Some are so obsessed with their glory days that they fall into the "Cyprus trap," and spend the majority of their time talking and thinking about the way things were. Others embrace the challenges inherent in being an officer, and excel at their new profession. Captain Michelson falls into the latter category. A dedicated family man, he talks often about his wife, children, and home life. He is maybe 40, with an open, sun-beaten face. He is a tall, large man who tries to hide his size with his posture. His face exudes good humour and kindness, and he feels his way through conversations with stock responses or funny say-ings. Once when his LAV broke down, we spent an entire operation together in the back of our command vehicle. We chatted at length while we ate rations in the air sentry hatch, and I found out all about his kids and his plans. I told him about how I wanted to build my own house when I got back from tour, and he responded that my best bet was probably a geodome. He explained a geodome design that he'd seen at the University of Brandon. The design is basically a sandbag igloo covered in concrete and insulation. Apparently it is simple and economical to make. Deep in my heart, I still harbour the goal of constructing my own geodome.

Captain Michelson is convinced that he has a cursed call sign. Two FOOs on previous rotations have been killed, both being call sign G13. He is call sign G23, but he replaced G13. He found the name of Captain Jefferson Francis etched above his bed in a bunker on the top of Sperwan Ghar. Captain Francis was killed by an IED in 2007 before we arrived.

I think that we all carry some manner of lucky charm with us, and a crucifix blessed by the padre hangs in the turret of our LAV.

After our charmed ride into Talukan the night Terry Street died, and the next day when an IED went off 20 metres in front of us, we feel that we have a lucky LAV. Intellectually, I'm aware that there is probably no such thing as luck, but I still knock on wood, and try my hardest not to tempt fate with my words or actions. On my dog tags hang two medals, one of Saint Christopher, given to me by my godparents, and one of the Archangel Gabriel, given to me by a friend from my unit. I'm not exactly a devout Catholic, but when I lost my Saint Christopher medal after the chain snapped, I had a tiny panic attack. Someone eventually found it and gave it back to me saying, "Don't you know that this doesn't do anything if you don't wear it?" I don't even know if it does anything if you *do* wear it, but I'm not taking any chances. Both medals are secured to my dog tags by a double-looped elastic band. I also have a length of braided string that Darcy made in 2005 tied to the dog tags. I feel an intense distaste for the idea of taking any one of these three things off, and by this point in the tour they are encrusted with filth and the metal has begun to oxidize.

The medics continue to work on Captain Michelson, and soon enough he is bandaged up and being prepared for his helicopter ride. He is talking and looks lucid when I poke my head into the UMS. I ask the doc how he's doing, and he says that the captain is going to be fine. I am immensely relieved. We hear the distant sound of an American Black Hawk growing louder. Captain Michelson is rushed out onto the HLZ (helicopter landing zone) by a party of stretcher bearers. I ask if I can help, but they have things under control.

The helicopter swoops in to land, and kicks up a massive cloud of dust that temporarily eclipses the sun. It is blazing hot, and we are all covered in another layer of dust as the helicopter takes off once again. I watch the dust cloud roll over the HESCOs, and wonder how the pilots can take off completely blind. The chopper makes a massive volume of sound, but it quickly diminishes. We see the helicopter hover for a brief second, and it disappears into the horizon accompanied by another Black Hawk. The ensuing peace makes us more aware of the sounds around us. I hear someone throwing out a ration into a garbage bag, and the rustle of kit being moved around. The army seems to enjoy alternating intense noise with intense quiet. The dust clears, and the sun reigns once again. I look up at the sky and wonder what clouds look like. I haven't seen one since the last dust storm almost two months ago.

Dust storms in Afghanistan are a unique and awe-inspiring experience. They usually bring rain, and black out the sky, like some kind of apocalyptic prophesy. Once, I was sitting in my room when the door sucked in and then banged out in quick succession. I had gotten off shift an hour before, and nothing had been out of the ordinary. I went outside to see what was going on and was greeted by a wall of dust that touched the sky. My ears popped, and it was incredibly calm. The light took on a different quality, as if someone were dimming the switch on the sun, and instantly our outpost was in the middle of it. I was alone for almost the first time on the tour, as everyone else was out at a routine meeting at Ma'sum Ghar. I frantically tried to batten down the hatches and tie down the tarps that we used as shade, but when the entire frame spiralled into the violent sky and I found myself having a hard time breathing, I decided that there was little I could do. I grabbed my goggles off my helmet, and wrapped a T-shirt around my face and kept trying to tie down everything that could fly away. Just then, the LAVs pulled in, and the rest of the headquarters section began to help me out. I pushed into the teeth of the wind, the sand stinging my face in a million places, and took a look at our antennas on the roof. One was no longer standing, and one was being held on by only the coaxial cable attached to the radiating element (or sputnik). I ran through the compound while the wind tried to destroy everything around me, climbed onto the roof, and pulled in the radiating element that was suspended in mid-air. I then tightened off the masts themselves, and only just prevented the other two from flying away. Ryan LaFontaine joined me on the roof, and we couldn't communicate even by shouting into each other's ears. I motioned with my hands at the guy wires that were about to snap, and we just barely managed to hold onto them until the dust storm passed. We were soaking wet from the driving rain, and every piece of exposed skin had been pulverized by sand. The storm lasted for about 30 minutes.

It rained only twice the entire time that we were overseas, and both times it was like that. Everything in Afghanistan is deadly, from the bugs (which we call the Afghan Air Force) to the snakes to the rainstorms. Everything is imbued with a quality of latent and deadly strength. It is an interesting place to live.

In Mushan, the heat is beginning to wane. The helicopters have disappeared into the distance, and it is about 1500, the time of day when the worst part of the heat is over and I can begin to relax a little more comfortably. We are told that we will be departing at 2000, after the sun sets. I don't really feel tired, so I try to stomach some more water. We set up a garbage can full of well water, and stick water bottles inside to cool them. We play cards while we drink the water. The game is Asshole, and six of us sit down—Smitty, Jeff Brazeau, a couple of snipers, me, and the doc. Everyone around me blatantly tries to cheat, and nobody takes the game seriously. It is mostly just an opportunity to smoke and unwind. I watch Smitty sit on the 2s that he gets when he is asshole, and hear the argument rage about whether or not he's cheating. I played this game often at university, and work on upgrading my position from vice-ass. Soon I am the pres. We continue to play for about an hour, until finally someone stands up, and we all realize that there are probably better uses of our time.

I sit once more on a chair outside our tent, smoke another cigarette, and drink another bottle of water. It is 1600, and we will be departing in four hours. I go to my sleeping pad, take off my boots and lie down. I'm not tired. I lay out my uniform and adjust my kit. I'm still not tired. I close my eyes and will sleep to come. Finally, I sleep restlessly on the sand for a few hours.

CHAPTER 7
SP MUSHAN TO COP ZANGABAD
18–19 JULY 2008

If all the ways I've been along were marked on a map and joined up with a line, it might represent a minotaur.
—PABLO PICASSO

PABLO PICASSO, regarded as the greatest artist of his generation, or perhaps of all time (although I'm still not entirely sure why), became obsessed with the Minotaur later in life. I had read a biography about him by Patrick O'Brian shortly before departing on this patrol. When I came to the section that explained his obsession with the image of the Minotaur I was confused, as I was by so much else in that book (I don't think I "get" Picasso in any meaningful sense). Why would Picasso care so much about a mythological creature, half man and half bull? I did a little bit of research (Wikipedia) but still didn't feel I understood. That changed during the patrol.

For me, and I believe for Picasso, the symbol of the Minotaur and the symbol of the labyrinth are inextricably linked. The Minotaur was born of Pasiphaë, the wife of Minos, the Cretan king, who refused to kill a sacrificial white bull given to him by Poseidon. In punishment, Poseidon made Pasiphaë fall in love with the bull and engage in carnal relations with it. Pasiphaë's progeny was a monster, half man and half bull, that served as a living reminder not to "screw" with the gods. The Minotaur was kept in the middle of a labyrinth. Virgins would be set loose in the labyrinth, where they would get lost and be eaten by the beast when they reached the centre. The Minotaur was eventually killed by the warrior Theseus, who is remembered in song and story. I believe that Picasso was drawn to the themes of this myth because he experienced them in his life. I hadn't had similar experiences until I set out from Mushan on this night.

Looking back on this patrol, it seems that we were lost as we tried to find our way out, and back to home and peace. The mud walls, always difficult to climb over, funnelled us onto routes that we might not have otherwise chosen. Wadis, riverbeds, and fear of IEDs forced us to follow a circuitous path that didn't seem to go anywhere. Although I could usually tell what direction we were travelling, based on the looming emptiness of the riverbed, which was always on our left, looking back it feels as if we were in an Afghan labyrinth, without any yarn to guide us. Even though time has passed, and hindsight has closed in on my experiences, I don't know if I will ever truly leave Panjway. It continues to present itself to my restless mind, and I'm not sure if a day goes by that I don't spend a little bit of time back in Afghanistan, back on patrol.

I sleep poorly in the sand, and am up well before we need to step off. I double-check my kit and smoke a few cigarettes. I feel restless and think about how much of this patrol is left. We start our move back toward Sperwan Ghar tonight, but we may be conducting a few more patrols in Zangabad over the next couple of days. *We've been out for . . . ?* My erratic sleep schedule makes it hard to remember. *Well, we left on . . . Monday? Tuesday?* I don't know. *What day is it today? Friday? Really?* I think about home, and going to the bar at the end of a long week of work. It doesn't seem real that a schedule like that could exist. I give up trying to remember how long we've been out, and think about how long we have until we get back.

Well, we'll be in Zangabad by tomorrow, and then we will sleep all day, so that's one day. If we conduct a patrol, we'll step off the next day after I get up again, so that's two days. If we head back to Sper at that point, then it will be three days. No, wait, we won't head back until the day after that, because we will need to sleep. We can't very well conduct a fighting patrol and a move back in the same day. *How many days was that again? Four? Five? I don't know. I guess that we'll get back when we get back.* Fatalism is the only viable philosophy for a low-ranking soldier. Things will either happen or they will not. You will find out when you find out.

As the sun dips behind the HESCO Bastions, and the shadows grow longer, I smoke another cigarette and brood. I don't have a specific focal point for my anger, but I'm pretty tired of this patrol, and there really is no way out of it. So I think about how much my shoulders are going to hurt. I'm not really used to sustained patrolling, and it is beginning to take its toll on my body. I guess it's like anything you ever do; it only gets easy when you do it a lot. I smile at the thought of some of the more difficult situations I've been in, climbing mountains in Alberta or running up and down hills in Shilo. Whenever I suffer, I always seem to forget about the pain and remember the good times, when all is said and done.

The sliver of sun remaining over the horizon has turned a deep, dark orange, and blue dusk begins to appear around us. I put my shirt on and get my kit ready to go. I smoke another cigarette, as I won't be able to have another until we get to Talukan. Tobacco has lost its appeal, but I still smoke slowly, holding it between the thumb and index finger of my gloved hand, flicking the ash into the sand with my middle finger. The habit calms me down and helps me get into the right mindset before we step off. The call to prayer echoes around us. Before I'm finished, I see people putting on their kit. We are on the go once again.

I wait until everyone else has started walking before putting on my helmet. I wait a few seconds more for the order of march to sort itself out, find the OC, and line up behind him. I go through the familiar motions and hear the muffled sounds of a patrol stepping off. This is going to be a long night.

As the lead elements of the patrol are swallowed up by the night, I follow them outside the wire, completely oblivious to the fact that this is a night that will forever be etched in my memory. I walk in the blissful ignorance of those that suffer righteously. I have no reason to think that tonight will be different from any other night. I am wrong.

Soon Mushan is once again a monolithic shape looming in the moonlight. I wish it well as it recedes over the horizon. We are making excellent time. The moon is almost full, and we have more light to see with than we've had to this point on the patrol. I think about what is actually happening with the moon; how it is reflecting the sun's light back onto the earth, how it is a sphere just as Earth is, that it is daytime on the moon right now. I think about the sun and the size of the universe. I think about how important this patrol feels to me right now, and how unimportant it is in the grand scheme of things. I feel small as I walk through the shadows cast by objects immensely larger then I am.

By 2100 we are once again on the riverbed. The sweat drips down my face, but I feel strong despite the pain my pack is causing. Every time we stop, I bend over and throw the weight of my pack onto my back. It relieves the pain for a few blissful seconds, but it makes me look bad to the people behind me. Who cares? It's just a terp and the FOO party minus Captain Michelson. Ahead of me, the OC does the same thing, and I'm filled with an irrational hatred. I can't really describe why I would be so hypocritical as to condemn the OC for doing the same thing that I am. It's probably just latent, pent-up aggression. The OC becomes the focal point for my anger. My eyes bore holes into his helmet as we march, but there is nothing I can say or do. I go back to concentrating on my spacing, scanning the area around me, and keeping my head up.

I quickly find myself lost in the rhythm of the patrol. The moonlight is bright, and wearing my civilian glasses I can see clearly in all directions. The landscape has once again taken on a surreal quality, and for a few moments I appreciate the beauty of patrolling at night along a riverbed that stretches forever in my imagination. I try to imagine a Cubist recreation of the flowing blue-grey lines and squat mud compounds of the landscape. I allow myself to escape into my imagination. I think about art, beauty, and aesthetics. Mostly I think about Darcy, and try to picture her face. I think about the sunny drive to the University of Calgary, and walking through the green fields that cover the campus. I think about how long it's been since I've seen a green field. Not since the opium harvest. I think about our desert uniforms, and try to imagine what green CADPAT looks like. Every few minutes, I'm jolted out of my reverie by the man in front of me stopping, or by some obstacle that I must cross, but for the most part I spend the move from Mushan to Talukan inside my head, thinking about better times.

We continue to walk quickly as we hear the good news over the radio: Talukan has eyes on our lead elements. I'm sweating and tired, but feel good. The majority of this leg of the patrol is spent in a fairly pleasant reflection, punctuated by painful moments and the taste of my own sweat. I smile for the first time tonight as we enter Talukan. I see Allan there, limping slightly, and we share a smoke. I ask him how his ankle is doing and he replies that it feels good, that it's taped up tightly by the docs, and that he's ready to finish off the patrol. I'm happy that he's feeling better, and watch him rejoin the engineer section. I see WO Abrahams, and he passes me a bottle of water. We bullshit and I tell stories about the fight we got into two days ago. I smoke another cigarette with him in the blissful cool of an Afghan summer night, without a helmet on.

"So there was a wedding last night, eh?" WO Abrahams looks at me, intent on telling his story. He recounts how an elderly

Afghan man had approached the COP a few days ago to inform the Canadians of his son's wedding. The man then politely asked if we would mind not "bombing him" while the wedding feast was going on. It is an Afghan tradition to fire off AK-47s when there is a wedding. We call these shots *Afghan fireworks.* (The fact that gravity will eventually return those bullets to earth doesn't seem to enter into their calculations; so be it, we are a culturally sensitive army.) He then asked WO Abrahams if he could pay the Canadians to fire off a few para-flares (man-portable parachute flares that we use to illuminate the night). WO Abrahams responded that it would be his pleasure to help this man's son on his wedding day, and the COP had fired four para-flares in honour of this new marriage the night before our patrol arrived.

"It's all about winning hearts and minds, eh?" WO Abrahams says, laughing and exhaling smoke. I smile. It's kind of a ridiculous situation, but we do have the best fireworks in town.

Soon enough and inevitably, we are on the move again, and I bid WO Abrahams farewell as I put my helmet back on. As I do up the clip and walk out into the moonlit night, he yells, "Hey, good luck tonight, eh, boys?" A quintessentially Canadian comment.

I smile as I continue to walk, but no one has ever really wished me luck before. I've done it to guys in my section if they leave on a patrol without me, but I'm always met with silence, and often a frown. I figure this is because no one wants to be reminded that they are in a situation that badly requires luck. We live in a scientific society, and the fact that science can't completely elimi-nate the threat posed by IEDs and enemy action bothers us at some level. WO Abrahams's comment makes me think about the risks of this patrol, the ever-present IED threat, and the possibil-ity that I won't make it back to Sperwan Ghar. I resign myself to the thought that I'm about thirty-seventh in the order of march, behind 4 Platoon and the ANA. It's a pretty safe place to be, relatively speaking. I get back to where Chris is sitting, put my smokes back in my chest rig, sigh, and prepare to carry on. It's not like I have a choice anyway.

Soon we have left Talukan behind and are walking along a tiny goat path beside a wadi. This is like many of the goat paths we have encountered that slowly narrow, threatening to dump us into the irrigation canal below. My steps are taken carefully; I'm ever mindful to keep my weight on the side of the mud wall, and not on the side of the drop. I've learned from my earlier mistakes. I take my time, and walk (or rather climb), trying not to guess how far down the drop is (probably only about four metres, but a sufficient fall nonetheless). It feels like I'm trying to walk along a balance beam with a bar fridge on my back. As I strain every nerve in concentration to keep myself on this path, which has narrowed to a boot width, I notice a strange sound. I hear drumbeats—actual beating drums, probably made from animal skin (I never saw them, so I can't say for sure).

The sound grows stronger as we approach, and in one of the compounds on the other side of the wadi, I see a fire and shadowy figures dancing to the incessant beat. It is the most alien sight I have encountered in my life. The drum continues to beat a slow, methodically rhythmic tone, and shadows swirl around the fire. The scene is lit by a strange, orange, fiery light, a colour that I haven't seen in days, and it casts deep shadows all around it. Outside the periphery of this light, figures sitting on their heels in the Afghan fashion can be made out smoking and conversing quietly. They seem completely oblivious to our presence, or they simply don't care that we are there. Afghans know the rules; they know that if they don't fuck with us, we won't fuck with them.

I doubt that the influence of opium and marijuana can be ruled out in the strange scene that I see as I hug a mud wall on the opposite side of the wadi; those sitting outside the circle of the fire are probably not smoking tobacco. Normally, the people we see on patrol stop and gawk at us as we walk through their villages in our stormtrooper gear. The fact that the spinning movement of other human beings continues not 10 metres from us, as we quietly skirt a wadi, pretending to be invisible, is completely surreal. It feels as though we are separated by more than a wadi. We are separated by the weight of our different traditions, histories, and purposes. I don't know if it's possible to be further away from another human being in any meaningful sense than I am from those swirling around the fire mere metres from me. I try to imagine what it would be like to sit on my heels, stoned, enjoying my weekly—what? dance party?—while an endless line of silently moving Canadians dressed in clothing that blends into its surroundings moves past me. It must have been a pretty surreal experience for them too.

The drumbeats fade as the goat path widens. We find ourselves once again in the village of Zangabad proper, travelling along a wide path framed by mud walls. The patrol regains its familiar flavour of sweat and pain, and we walk very quickly toward the COP. At this point, my whole being is consumed with trying to keep up with the man in front of me. My earlier philosophical thoughts recede from my mind like the beat of that alien drum. Once again, I concentrate on keeping up and begin to breathe harder.

In high school I took a class called Outdoor Education (OE); basically, it taught us how to survive in the Canadian Rockies, and we did quite a few trips into the remotest areas of Kananaskis and Rogers Pass in the fall, winter, and spring. I learned valuable skills, such as how to purify water, read a map, use a compass, pack enough on my back to survive three days, and cook in the wilderness. I remember that near the end of one particularly long trip, the pace increased remarkably. We were walking faster than we had for the entire trip, as the end was only one-and-a-half kilometres away. My OE teacher, who was walking in front of me, explained that it was always like this: "Like a horse to water, Ryan, we always move quicker when the end is in sight."

Less than a kilometre outside of Zangabad, these 80 Canadian soldiers are 80 horses who scent water. We move faster than we have since the patrol began, as the prospect of rest looms just over the horizon.

All of a sudden, the world flashes, and for milliseconds it is illuminated like daylight. I feel as if someone has taken a flash photograph of us. I am stunned by the light, but it is instantly dark again. Before I can process the flash, I feel the concussion of the blast and hear its boom.

I stand stunned for a second, and then drop to a knee. *What the fuck was that?* Most of the explosions that I've heard in the military have been planned, and for a second it feels like the explosion was supposed to happen, as if some captain in Wainwright decided to test how we would respond to coming under fire. But then the logical part of my mind realizes that we are under attack.

Was it an RPG? No, I would have heard the whistle as it flew through the air. Was it a mortar? It could have been, I guess. I rest my weapon on my thigh and again the world flashes for a moment. Again I feel the concussion and hear it echo through the landscape.

It must be a mortar attack. Why else would there have been two explosions in a row? It couldn't have been an IED, it had to be a mortar. My mind recoils from the thought of an IED. *It couldn't have been an IED, it must have been a mortar.* We'll find the base plate, isolate it, and call in artillery. I've heard it done over the radio countless times. It was a mortar.

The night is now exceptionally quiet. I wonder if there is something I should be doing and look at Chris. He has taken a knee and is scanning our moonlit surroundings. I do the same. I move my NVG in front of my eye and scan the green world as I wait for something to happen. Everything looks calm and silent.

"29er, this is 21, IED contact, we have casualties, wait out." I hear the voice of Lieutenant Chang on the radio. He sounds tense but professional. We all know what this means. Improvised explosive devices are the number-one killer in Afghanistan.

In a few seconds, I hear the doc and the sergeant-major push past us. They are walking quickly, trying not to tread on any terrain that might have another explosive buried underneath it. The engineers are already working farther ahead, clearing a route to the casualty. The doc's job is to stabilize the casualty prior to helicopter evacuation, and the sergeant-major's job is to coordinate the extraction process, establish a helicopter landing site (HLS), and get the right people moving to the right places as quickly as possible. My role is to stay put and ensure that radio traffic is passed quickly and accurately. I have done this plenty of times in training. Now it is different. I would like nothing more than to push up with them and help stabilize the casualty, but we are not moving. That is not my job. I look at Chris, to see what he is doing, and he stays put, looking stoically out upon our surroundings. I do the same. My radio squawks with the sound of oddly calm and intense traffic aimed at getting a helo spooled up as quickly as possible. I have absolutely nothing to do, so I go back to scanning the horizon with a greater intensity. My stomach feels heavy and sick.

We wait, kneeling down, looking out into the darkness, trapped in our own thoughts. I can feel my senses heighten and hear my own heart pounding in the cool night. My calves begin to ache; I am unaccustomed to taking a knee for an extended period of time. My pack straps dig into my shoulders, and I feel the weight of my kit once more. I find it hard to focus on our surroundings; I should be looking for movement that indicates there was a person who remotely detonated the IED, or connected some wires to a car battery as they watched our patrol pass. Someone might be there watching us, congratulating himself on successfully detonating an IED, sitting in the shadows quietly with a smug beeb smirk. Or it could have been a VOIED—"victim operated," the military's euphemistic term for a mine that is set off inadvertently, usually by someone stepping on it. If that is the case, then I am staring at nothing. But the image of some beeb sitting happily in his compound, probably stoned on hash or poppy, smiling at the thought that he might have killed one of us fills me with rage. My knee starts to ache so I decide to stand up. By this point, the echoes of the explosions have receded from my consciousness, and some small part of my brain wonders if any of it really happened, if someone really is injured, bleeding and choking no more than 100 metres from our position. It seems unreal, but it is not.

We get the word over the radio that there is no suitable site for an HLS near the blast seat. The sergeant-major says that we should push up to Zangabad, which is only 400 metres away, and that we should get the LAVs to come out and meet us. The OC decides to move up and make the call on the ground. Zangabad, under the command of call sign 24, decides to push out the LAV slowly, as far as the towers can cover it, theoretically immune from IEDs. This is, intellectually, a dangerous decision, as there is a possibility that the Taliban have managed to plant another IED under the nose of the tower, but it is difficult to convince oneself viscerally that there is a threat that cannot be seen or heard or identified, especially when the LAVs are needed as quickly as possible. Chris walks confidently and carefully in front of the OC as we begin to move forward. I follow behind him along with the terp, and realize too late that the entire line has begun to move. I have forgotten to tell the person behind me to stay put. I stop, turn around, and whisper furiously at an artillery observer named Burhoe who is hard of hearing.

"Stay here," I say and watch him cock his helmet to the side. He walks quickly toward me.

"What?" he says in a conspiratorial whisper.

"Stay fucking here," I whisper louder, but again his head cocks inquisitively to the side.

I hold up my hand, palm out, pushing it back and forth for emphasis. I embellish this gesture with "*Stay fucking here!*" I turn around again and see Chris, the OC, and the terp about 20 metres ahead of me. I have to hurry to catch up. I walk more quickly than I should.

As we walk through the dark landscape, we pass kneeling soldiers on both sides of the track. They are looking outward for any sign of movement, hoping against hope that the enemy might show himself. We want nothing more than to put a face to our suffering. Unsurprisingly, if there are any Taliban watching us, they keep their heads down inside a compound; there is no noise, no movement, and no hope of engaging the enemy as we push forward.

We continue to walk for about 50 metres before rounding a bend. Here the silence and darkness of the night disappear, and I turn to see the medics working on a soldier, amid buzzing activity and light. Whereas until now my eyes have had to strain to perceive the mud walls around me, and my ears heard only the rustle of my kit, here movement, light, and sound prevail. The medics work quickly, talking to each other in a steady rhythm. Medics usually carry white LED headlamps with red filters, because red is the frequency of light that travels the shortest distance, and thus is hardest for the enemy to see at night. Those working on the casualty are using white light, so that they can differentiate between sweat and blood. Others have neglected to flip off their red filters. A few people carry green and blue flashlights. In front of me is a kaleidoscope of colour.

We have stopped about 20 metres away, and I try to take in what is going on. There is a bright silver space blanket wrapped around a stretcher. At the top there is the outline of a helmet, and below what looks like a very short person. Protruding from underneath the blanket is a pale white shape covered in glistening dark red. All of a sudden it dawns on me that I'm looking at shards of bone, and that the glistening red is blood.

I stare at the scene, unable to look away, and watch the play of the lights off the space blanket, the ground, and the mangled flesh. No thoughts enter my brain, and I feel completely numb. It is as if my mind has gone into screensaver mode, or has become a camera, taking in the images around me but failing to process them. There is no shock, no emotion, nothing but the sound of the blood rushing in my ears and the beams of light moving chaotically in front me—and the blood, so red.

"We need stretcher bearers!" I hear someone yell. I'm not sure who it is, but I unthinkingly start to walk forward. I need to do something. Chris stops me and looks me in the eye. "Stay put, man, the OC needs you." I don't know why he stops me, perhaps because he is afraid that I can't carry the load, or because the platoon should be allowed to carry its own wounded. Or maybe he thinks the OC may need my radio. Chris points at the fork in the road where we've just walked and tells me to remain there, directing others to go around to the left, along a cleared route. As the stretcher bearers pick up the casualty and start to move him toward Zangabad, I give directions. I am talking in a normal voice, but it sounds strange in my ears, gravelly and low. I wonder what everyone else is thinking. The line slowly snakes past until Chris comes and taps me on the shoulder. We move off in our original positions, being sure to keep to the left. I wonder if everyone else will stay on the correct path without me there. I wonder if it even matters. I feel nothing as we walk and listen to the familiar sound of a LAV pulling up, stopping, and dropping the rear ramp. Its quiet engine sounds like a school bus as it drives toward Zangabad, and I hear the familiar whine of its belts. I hear the sound of helicopter rotors in the distance, growing louder by the second. The OC has gone on ahead, and Chris turns around, glaring at me. I can see anger in his eyes. I'm following too close again.

Soon we hit the tracks that the LAV left, and make sure to stay on them until we reach Zangabad. It is a short walk, and we arrive at the COP just as a Black Hawk helicopter lands, kicks up a cloud of dust, kisses the ground, and takes off again, all impossibly fast. Someone tells us that the casualty has died. Chris is in front of me, and he whispers, "Who was it?" to one of the guys framed by the open back ramp of the LAV, which smells of blood.

"Arnal from 21," someone responds. As the word spreads, I hear a furious scream, impossibly loud, and the sound echoes in the Afghan night. I watch a soldier throw his helmet as hard as he can at the ground, and see the moondust splash up around it.

We finish moving back into the COP, and I sit down on the sandbags that are arranged in a seemingly perfect circle around the mortar pit. The OC walks directly into Zangabad's CP, and I am left alone. I watch the rest of 21 filter into Zangabad; they are stopping just after the entrance and it is difficult to make them out in the dark. There is nothing that I can do to help. Around me I can hear the beginnings of sorrowful conversations about Corporal James Arnal. I feel alone. I walk over to the rest of my section, and listen to people talk about how they knew him and good times that they had together. Voices laden with emotion, they try their hardest to laugh. I don't think that I can picture his face.

I drop my kit on the sand and find an open box of rations. For some reason I am hungry. This is not the normal hunger associated with finishing a leg, but full-on ravenousness. I take a ration back to the mortar pit and rip it open. The food becomes my only focus and I tear at it, throwing cardboard and silver packaging onto the ground. Soon I am thrusting spoonful after spoonful into my mouth. I feel hot tears push into my eyes. My body has no conception of what to feel, or how to feel it, so I eat and hold in tears. I feel an intense need to hide from those around me the fact that I'm eating; I hope that the darkness and the sorrow are sufficient to cover up my actions. My hands shake, and I finally identify what I am consuming: Chicken Carbonara. I will never eat it again.

I finish, and the tears try again to push their way out of my eyes. I refuse to let them. It wouldn't be proper for me to break down in front of all these stoics who must feel a much greater depth of sorrow than I do. I throw out my ration and go back to sitting. My hands shake. Numbness returns. The night is dark and cool and I feel nothing.

Word is passed: the OC is going to make a statement. We shuffle over to where he is standing and form a horseshoe around him. I stand at the outskirts of the crowd. I try to force myself to think about what has happened, and what we've gone through, but nothing comes to my mind.

"What can you say about a guy like Corporal Arnal? He was a real soldier," the OC begins. I don't remember the rest of the speech. I didn't really process anything that he said. I stood there sullenly with my arms crossed, seeing and hearing nothing.

The OC concludes by saying that 4 Platoon will be evacked by choppers tomorrow, and that this is good news. I don't grasp the immediacy of what is going on around me, and when everyone else starts to go back to their sleeping areas, I follow in a daze. Looking back, I don't know if anyone could properly explain what they felt on that cool and quiet night, while the OC tried to console us for the loss of someone who had stood upright, walked, laughed, hated, loved, and fought with us less than an hour before. I don't know if there is anything anyone could say that might mitigate that reality. Maybe it was enough to stand in the cool silence of the night and listen to one man talk. I don't know.

I find Allan, who is staying in the engineers' area on the north side of the camp. I sit beside him and pass a cigarette; we smoke in silence. I try to say something negative about the OC's speech, but nothing comes to mind. I try to think of something funny to say, but can't. In the end we sit quietly, leaning against a HESCO Bastion, and looking at the clear night sky, which is filled with millions of stars. I stare at the moon for a few minute until a cloud comes from the south, moving quickly to eclipse it.

"Hey, man, check that out, it's a cloud!" It's not poetic, but it's what I say. I try to remember the last time that I saw a cloud; I can't think of a single instance in the pure blue or black skies of Afghanistan. We watch the cloud cast shadows across Zangabad, and think about nothing. After a while, Allan says that he feels like he has a 50-metre bubble around him where nothing dangerous ever occurs. I agree, though my bubble is much smaller.

After what seems like a long time, the engineers start to funnel back to their cots to sleep. I realize that I should probably be doing the same, and wish Allan a good night. I go back to the area where HQ is sleeping and find my kit piled in the moondust. Most of the rest of HQ are lying on their cots talking quietly or sleeping. I find an open one and go through the familiar process of laying out my ranger blanket and sleeping pad. I rest my pack against a HESCO Bastion, and put my chest rig, flak vest, and rifle in a neat pile in front of it. A cool breeze blows, and I feel cold in my sweat-soaked shirt. It is surprisingly refreshing to be cold. I take off my shirt and lay it on top of my pack. I unzip my boots, take off my socks, and lie down in my cot. I take off my glasses as an afterthought, and put them in my boot, a trick I learned long ago on basic training when I lost my glasses one morning. It has been seven years since I completed my basic training, and nothing is the same; only those little tricks drilled into a sleep-deprived mind, never to be lost again. On the surface everything may feel the same, but it never will be. Something inside of me has changed. I have found the Minotaur.

I close my eyes and am lost once more to oblivion. Later, I would write the following lines;

Lights,

The unexpected procession of perception,
Flash before Bang,
Flash before Bang.

Hit the ground;
Mortar? RPG? Heart-sinking IED.

Lights,

A kaleidoscope of colour,
Attached to heads and hands.
Attached to newly unattached.

Lights,

Reflecting omnipresent tan
And bright silver heat
And red, so red.

Lights,

A glimpse,
An instant of photons and pain.

CHAPTER 8
COP ZANGABAD
19 JULY 2008

But who, if he be called upon to face
Some awful moment to which Heaven has joined
Great issues, good or bad for humankind
Is happy as a Lover;
and attired with sudden brightness, like a Man inspired
—WILLIAM WORDSWORTH, "THE CHARACTER OF
   THE HAPPY WARRIOR"

IT IS ABOUT 0200 WHEN I PASS OUT in COP Zangabad. Alberta
is 10 and a half hours behind Kandahar, so in Calgary it is 1530. As
I fall asleep on the other side of the world, my girlfriend is sitting
in class at the University of Calgary. The grounds of the U of C in
summer are beautiful. The fields are green and the trees are bursting
with leaves. There is a faint fragrance of flowers intermixed with fast
food when one walks past Mac Hall, the central point of campus. On
sunny days like today, students sit underneath the Prairie Chicken,
a massive abstract metal statue. They nap, or discuss their classes, or
their pastimes, or their ideas. White notebooks and blue pens con-
trast sharply with the green hill that invites all who pass by to relax
and take a break. A little farther along, there's cheap food and beer at
the Black Lounge, where students absorb the sun on the patio.

Before they banned smoking I used to sit there and read philosophy, or history, or fiction while drinking beer and water, and
working my way through a cigarette pack. I can remember reading

Sartre, Camus, and Fussell on the patio. I remember thinking that I understood the world when I read these books, that I was narrowing in on the answers to the big questions, that I could give an intelligent opinion about whether existentialism was a valid school of thought, or whether Napoleon should have invaded Russia or changed his tactics at Waterloo. I remember thinking that all this knowledge was good and important, and that I could change the world, if only given the opportunity.

As I sleep on a cot in Zangabad, my girlfriend sits in her class in Murray Fraser Hall and listens to her prof speak in an enlightened fashion about the development and practices of Western religions. She is planning on writing her term paper on Islamic wedding practices, and before I left on patrol I e-mailed her a few suggestions about how to research the topic. Goths, preps, keeners, hippies, hipsters, and Albertan conservatives sit beside each other and try to make sense of the world around them and the development of Western religion while I sleep under the Afghan stars. Students frantically write notes on lined paper and try not to lose the thread of the prof's argument. They type quickly on laptops while carrying on virtual conversations with their friends. Outside, the Black Lounge promises cheap drinks and good times. The Canadian flag flies proudly above a small pond two swans call home. In Zangabad, two sentries stand underneath the same flag and look through NVGs and thermal optics at the landscape around them. In Calgary, a reference to the origin of the term *jihad* makes my girlfriend think of me for a few seconds. She refuses to worry, however; she is proud of me and thinks that I am trying to make a difference. "Either way, he could be hit by a bus tomorrow. At least this means something to him." She stops thinking about me and resumes doodling on her page and trying to pay attention to the lecture. At the Black Lounge, a waitress serves a student his fourth beer while he tries to come up with a witty way to introduce himself to the pretty girl sitting at the next table.

In Shilo, the news of Corporal Arnal's death is travelling quickly along predetermined channels. Secrecy is paramount, as no one can know the horrible news before the family. The military has gained a lot of experience over the course of seven years in Afghanistan, and the padre, the assisting officer, and deputy commander are putting on their dress uniforms to make a trip they wish they did not have to make. In Shilo, the order goes out to the duty sergeant: fly the flags at half mast, you will get more information when the comms blackout is lifted. There can be no personal communications in or out of theatre until the family has been notified. In Zangabad, we sleep while the machines and systems that sober, intelligent people have put in place begin to do their honourable work.

Sandflies trapped in our ranger blankets eat our flesh as we sleep. In Calgary, my girlfriend goes home to my parents' house for a barbecue supper. The young student sitting at the Black Lounge drinks enough beer that he feels confident enough to talk to the pretty girl at the next table, not realizing that he has drunk too much. He returns to his table dejected, frustrated with all women everywhere, and listens to the chorus of jeers from his friends. The sentries in Zangabad stand sleepily underneath the Canadian flag, looking at a landscape that they long ago memorized in detail. The car filled with sombre men in dress uniform departs the base, and its occupants worry about the task they have been called on to perform.

In KAF, the night duty officer liaises with his American air force counterpart to arrange helicopter transportation to Zangabad the next day. He has no luck with the Americans, so tries the Dutch, who are flying Chinook helicopters sold to them by the Canadian government in the 1990s. He manages to book transport for the following day; forms are filled out and signed, operators tap furiously at keyboards, and flight manifests are organized. As the world turns, so too does the military machine. The message is sent to the battle group command post, which sends it to the company command post, which sends it to the Zangabad command post. At each point operators log the data, and make a note to inform the duty officer when they wake up in the morning. Battle group is nervous that the Dutch will change their minds and cancel the transport. Company is nervous that battle group will fuck things up again. Zangabad has no faith left in either and accepts the presence or absence of the helicopters as the whim of God or lieutenant-colonels, both of whose logic is utterly impenetrable.

In Calgary, it is midnight. Darcy has had supper, gone for a run, done a little bit of research for her paper, and checked her e-mail one last time in vain. She is now asleep. At the Black Lounge, the young student has now been drinking beer with his friends for eight hours. He is no closer to hooking up with a pretty girl. In Zangabad, it is 1030 and already blisteringly hot.

Until the sun comes up, I don't move an inch. By 1030 I've lost my battle to remain asleep, and wake up in a pool of my own sweat, which has collected at the bottom of the cot. I blink in the bright sunlight and feel hungover. I sit up, throw off my ranger blanket, look disparagingly at the sweat and salt stains that have soaked the green fabric of the cot, and put on my boots. Around me life carries on as normal. Some of the infantry are engaged in simple tasks, like re-sorting the mountain of bottled water to our left, or improving the tents that are strung along the HESCO Bastions, ensuring that they provide the maximum amount of shade. Most are sitting around and demonstrating a casual disregard for normal standards of dress and deportment. Many lounge in their underwear. Tobacco is chewed or smoked, water is sipped, and rations are passed. There are pictures of women in various states of undress taped to the table outside the CP. It feels like just another day in sunny Afghanistan, but at the same time it is different. The laughter is a bit too strained, the jocularity a bit too violent. Although 24, who have been in Zangabad for almost a month, seem relatively nonplussed, 4 Platoon is for the most part sitting quietly under their tents, speaking in hushed tones. Arnal was immensely well liked.

I grab my toothbrush and bar of soap and stand up. I'm wearing blue underwear, the socks that carried me from Mushan, and unzipped boots. I make my way over to the ablutions area, stumbling as if I were drunk. I find a bottle of warm water and brush my teeth before washing my face in a basin. I look at myself in the mirror, which was once the rear-view mirror of a LAV before it was blown up nearby. I'm surprised to see that I look like the infantry. My hair has grown long and is matted with dust and grease, my face is dark brown, and my hands are blistered and cut from numerous encounters with the Afghan vegetation. I make a stern face at the mirror and try to remember what I looked like before I deployed; fat, puffy, and white, if I recall correctly. For a second I am consumed with hatred for what I used to be, and pride with the way I look now.

Masculinity, chauvinism, and vanity all play an important role in the makeup and outlook of the average infantry soldier. These three elements, when combined with camaraderie, form the worldview of the majority of those around me in Zangabad. It is important to bear in mind that the group of people that I'm standing with, and washing myself beside, are here because they wanted to be. They didn't just want to be in the Canadian Forces, or Afghanistan—they wanted to be at the front, the tip of the spear. They wanted to fight. As much as bringing stability to Afghanistan and promoting the development of the country are important factors in their motivation, an infantry NCM only has one primary job: to close with and destroy the enemy with maximum speed and aggression. Not only do the majority want to fight, there are better-than-even odds that they will. At some point they will probably come under enemy fire, if not on this tour then the next, or the one after that. They have to be better than their enemy. The mindset that leads an average person to want to excel somewhere like Zangabad must inherently be aggressive. Masculinity and chauvinism naturally come to the fore in an environment that is almost utterly devoid of women.

Most infantry soldiers have devoted a large portion, if not all, of their lives to excelling in combat. They are not vain in the traditional sense; rather, it is a love of "being hard" that motivates them, a pride in the suffering and hardship that they endure, often with a smile. A casual glance in the mirror does not necessarily lead to a flexing of muscles (although it is known to happen), but rather to a grim appreciation of and pride in the man who stares back. More often than not, this appreciation is contrasted with the "other" military, those who do not fight or train to fight. It is vanity that allows us the luxury of being able to look down at the rest of the world, those who don't do what we do. It is pride that allows us to suffer cheerfully, bitching all the while. This outlook is at the core of any fighting formation and has been present to a lesser or greater degree in every army that has ever existed. The army can spout its doctrine that "we are all one team" as much as it wants; the fact remains that the combat arms generally, and the infantry specifically, will always act as if they were a breed apart, especially when they are engaged in actual combat.

As I catch a glimpse of myself, I am surprised at the man who looks back; I feel as if I were one of that breed apart and feel a surge of pride and vanity.

On my way back to our sleeping area, I see Kevin Lowe talking to some other members of 24. I go back to my cot and pick my soiled

T-shirt out of the pile of dirty clothing I used for a pillow. There are fresh sweat stains, and the shirt feels wet as I pull it over my shoulders. I sit down beside Kevin and light a cigarette. He scrounges me a breakfast ration, and I open it with the smoke hanging out of my mouth. The ritual of opening rations exists even here, and I hope against hope that there is going to be a chocolate bar in my breakfast ration even when I know that there never will be. I cut what the army laughingly calls *bread* in half. The French words printed on the package are *petit pain;* or "little pain"—which basically sums up rations in general. I spread mustard on one half with my Gerber, and take out three of the four sausages from the pack. I place them on the mustard side, wipe my Gerber on my pants, lick off the remaining mustard, close the sausage sandwich, butt out my smoke, and dig in.

Little rituals such as this are an important element of army life. If I threw a sausage ration at a civilian or a brand-new soldier, they would look at it, read the labels, slowly and cautiously open the packages, and take tentative bites of what they find inside—all the while expecting to be disgusted. Seven years in the reserves, and one year of training and deployment with the infantry, have taught me how to make a functional sausage sandwich in less than a minute. Strange little skills and actions like this have a calming effect on soldiers. Moreover, it is these unique skill sets (eating a ration, packing kit quickly, cleaning a weapon) that separate soldiers from civilians. From the first day on basic training, seemingly bizarre lessons are taught, and their importance is continually reinforced: the folded-over portion of your top sheet must be exactly 30 centimetres long; your hangers must be separated by precisely the width of a credit card; your weapon must be disassembled and placed in exactly the proper order on your bed; your beret must be worn at all times outside, but can never be worn in a mess hall. As the soldier masters these bizarre skill sets, he begins to look down on those who cannot perform them properly. Officers who salute sloppily or in the American style, flailing their arms like birds' wings and with their hands at a 45-degree angle downward, are derided quietly behind their backs. Courses who march improperly are "all fucked up," and judgments are instantly made about those whose berets are improperly formed. These skills can be acquired only through difficult and often painful repetition. They propagate themselves throughout the generations, and strange historical terms like *reveille* and *mufti,* whose origins predate the First World War, are still used every day. Those who are on the outside cannot know these skill sets, or these insider jokes, and will always remain on the outside, no matter how many war movies they watch. Those who are on the inside and are being true to their army selves usually look down on all those who are on the outside. It is the little things that separate soldiers from civilians, and the same that separate fighting soldiers from those we call WOGs (soldiers who do not fight). The world of an infantry NCM is very small, often confined to his platoon of no more than 40 people. To a greater or lesser degree, all those outside this group are the "other." When an infanteer is suffering in a COP, with no air conditioning, no fresh food, and constant danger, can he really be blamed for begrudging those who made different choices? I don't believe so; it is only fair that the infantry are allowed their vanity and pride in exchange for their suffering.

Kevin and I start to play chess as I light another smoke. Again, I begin to lose as we split a pack of Prince, chain-smoking and carrying on conversations with whoever happens to sit down. I drink as much warm water as I can tolerate; I know that I need to rehydrate, but all I can think about is the taste of cold water. I play distractedly and lose spectacularly, which doesn't affect my mood. There is a slightly different vibe in the camp; those around us are quieter.

An outsider might not notice a difference, but there is no joy in anyone's conversations. There is no laughter that is not strained or slightly manic. Around me, soldiers go about their daily business, be it going on sentry, sorting out kit, or chewing tobacco and bitching, but there is something missing.

Kevin has to go on sentry, so I walk back to my cot and lie down. Beside me, Murphy tells stories about the good times he had with Arnal; he talks about going dirt biking with him around Shilo, and the conversation turns to dirt bikes and motorcycles. I have nothing to add, so I sit, drink water, and smoke cigarettes. I listen to Chris tell a story about how he stores his Harley in the kitchen during the winter.

"So my roommate's girlfriend is freaking out. 'That thing can't stay in here!' she's yelling at me. And I say, 'Listen, my relationship with this Harley started before your guys,' and let's be fair, it's probably going to last longer. So either shut up or get out.'" The group smiles and thinks about home and their girl or their bike, whichever is waiting for them.

"I even started her up inside—it's good for the engine and it pissed that chick right off. I mean, I'd open the door." Chris has a wistful look as he talks about his Harley. I think that he misses the freedom to ride wherever he wants whenever he wants most of all. "As soon as I get home I'm gonna hop on my bike and ride into town. Then I'll get some new tattoos," he says.

"Yeah, I can't wait to ride in my truck" someone else pipes in.

I just hope that I get home.

At this point, thoughts of home have become ideas more than memories. It is less that we miss what we had than that we make home into something infinitely better in our imaginations. Some will be shocked upon their return to find out that home isn't as happy as they imagined it to be. Some will have to adjust their imaginations. I wonder which group I will fall into.

The events of the previous night hang like a shadow over our conversation. No one seems to know exactly what to say, and there is more silence than usual. But there is nothing that we can do to change the past, so the monotony of our daily lives returns and is greeted like an old friend. Smoking, bitching, drinking water, bullshitting are all easy and safe activities. The familiar routine is an escape from the horrors that we have witnessed. The future is uncertain, and we still have a long road back to Sperwan Ghar, and a longer road to Canada. So we escape into what we understand, and push the previous night out of our minds. This is why soldiers will always be conservative by nature. Who knows what the future holds? The only thing that we can control is the present. We will wait to process the past when we are at peace and alone.

At some point, the conversation turns to the fact that we are not going to be going on a clearing patrol around Zangabad. We all feel like we should do something to avenge the loss of a Canadian soldier; we should go out and face the enemy and fight and find the IED cache and win. Unfortunately, these sentiments belong to another war, or at least another company. We can only be sure that there are more IEDs waiting for us in the surrounding area, and that whatever Taliban planted them are long gone, or doing their best civilian impression. Any clearing patrol would be an immensely dangerous and most likely fruitless effort. But that doesn't change the fact that we want to do something, not scurry back to Sper with our tails between our legs. Maybe a strong leader would allow us to do something, or maybe a stronger one wouldn't. I'm not sure. I do know that each of us, to a man, sitting around smoking, or dipping or bullshitting, would like to do something to strike back at the enemy. But none of us are in command; it isn't our call to make. In the end there's only one place to direct our anger.

(Shortly after our return to Sperwan Ghar, behind the seat of a porta-potty on the west side of the camp, some anonymous scribe recorded our mood with an indelible black marker. He wrote "29's Battle Plan" in large letters, with an arrow pointing downwards. In another porta-potty on the other side of camp, someone had taken a blue pen and described our feelings more generally:"Harder than it has to B Coy." In Sperwan Ghar, if you wanted a clear picture of our morale you only had to go to the bathroom.)

Like Mushan, Zangabad has a few things that the engineers need to blow up. A few IED components and unexploded shells have been turned in by the locals to the COP, which has no means to dispose of them. Now that the engineers basically have the day off, they undertake the task of blowing (or BIPing) these munitions. For those counting, that's two things that they've gotten to blow up in four days.

Engineers practise a truly underappreciated trade in the Canadian military. No matter where they are in a war zone there is interesting work to be done. Occasionally that work involves finding mines, but it just as often involves building furniture or structures, using chainsaws to clear trees, or blowing things up with high explosives. I am not sure why the majority of those around me joined the military, but wanting to blow things up probably wasn't at the bottom of their list. Everyone loves explosions. I mean, really, who doesn't like the idea of blowing something up—ask any stranger walking down the street if he or she would like to pull the trigger of a controlled detonation. I bet I know the answer. For the engineers we are working with in Afghanistan, blowing things up has become so commonplace that it's almost boring—*almost.*

We all remember the incident with Captain Michelson, and so this time, as the engineers prepare the charge, we sit closer to our kit and get ready to put on our helmets. While the engineers put the finishing touches on their charges, I hear the sound of automatic gunfire coming from behind the HESCO Bastions. Again, it takes a few seconds to sink in. I see people sprinting and wonder what they are doing, as I lean halfway up on my cot. Then I hear the startlingly loud sound of unexpected rounds being fired from a machine gun directly over my head. The enemy is not finished with us, and we are already returning fire. I sit stunned for a few moments, wondering what has gone wrong with the engineers' BIP before I realize that the COP is being shot at. I stand up and grab my weapon and helmet. In front of me, what at first appears to be a chaotic rush resolves itself into order, as people dash for their kit and run to their fighting positions along the walls of the COP. The scene reminds me of watching a rugby game before I understood the rules; there was obviously some sort of organization, but looking at any one individual on the field, you would see only chaotic running. I look around to see what I'm supposed to be doing, and notice those who are not running to the finite number of fighting positions are moving toward the security of the sea can near the centre of the camp. They are doing so in a grudging fashion, slowly putting on their kit and doing their best to look as if they would rather be moving to the fighting positions. No one wants to be seen to panic or cower under the threat of small-arms fire. I hear an RPG or two whistle through the sky and explode, most likely against the side of the HESCO Bastion, but I can't be sure. I do my best to imitate the slow walk to the sea can, but I certainly don't feel as nonchalant as I try to look. I have hastily put my helmet on my head, and move with about 20-plus kilos of my remaining fighting kit in my right hand and my weapon in my left. As I walk, the weight in my right hand becomes heavier and heavier, forcing me to focus on squeezing my fingers as hard as I can so that my kit doesn't slip out. As the machine gun behind me continues to let out burst after burst, and the orderly chaos continues to unfold around me, I can focus only on trying not to drop my kit in the sand.

My hand is throbbing by the end of the 20 metres that I have to cover to the sea can, and I walk the remaining five in a strange, swinging wobble, like someone carrying a very heavy suitcase in one hand and nothing in the other. I also have to keep my head straight up so that my helmet doesn't fall off, all the while trying to look as calm as possible. I drop my kit in the sand behind a miniature HESCO Bastion and take a deep breath. I continue to stand as I put my flak vest on, and swear silently at the Velcro that, due to the ever-present dust, has stopped fastening. I do up my helmet strap, and try to put my chest rig on, struggling to do up the clips. This movement requires dexterity and flexibility, and I don't possess either at this moment. After a minute of struggle, I finally hear the reassuring snap of the clip falling into place, and am able to look around again. The machine guns are silent by this point, probably only moments after they started firing. Now that I am ready to fight, it would appear that the brief encounter is over—another shoot and scoot. We can't leave the relative security of the sea can, so I pull out my cigarettes and pass them around. Most of the faces are unfamiliar, and we all try to look as unconcerned as possible. It is very quiet.

The Taliban have left for now. We stay through two cigarettes and one strained conversation until we disperse. If war can be described as brief periods of intense activity followed by long periods of tedium, we are walking back to the tedious. The camp is quiet, the adrenalin has mostly worn off, and we go back to sitting, smoking, and bitching.

"I bet those choppers won't be coming," someone says. I lie with my head flat on my cot and look up at the waving green piece of modular tent above us. Everything in the army is green, brown, or tan. It gets depressing after a while. I realize that I probably haven't seen a colour other than tan, green, or dust in almost a week, except for one brief glimpse of red.

"Who's flying 'em?" someone asks.

"I heard it was the fucking Dutch," the first voice responds.

"Ah. They'll never show up," a third voice agrees. I think about my time in Amsterdam with Darcy, and it doesn't seem entirely real that I was there.

"Yeah, it's hard to get shot at while you're sitting at the Green Bean." The Green Beans Coffee Company is an American coffee shop in KAF. It is basically an army version of Starbucks. Instead of jazz music CDs and stylish decoration, its walls are crowded with the insignia of the units that have patronized it. There is also a long list of other Green Beans locations around the world, such as South Korea, Iraq, and Kuwait. Their motto is "Honor First, Coffee Second." They make a fine mocha frappuccino.

The possibility of Dutch helicopter pilots is thus derisively dismissed. I didn't even know that they had helicopters.

"You ever been to the Dutch PX?" The question is aimed at no one in particular.

"I buy all my smokes from there; they're the official cigarette of Prince A/S." I respond while taking one out.

"Who the fuck is that?"

"I have no fucking idea. He must be someone important."

"Yeah, and he's got all the hookers in Amsterdam." I try to imagine all the hookers in Amsterdam in one room, organized by nationality and hair colour. I enjoy the image and smile up at the sky. I continue to smile with my eyes as I take a drag off one of Prince A/S's cigarettes.

"That would be a sweet go," I say, exhaling smoke between words.

"Yeah." The conversation trails off.

"I bet the choppers aren't going to show up."

"We'll see."

In the army, *go*—as in a "good go" or a "rough go"—is applied to any conceivable occupation, attempt, service, or time period. For example, if I were to give an impromptu history lecture, it would be perfectly acceptable for me to conclude by saying, "As you can see, the Second World War was a pretty fucking rough go." This remark would most likely be met with nods of approval in a crowd of soldiers. A go, not to be confused with the British term for "have sex," is something that soldiers can understand. It is an event that is finite in its duration and understandable in its description. As such, life can be broken up into a series of good gos and rough gos. The fact that we are sitting in the middle of a rough go doesn't really matter; Cyprus is going to be a good go, and HLTA was a good go, so we always have something to look back on and something to look forward to.

We sit and smoke and drink water in our sleeping area for a while; there is absolutely nothing to do. By the time we are talking about "buddy's wife" and her extramarital affairs, movement around the camp becomes perceptibly more hurried. In the CP they have received word from the voice of God, call sign 2, who has confirmed that helicopters are inbound and will arrive in approximately 40 minutes. It is 1400 and above 40 degrees. I barely have the energy to sit up. I smoke another cigarette and enjoy the feeling of it between my thumb and forefinger. Word spreads around camp that there will be two Dutch Chinooks with a British Apache covering them. Outside the Zangabad CP, the groups that will be getting into the helicopters are lined up, counted off, sorted out, and double-checked. These men sit in a long line in the sand and wait. 4 Platoon will be loaded onto the first chopper and before the dust cloud has settled, the second chopper will come in and make a combat landing literally on the heels of the first. Allan is at the front of the line for the second group. They are stretched out in a mostly orderly fashion, prepared to make the short dash to the HLS. The soldiers are experienced enough to know that they don't need to move for a few minutes, until the blades cutting through the air can be heard in the distance; they sit with their kit on, smoking or talking, maintaining their place in the line. The sense of urgency that reigned when the orders were being passed and the men were being lined up has washed away and been replaced with idle speculation on whether the choppers actually will arrive, or if it was all just a clever ruse to get them out of their cots.

I have no part in this operation, as there is not enough room on the Chinooks to lift everyone back. The call has been made that only 4 Platoon and those who were injured on the march (including Allan) will get on. They are leaving to attend Arnal's ramp ceremony. 29 Tac will stay and walk the rest of the way back to Sperwan Ghar, a prospect that no one relishes. I watch the men relax in the dirt, leaning back against full packs, talking quietly. I don't envy them; they all deserve the spot on the chopper more than I do. I wait for the sound of the helicopter blades in the distance, wondering if call sign 2 is going to get a message from call sign 0 that the choppers have been cancelled for some reason. It wouldn't surprise me.

The sound of the helicopters starts softly, growing louder as the Apache tentatively pushes its way into the vicinity while scanning for targets. The security of the Chinooks is the Brit's primary concern, so he takes his time attempting to establish whether or not there is a threat. Unfortunately, there are some places that not even the best thermal imaging sights can penetrate. The helicopter hovers well above us, appearing as a dot on the horizon and resolving itself so high that it looks like a toy suspended in the air. We have grown used to close air support by the Americans, who try to fly anywhere the infantry can walk. We are surprised by the seemingly standoffish approach that this chopper is taking. It sounds like a riding lawn mower outside a building on a spring morning. As the sound's volume increases, so too does its violence, and the graceful image of the helicopter suspended in the air seems disconnected from the unconscionably loud noise.

I grab my camera and after some violent cajoling I manage to get it working. One of the Chinooks swoops in for a landing, seemingly from nowhere. A coloured smoke grenade is thrown onto the HLS to help guide the pilot and give him an idea of the winds on the ground. I watch it pour its brilliant red fumes upwards over the HESCO that separates the camp. The immense bulk of the aircraft is briefly visible as it swoops toward the ground, the wind from its blades washing over us. A dust cloud envelops it almost instantly, and I manage to get a picture only of that brown plume. The soldiers who moments before had been sitting casually are now running into the swirling inferno of dust. I watch them disappear individually and wonder how they can possibly find the ramp. Within a minute, the pitch of the rotors changes and the Chinook is gone, turning toward KAF and hugging the earth as the soldiers aboard frantically try to find something to hold onto. In the second group, Allan waits for his turn.

We are surprised that the Taliban didn't take the opportunity to shoot at the first chopper. For the few seconds that it sat there, it must have been an enticing target. We had expected any surviving enemy in the area to at least take a few potshots. Maybe they were killed in that brief firefight, although that seems unlikely. Maybe they left the area, or are stoned on hash. Maybe it's just too goddamn hot for them. A grizzled 4 Platoon sergeant standing next to Allan has the answer.

"It'll be the second chopper," he says, as he looks into the middle distance. "It's always the second chopper." Allan looks at him and realizes that he is completely serious.

The second chopper swoops in to land in the dust cloud of the first. A work party with scarves covering their faces rushes to help offload the rations and water that the Chinook has brought as an afterthought. Allan's group waits beside the HESCO Bastion, waiting for someone to tell them to move. A loud boom is heard over the din of the rotors. We are being mortared. I look up and see two of the sentry towers pouring machine gun fire toward suspected base plate positions. They appear to be shooting directly over top of the Chinook. The CP is getting reports of a suspicious van approaching the COP, and it is possible that the Taliban are moving something big in, a recoilless rifle or an RPG team. No one knows what is going to happen, and the cacophony makes it hard to hear my own thoughts. I watch the scene while being buffeted by the sand from the Chinook. Another mortar explodes, and it sounds louder this time. Someone starts yelling to get our kit on, and I run toward the sea can. Around me organized chaos reigns again. Another mortar explodes and sounds closer still. The rotors continue to spin. Why hasn't it taken off?

Allan stands transfixed, convinced that the helicopter is going to explode where it sits, raining debris all over. He is also convinced that, failing to explode, it will take off as soon as it can. Someone from the CP comes running out with no helmet or flak vest, screaming, "Get the fuck on the chopper!" Allan runs into the cloud of dust, and I see the whole line disappear in unison. The pain in his badly sprained ankle does not slow him down as he sprints toward the chopper. The machine guns continue to fire. Before the ramp is closed, the pitch of the rotors changes again, and the Dutch Chinook lifts off. The door gunner doesn't get a chance to fire a single round. While the soldiers inside scramble for a place to hold onto, the chopper begins its violent ride toward Sperwan Ghar. Another mortar lands; this time it is farther away. It will prove to be the last one of the day.

———————

The memories of this day once evoked in me an overwhelming sensation. I could not think about it without remembering the crash of the mortars around me. My feeling of strange calm as I lived in the moment, and grabbed my helmet. The tactile grit of the shoulder pad of my flak vest as I closed my hand on it. The feeling of my heart pounding in my chest as I looked at those around me and tried to keep my face impassive. The echoing boom of the second mortar, and the strange realization that I hadn't heard a whine. These images would rush into my brain with almost the same intensity as when they were actually occurring. But over the years they have begun to fade. Today I have to stop and think about which hand I grabbed my flak vest with, and whether I actually had my chest rig with me. My heart no longer pounds as I relive the experience in front of my computer screen. My memories no longer terrify me.

This is probably because the number and quality of the images that I was forced to deal with was, for the most part, limited. I caught only a glimpse into the black maw that is warfare, and unlike some, I recoiled from it. I didn't have sufficient experience with the reality of warfare for it to retain its power over me. Perhaps this is what separates me from those poor souls who continue to live in their memories after their war is finished. None of my memories were strong enough to survive the influx of newer memories: seeing the look on my bride's face as she walked down the aisle; training a new puppy to sit; drinking beer in the Black Lounge on my first day of graduate school. My tour will always be with me, will always be part of me, but the memories have lost their power.

Nothing can prepare you for the reality of bloody, concussive warfare. Some excel at it, living for the glorious excitement and clarity of the moment. Others, even the most masculine of men, realize that they are truly afraid of it. Some learn to cope with the fear, but others do not. Those are the ones whose memories will always control them. In the end, you either like war or you don't. No one can know until he or she has experienced it first-hand. Those who like war are aptly named *warriors*. They are the brave adventurers of our society. In my experience, they are not often zealots and are quiet in their unshakable convictions. Even when they are loud, they are usually calm in their actions; they've learned over time to be deeply restrained. It is they who should rightfully stand guard over our nation, for that task requires warriors to succeed at war. In representing Canada, they embody some of the ideals and ethos of our country. Although the mirror that they hold up to society is somewhat distorted, Canadian soldiers are still Canadian. If a society can trust itself, by and large it can trust its soldiers.

Some, like me, are fated never to be warriors, as we are more afraid of war than fascinated by it. But I have the consolation that I have walked with them and know what kind of men and women they are—what kind of situations they face. I know that danger doesn't always seem dangerous. I will never be a warrior, but I have known war. Now, as I walk amongst a population who has not, I am separated from them I am happy to say that on that hot, dusty day in Afghanistan, I stood amongst Canadian warriors, ready to do my job.

The excitement fades with the retreat of the Chinooks. Once again the silence is deafening, and I wonder what exactly just happened. The old routine remerges, and I lie down to try to get some rest in the heat. We will be walking all night. I force another bottle of water down my throat and fade in and out of a fitful sleep while people around me talk softly. We will be leading the last leg of this patrol, and that significantly increases our chances of having an encounter with an IED. I sleep in the underwear and T-shirt that I've worn all day.

CHAPTER 9
COP ZANGABAD TO PB SPERWAN GHAR
19–20 JULY 2008

Oh, what can ail thee, knight-at-arms,
Alone and palely loitering?
The sedge has with'red from the lake,
And no birds sing.
—John Keats, "La Belle Dame Sans Merci"

WAKING UP IN A PUDDLE OF MY OWN SWEAT has become a monotonous reality, but I still do not like it. I wake well before the sun dips below the horizon, sit up in my cot and look at the orange light and elongated shadows of the early evening. It is still hot. I look down at my cot and notice the new white salt stains that cover it. Once again, I feel hungover. I pull my boots on, grab a bottle of water, and appreciate the fuzzy dumbness in my brain. As I sit, I let my head hang down and my mouth hang open; I would really rather not walk the rest of the way back to Sperwan Ghar. Oh well, ours is not to question why. Around me people are sorting out their kit for this last leg of the patrol. I guess I should do the same.

I root around in my pack and find a clean pair of socks and my only spare clean pair of pants. Unfortunately, I'm out of T-shirts, so I'm forced to wear the one that got me through the first two days of this patrol. It is still wet with five-day-old sweat. I guess that it will have to do. My pack smells like a hockey bag. I relish the feeling of my last pair of clean socks, and wiggle my toes in them. I finish putting on my T-shirt and pants before blousing my boots. I tuck in my shirt, do up my belt snugly, and for the first time in days feel clean and happy. I wash my face and notice that the water turns brown. Clean socks go a long way to allowing me to forget the situation that I'm in, and I begin to feel optimistic. As I repack my kit, I whistle "The British Grenadiers."

Two guys from HQ will lead the last leg of the patrol. They understand the risks involved with being first in the order of march, and unlike much of the company, they don't have a lot of experience on the ground around Zangabad. That's real bravery: understanding that one is in a truly dangerous situation but continuing to do one's job as a professional soldier. This is the quiet unspoken bravery that Hollywood will never portray.

The sun drops quickly, and I hold my fifth cigarette in my mouth as I do up my shirt and put on my flak vest. I then put on my chest rig and sit down against the mortar pit. There is a much more cautious feeling about tonight's patrol. What for me was a purely intellectual awareness of the life-and-death reality has shifted into a cold understanding that we are discussing real men's lives, their flesh and their blood. The ravages of IEDs and enemy action had, up until yesterday, been filtered through a radio, little more than a disembodied electric voice calling for help. Today I understand the reality and the risk.

If you could do it all over again, knowing what you know now, would you? The question rings through my brain as I think about the road ahead. *I don't know. We'll see how this thing turns out, I guess,* comes the answer. And then, a little more optimistically: *I guess it is better than sitting at home jerking off. At least it's something real, so long as I make it back.*

I look around instinctively for a piece of wood to touch. Before I can find one, I see those in front of me standing up. We are off once more into the dark Afghan night and an uncertain future, but it feels different this time. I throw on my pack and helmet, pick up my weapon, and wrap the sling around my forearm. A lit cigarette glows in my mouth as we start to move, and before we exit the wire, I throw it at the moondust.

Before our shortened patrol can finish leaving the wire, our terp intercepts a communication between the Taliban. They know where we are, and pass on to their friends the route we are taking. They are watching us file orderly out of the camp. In one of the mud compounds surrounding the COP, evil men are plotting to do us harm. We will probably never know which building they are in, and even if we found them, we wouldn't find any weapons or IED components. The Taliban are too wily for that. We are forced to hope that they haven't laid any IEDs on the route, and walk out while they watch us with dark eyes and a dark purpose.

Our plan for the final leg of the patrol is to take no route whatsoever. We are going to bush-bash through farmers' fields, staying off the road unless absolutely necessary. Unfortunately, we are not the only ones who know when it is absolutely necessary. As I take my first step outside of COP Zangabad (this time being careful to walk around the coiled razor wire, as opposed to through it), I feel like I am walking into a minefield that stretches all the way to Sperwan Ghar. In an almost literal sense I am. I have to work hard not to stare at my feet and to keep looking up and scanning my surroundings. In the end, either something bad is going to happen, or it won't. I can mitigate the risk by the way that I walk, but can't eliminate it completely.

I look at the ground and sigh; there is nothing that I can do about it, so I try to force these thoughts out of my mind. I'm not entirely successful, and as the weight of my kit begins to once more make itself known, my sweat feels cold and clammy on my skin. I wonder what it would feel like to have an IED explode underneath me. I wonder whether I would understand what had happened. These questions lead my mind down a dark path, so I force them away from my consciousness. I focus on keeping the proper spacing, watching where I step, and scanning my surroundings. There isn't too much else I can do.

We walk down a wide mud road, attempting to find a path into a farmer's field. As the road twists and turns, and as compounds and walls loom around us, we are forced to walk outside of the sight of COP Zangabad's towers. The Taliban could easily have laid an IED here. My senses are heightened and every sound becomes louder. I flinch when a dog barks from behind the metal door of a compound to my right.

We can't seem to find a convenient farmer's field, and eventually choose to skirt a wadi. As we walk along the edge of it, the terrain changes and we find ourselves in the middle of a grassy avenue that runs parallel to the irrigation canal. The grass is green and relatively sparse, but grows high in the moondust. I cannot recall ever having seen grass in Afghanistan, let alone walking through anything like this. The thought dawns on me that there is probably a reason why this grass is uncut—the villagers are most likely afraid to walk here. I focus on walking only where the grass is trampled down.

Ahead of me, I hear the OC having problems with his radio. He cannot reach call sign 2. I walk up behind him and pass him my handset. He still has no luck. I undo the Velcro strap holding my antenna down, and now he meets with limited success. The OC is trying to arrange for us to have eyes in the sky, an unmanned drone that can scan our route and look for any ambushes or triggermen. I pull out the faceplate to the radio and switch the frequency, hoping that our lower backup frequency will reach Sperwan Ghar. This solution works perfectly for a few seconds before the connection cuts out completely. We are standing in a deep depression surrounded by dirt walls, not ideal for communications. The OC glares at me, as if I am somehow personally holding back the necessary photons. There is absolutely nothing I can do to remedy the situation short of moving to higher ground. I tell him this, but he decides to relay our messages through Zangabad, a more time-consuming but safer approach.

As the OC talks, he continues to walk forward slowly, effectively pulling me on a leash as he does so. I am concerned that we are walking too close together and that he is not fully concentrating on where he is stepping. He is, after all, engaged in a conversation while trying to use a map and GPS simultaneously. By the time the end of the grassy avenue is in sight, the OC is finished with his transmission and hands back my handset. I clip it to my shoulder strap and fall into position. I also change the frequency back to normal, and put the faceplate in its pouch. The patrol continues forward.

The lead elements find a mud wall that is low enough to climb, and we begin to work our way over it. We pause beside the road, moving forward one at a time as those in front scale the wall. As I step on the road, I hold my breath, a wholly ineffective and unreasonable thing to do. I pass off my weapon to Chris, who is waiting on the other side of the wall, jump, kick one leg onto the top, and perform a semi-coordinated roll onto the other side. As my feet touch the ground, the hard weight of my pack catches on the wall and pushes me forward, forcing me to jog out of the fall. I take my weapon back, clip it up to my sling, and let it hang down. I turn around and grab Burhoe's weapon and watch him navigate the wall. We are now in a grape field that has been flooded for irrigation. The ground is wet, sticky, slippery mud. Sweat pours off me and I breathe hard from the effort of getting here. I manage not to fall down as I take a tentative step forward.

When in bloom, grape fields are lush with leaves and green tendrils that brush against you as you walk. Around the perimeter of these fields is inevitably a mud wall, and a small space that allows the farmer to circumnavigate his field. We are walking in this small space. The wet mud again makes my boots feel like skates, and I walk unadvisedly fast to try to catch up to Chris, before unintentionally attempting to do the splits. I recover, only to perform my impression of a running man, with both my feet slipping out from under me as I try to move forward in the slippery mud. I fall to one knee, and can stand up only with an effort, like a horse standing up with a rider on its back. Lead elements are again looking for a good place to scale the wall, and we walk around the entire perimeter of the field. Throughout this, my exposed skin (of which there is blessedly little) is scratched by branches and thorny bushes poking out from the ground and walls. I keep my right hand on the pistol grip of my weapon, so I can move branches aside only with my left. The result is that whenever a branch reaches out from the right side, I have to make an awkward decision to either switch hands with my weapon, which is difficult in the closed in terrain, or to let the branch hit me, which I usually do. My uniform is also grabbed at by every plant that we pass, and after a few minutes I begin to feel like the entire landscape disagrees with my presence here.

When we reach the far side of the grape field, the patrol pauses. Sweat is pouring out of me in the warm Afghan night, and I take out a bottle of water. I sit down on top of a thorny bush, and adjust my weight as silently as I can. Looking through one of the rows of grapevines, I see the other end of the patrol, about 20 metres away. We could have simply walked in a straight line to get this point, but instead walked the entire perimeter. The worst part is that to stay in the proper formation, the remainder of the patrol, who can see the front clearly, will have to walk the same distance through slippery mud and angry grapevines. Those in line looking at me realize this, but can only sigh and carry on moving forward. A civilian would walk in a straight line; a soldier understands that maintaining the proper order of march and route discipline is more important than being comfortable. The lead elements of the patrol have realized that the only way in and out of the walled grape field is through a compound that its owner and his family sleep in. On the other side of the compound is the main road that we are trying so desperately to avoid. It probably wouldn't help the locals' perception of us if we sent a large patrol through their house in the middle of the night, especially if women and children were sleeping there. That is just the kind of thing that Taliban propagandists love to blow out of proportion. What would be a simple desire to get outside of a walled-in compound could be turned into an accusation of rape and murder by the Taliban the next day.

After some deliberation, we decide to try to scale the wall. It is not quite three metres tall, higher than I can reach. At one point, there is a walnut tree that grows beside the compound. I watch the lead man on the patrol use it to climb to the top of the wall, rest there for a few seconds, and then drop down into the adjacent field. On the other side is a marijuana field, and the moist stench of drugs is thick in the air. I wait my turn to cross. We have been in the field for almost half an hour.

Now, you might think that the hardest part would be getting to the top of the wall, but this is not the case. With the aid of the tree, I shimmy to the top relatively easily. There is a gap between the wall and the tree, however, and I have to throw myself onto the top. When I look down, I realize that the drop is even farther on the other side. It must be at least 3.5 metres. I spend a couple of seconds trying to figure out a way to lower myself at least some of the way, but unfortunately I am poised pretty precariously with 65 kilos of kit balanced on the top of a wall 30 centimetres wide. I eventually manage to position myself so that my feet will fall first, pass off my weapon and jump, or more accurately drop, to the ground below. As gravity takes hold I have time to briefly register the freefall between the top of the wall and the bottom. I land awkwardly and allow my body to crumple as I hit the ground.

Although my drop is not graceful, I am able to stand up unin-jured. I take back my weapon and watch Burhoe perform the same awkward manoeuvre.

The field that we stand in front of is blessedly dry. The plants have not yet grown to their full height, and they reach to only about our waists. There are no obstacles to human movement inside the field, and we walk by crushing the plants in a line for others to fol-low. Unfortunately, we are as trapped in this compound as we were in the last one. It is also bordered on all sides, allowing entry only through locked metal doors that lead to the road and a compound where the locals reside. Luckily, at one corner there is a low wall. Piled up below are dried sticks that are probably used for cooking fires. When we get to the corner of the field, we walk over these sticks to reach the wall. The snap of breaking wood echoes through-out the landscape, and it occurs to me that I have never heard a louder sound in my life. If proper patrolling can be likened to a delicate ballet, what we are doing approaches *Stomp*.

It has been two hours since we departed COP Zangabad, and although we have walked three kilometres (as someone's GPS informs us), we have progressed only 600 metres as the crow flies. By this point it is almost 2300, and we won't reach Sper for another seven hours. For the next hour we bash through Afghan fields, constantly harassed by the sound of barking dogs that can hear and smell that something is amiss. When necessary, engineers use sledgehammers to break down the walls. The packed mud proves to be almost impossible to knock over, however, and we usually scale the walls at their lowest point. By the time I get over the last wall, I am cut up from the grape vines, bruised from falling over the walls, covered in mud from slipping in the wet fields, and drenched in my own sweat. What had been, at the begin-ning of the night, my last clean uniform has become soiled and ripped from my exertions. Eventually, I tumble over a wall and find that there is not another field, only a wide open space with the Arghandab riverbed behind it. Between us and the riverbed spreads a graveyard.

Afghan graveyards are usually not marked or delineated in any particular way. Bodies are buried under piles of stone that are taller or shorter depending on the importance of the person who lies underneath them. Above some piles, brightly coloured prayer flags wave softly. They are tied to long, thin branches that are driven into the ground at the head of the grave. Some say that these flags are reserved for those Taliban who died fighting against us, but I can't say if this is true. One thing that Afghanistan has no shortage of is death. The graveyard stretches on for almost a kilometre before reaching the depression of the Arghandab riverbed. It is almost impossible to walk without stepping on someone's final resting place.

The patrol continues through the open space, and it feels good just to be able to walk without hitting an obstacle. As we go, we pass a short mud hut. Someone notices legs sticking out. We cannot be sure if the people are dead or alive, so we throw pebbles at them. To our surprise, the bodies begin to move, and an angry Afghan man and his son arise from the hut in the middle of the graveyard. They claim to be gravekeepers, but we cannot be sure they are not Taliban taking a nap while waiting in ambush for us. We search them and their hut and find nothing. Turns out they probably really are gravekeepers. Something is strange about the whole exchange, and I can't quite put my finger on it. Finally, I come to the conclusion that talking to Afghans at midnight in a graveyard is a strange thing for anyone to do.

I think that they are almost as upset with the group of soldiers from the other side of the world waking them up as I am to be walking through a graveyard in Afghanistan. We carry on, our boots treading over the final resting places of Afghans who may have been killed by us. It is the only way back onto the riverbed that doesn't involve bashing more holes in walls.

We reach the wadi system that runs parallel to the Arghandab, and cross it by walking down one side and up the other. I manage not to get my boots wet and smile at my tiny victory. My whole body aches from our exertions to get to this point. The wadi system falls off steeply to the riverbed and we are forced to walk past the same smashed compound that we passed on the first day of the patrol. It is about a metre high, and a few slits in the mud walls indicate that it may once have been a house. It is illuminated by the moonlight and is strangely beautiful. The Arghandab spreads out around us as I push past the compound.

Again, the flash of the IED hits me first, followed quickly by its shockwave and the sound of the explosion. Again, I think that it is a mortar, hoping against hope. Again, I feel sick to my stomach. I take a knee and begin scanning, knowing that this is my only responsibility. I look south toward the compounds on the other side of the wadi, but they are as black as night. I pull down my NVG, but it fails to give me any more information. The green light glows as I wait for the radio to begin spewing out information.

"29er, this is 29W, IED contact, wait out."

It is the call sign of our weapons detachment commanded by Jeff Brazeau. I hold my breath; I have lived in the same room with everyone in that call sign since I got to Afghanistan. I know them better than I know almost any other group of people, and like almost all of them. I set up and programmed the radio he is currently talking on. For the second time in five days, I pray, this time that everyone is okay. Maybe it was the ANA that got hit. I try hard not to wish for that, but do anyway.

An ominous quiet weighs us down while we wait for information. I can feel my heart pound in my chest. The weight on my knee begins to throb, but I force myself to continue to scan our surroundings.

"29er, this is 29W, be advised, all okay. I say again, all okay. Request Echo assets push up to help exploit the blast seat, over." The IED must have been remotely detonated. Everyone is okay. I exhale a breath I didn't know I was holding.

"29, roger, 2, E21, acknowledge."

"2, roger." We have good comms with Sper over the open space of the Arghandab.

"E21, acknowledged, on our way, over." The engineers begin to push up to the line, walking carefully to avoid any secondary devices. The sergeant-major and the doc push up behind them, just in case. I concentrate on ignoring the pain in my knee.

I move to the OC's side and pass him my handset. My more powerful radio can reach both Zangabad and Sper, and the OC uses it to coordinate an aerial sweep of the area. The engineers quickly determine that it was a command-wire IED, initiated from the north side of the river. Somehow, in the last few days, the Taliban had both dug in the IED and run out a long, thin wire over the intervening space. I immediately start scanning the north side of the river. All that is visible is a group of compounds. Whoever detonated the IED must have used the destroyed compound as an aiming marker, waiting for us to appear from behind it, and timing our passing. Luckily the triggerman had missed the timing slightly. It had exploded in between an ANA soldier and Jeff Brazeau, missing him by only a few metres and knocking him back. Somewhere, on the other side of the river, less than a kilometre away from us, someone had tried to kill my friends and failed.

"Another roll of the dice," is a saying I heard often on tour. "I've rolled the dice enough times," was another common phrase when people talked about getting out of the military. The engineers painted flaming dice on a piece of wood with their call sign below it, E21. It wasn't until this patrol that I realized how literally this phrase was meant to be taken. The simple fact is that there is no safe way to patrol in this country, but it has to be done. Every step is a roll of the dice—every bullet fired more dice being thrown. The good news is that we have extremely good odds. The bad news is that those odds will hold for only so long. Take enough steps and eventually the odds start to turn against you. The house always wins.

About a week after this patrol, I was sitting in the CP on radio shift. Another IED had struck a vehicle, on the major highway north of the riverbed. The same scene had played out so many times by that point that it almost didn't faze me. I didn't recognize their call sign, E21B; they were engineers, not infantry, so I probably didn't know them. And they were operating on another radio net, so I didn't hear the calls for help, calm but intense. I just watched the silent information scroll onto a computer screen to see if there were casualties. North of the river was someone else's problem, so although I logged the incident, and told the duty officer, I didn't need to do anything. The impersonal information about people's lives and deaths scrolled across the screen—three people killed and a few more wounded. *That must have been some big IED*, was all that I thought.

The next day I saw Allan, and his face was crestfallen. He had been close friends with all three of the engineers who had been killed. We were leaving on the largest operation thus far on the tour, so I didn't get a chance to talk to him before I loaded up into my LAV to go to the staging area at Ma'sum Ghar. While we were there, we got word that the LAV that the engineers had been killed in had been towed to MSG, and I went to look at it. What I saw wasn't really a LAV; it was a blackened, charred wreck that hardly resembled an armoured vehicle. The turret had been completely shorn off, and the vehicle had rolled, instantly killing the occupants. It was a lot harder to be dispassionate when I stood looking at the vehicle that had once held Canadian soldiers. I couldn't look away, but I felt nauseous. The following morning we rolled down the same road, second in the order of march. If the engineers hadn't gone the day before, it could very well have been our LAV being towed to MSG, a charred, blackened mess. After that IED, the engineers no longer used dice as their good luck symbol.

About a year after the patrol, Allan came to visit me at home in Calgary. We drank beer and wine, and talked about old times. The conversation wandered, and we eventually started talking about the field exercise in Wainwright and the training we'd done there prior to deployment. I remembered running out of cigarettes with four days left on the ex and how I had almost lost my mind. At one point, I was helping sort out some communications problems in the engineers' LAV and was sitting enjoying a bottle of water and a bummed cigarette in the back of their vehicle. We weren't really talking about much of anything at all, and it came up that I was out of smokes. One of the engineers fished around in his pack and pulled out a pack of Export A Gold, my brand. "Here, take 'em, I've got lots."

I couldn't believe this guy's generosity. I'd never even met him, it was just a random act of kindness. I smiled and accepted the pack, walking away with my faith in humanity somewhat restored. I described the guy who gave me the smokes to Allan.

"Oh, yeah, that was Sergeant Eades."

"Yeah, I think he was a sergeant. Hey, if you ever see him again, give him a pack of smokes for me."

"I can't. He was in E21B's LAV."

The engineers finish "exploiting" the blast seat, and determine what type of device was used. They fall back to their position, and we continue with the patrol. Soon we receive reports from Haji that they have eyes on our position. This is good news. I instantly feel safer. The patrol as a whole hunkers down and moves more quickly toward the COP. The distance to Sper no longer seems insurmountable. We walk quickly in the Afghan night, expecting to see the razor wire of Haji any moment. After a half-hour, I become annoyed that we are not yet there. After 45 minutes I begin to think that we will never see Haji, and that it does not actually exist, except in my mind. Even though I can see the man in front of me clearly, I feel completely alone, slogging through the work and effort of walking. After one of the longest hours in my life, I finally see the diminutive COP on the horizon. The south tower looks squat and square, and I can clearly make out the columnar shape of the HESCO Bastions crowned with razor wire. I breathe a sigh of relief and am soon walking up the steep hill that separates the riverbed from the COP. We have made it halfway back.

I get to the area just outside the COP where Chris had yelled at me for throwing away my water bottle a few days before. So much has changed since then. I succumb to gravity and relax for 15 wonderful minutes with no pack and no helmet. Someone passes me a bottle of water that the COP provides, and I smoke a cigarette. I close my eyes and relax every muscle. Near me I hear Jeff quietly tell the story of the IED strike. I let my head lie back and soak in the few minutes of doing nothing. When I finish the water, I throw the bottle away.

"Kit up." The dreaded word is passed, and I put my pack on and stand up. Again I experience the amazingly disgusting feeling of my own cold sweat dripping down my face after I put on my helmet. The pain in my shoulders is gone, and I try to focus on enjoying that for as long as it lasts.

We move out of Haji onto a wide open road and soon lose sight of the COP. Again, the ground looms up in my mind. We are close to Sper now, only about three kilometres away, but it feels like it is much farther. We walk through the village of Haji, and the mud walls and compounds rise on either side of us. We reach a clearing bordering a wadi, and I look for Sper in the distance, but see only the dark mountains around it. I continue to look for it when we stop, and eventually I notice a tiny dot on the horizon with a single light on the top. This is my home, and it suddenly feels like I will not be physically capable of getting there. Every step is a challenge, and the weight of my kit is unrelenting, digging into my shoulders. As we stand up from our short halt, I have difficulty straightening my legs.

In the summer of 2005, I went through what is called the Primary Leadership Qualification (PLQ). This course is designed to teach soldiers how to lead troops in the field. It starts of with instruction on how to instruct, before moving on to military writing, ethics, and physical fitness. Before deploying to the field on our confirmation exercise, we were instructed on what is known as *fieldcraft*. One of the lectures that stood out for me dealt with the "patrolling spirit." The idea is that a person can be physically fit, capable as a soldier, a good shot, and a good friend—but if he or she does not have the patrolling spirit, that person will eventually fail. At the time, I dismissed this class, as I did the vast majority of military classes; this was an outmoded Second World War idea that no longer applied. Looking back now at this patrol, I know what the patrolling spirit is. It can not be taught in a classroom, it can only be lived.

The patrolling spirit is fundamentally a desire to be there. I remember someone saying that "when it sucks, all you can do is smile." I didn't realize it at the time, but that is literally all that you can do if you hope to be successful as a soldier. Those who have the patrolling spirit also have a desire to embrace the challenge, a desire to be hard. It would take a strange person to want to walk an IED-infested riverbed, but real soldiers understand that there are only two choices; to want to be there or not to want to be there. If you choose not to want to be there, it won't change the fact that you are there, and it won't lessen the stress one bit. In fact, once you admit to yourself that you do not want to be there, it only makes the road much longer.

Patrolling spirit is what separates those who succeed from those who fail. I realize now that I possessed that spirit for a long time, but began to lose sight of it on those last long kilometres separating us from Sperwan Ghar. I was afraid, tired, sore, dehydrated, and dirty—but that was the first time I truly did *not* want to be there. It was a sobering experience and gave rise to a long process of self-reflection. This would not be my last patrol, and I would have to find a way to deal with my feelings every other time that I stepped outside the wire. I was not alone in this; I think that everyone had to come to terms with their own private battle of fatigue and exhaustion versus pride and strength. The best of us used their darkest hour to improve as soldiers and develop their spirit. Only time would tell what would become of mine.

As we continue to work our way through the village of Haji, I slowly close further into myself. My breathing is laboured, and I have a hard time concentrating on anything other than my shoulders. I drink all but one of my bottles of water before we exit the village. For the first time, a new emotion creeps into my mind like the slow advance of a dark tide: despair. It is born of the opium field that will never end, soon leading into the kilometre that will never end, and the leg that will never end. This new feeling of despair comes from the stress of the last five days on patrol, and the last five months in-country. The inner strength that I felt when we stepped outside the wire at Haji has all but evaporated. Mostly, it is the tension of the patrol that wears me down, the constant anxiety that refuses to abate.

I don't know if I can push my exhausted body through the remaining kilometres. My universe has shrunk to the man in front of me, and the terrain that my feet must tread upon. I look around with only fleeting glimpses, but mostly I concentrate on the gravel and the angle of the short slope in front of me. I calculate the odds of someone having laid an IED where I am about to step, in between the moment I lift my foot up and when I put it back on the ground. I try to trick myself into believing that there is no danger, as I find it easier to walk when I do that. I lie to myself and say that I am sure that someone has already stepped here, or that no one would lay an IED at the bottom of a depression, only at the top. I never step on the crest of any mound of earth, no matter how small, and I never step on the intersection of any two paths. The process reminds me of "step on a crack—break your mother's back," the superstition that caused me and my sister to watch where we stepped through-out childhood. Inevitably, I cannot follow my own rules, and I end up stepping somewhere I don't want to. At these moments I hold my breath and tense up my body. The rational part of my brain reminds me that I doubt I would see it coming if I stepped on an IED. There are simply too many spots to hide them, and too many steps to take. I am glad that I can feel my St. Christopher medal dig into my chest under the weight of my flak jacket

We take agonizingly slow steps forward, and in the distance I hear a familiar sound. LAVs are moving from Sper to the edge of the riverbed to pick us up, saving us a few kilometres of the patrol. There is an ANA checkpoint named Brown that lies at the end of the road between Sper and the Arghandab. This dusty collection of HESCO Bastions, with an Afghan flag flying above it and a tan-painted Ford Ranger in front of it, is effectively the beginning of the Afghanistan that is friendly to us. The sound of the LAV engines carries extremely far in the cool, quiet night. It is nice to hear the reassuring diesel rumble after so long with only the sound of distant dogs, the rasping of our breath, and our own hearts beating. We can hear the engines rev as they drive over the berm that separates CP

Brown from the Arghandab, where they will wait for us, scanning the dark night with their thermal optics. I imagine the massive bulk of the LAV, which I've always thought looked like a green-painted armoured RV with a 25mm cannon sticking out of it. That thought reminds me of the movie *Stripes*. ("We got one heavily armed recreational vehicle here, man.") I laugh, feeling grateful that their hulk is watching over us.

As we walk up the steep slope of the riverbed, it is obvious that the patrol as a whole is slowing down. I look at my watch, and it is 0300. We have been going for over eight hours. The patrol pauses often, and we finally reach a compound surrounded by wide, dried-out opium fields that seem to stretch over the horizon. As we progress through this field, the sound of the LAV engines grows louder, but I still can't seem to make them out. I can not believe how far the opium fields stretch, and we seem to take a break and sit down every five minutes. There is a large mud compound between us and the Arghandab, and outside it sits an old tractor and a van. I catch myself thinking that this is a really nice house, when I realize that it is a mud compound on the edge of a war zone. I have been surrounded by the abject poverty of the villages west of Sper for so long that I truly believe that this large, unpainted mud compound with vehicles sitting in front of it is the height of personal accommodation, that it should be featured on "MTV Panjway Cribs."

Finally, we descend to the bottom of a short ditch, before climbing up the other side and finding ourselves in the midst of the laager. The sound of the LAV engines idling is almost deafening to my ears, which had become accustomed to the silence of the march. I walk in a daze to the centre of the vehicles and stand there, not knowing what to do. Eventually someone comes out and directs me toward an ANA truck that is waiting to take our kit. I am halfway through a smoke, and it does not register that the patrol is over. Instead of the elation that usually comes with the end of a patrol, I feel utterly exhausted and mostly numb. I drop off my pack in the back of a large transport truck, and it is taken by an Afghan soldier wearing green camouflage pants and a tan T-shirt. He strains under its weight.

Although I don't realize it yet, the fear and despair that gripped my soul on this last leg of the patrol will remain with me throughout the tour. It will even remain with me in Canada, when I wake up drenched in cold sweat, convinced that the ground underneath me has fallen away, or that I have lost the rest of the patrol and am alone. On this last leg, drenched in my own sweat, covered in dirt, weighed down under far too much kit, walking on blistered feet, and bleeding from a cut on my face, I lower my head and will never raise it fully again. Maybe every soldier has a moment like this—or maybe not.

"Okay, 1, 2, 3, 4, 5, 6, 7, 8." Someone counts us off. "You guys go to the back of that LAV." I don't see where he is pointing, but follow the crowd and eventually see an opened rear ramp leading to a dark interior.

By the time I make it to that LAV, the first six have already gone in and it is almost overflowing with soldiers. The benches comfortably seat six, three on either side. I am the seventh, and three more people push into the back as if this were a Tokyo subway car. Chris is in my group, and I see him as we cram into the LAV. I feel the press of other people's armour, kit, and bodies as we each try to wiggle into a somewhat comfortable position. A few are smoking cigarettes and the air is cool and humid and full of tobacco. Someone comes to the back of the open ramp and asks if we want cold water.

"Fuck, yes," is the reply, and the box is handed to Chris. He rips it open and starts handing the water out. I take a bottle with my gloved hand, excited at this treat. As I squeeze the bottle I realize that it is completely frozen. I open it and get a few ice-cold drops from the top, but nothing else. The bottle is too cold in my hands and eventually I replace the lid and drop it behind the blast blanket that I'm leaning against. The box is sitting on Chris's lap, and he complains that his crotch is freezing. I help him take out individual bottles of water and throw them unceremoniously to the side of the carrier.

"That's fucking retarded," is all I can think to say. I finish my cigarette, tap the air sentry on the leg and pass it to him to throw out into the moondust. The ramp closes with a hiss of air and a metallic *thunk* as the heavy latches move into place. It sounds like the closing of the doors on the Death Star. There are yellow stickers on both sides of the door warning people not to put their hands where the latches close. They depict a black silhouetted hand being mangled into unnatural shapes by the gears.

I feel safe once again, and lean back against the blast blanket, take off my helmet, and close my eyes. Around me, most have given up on the frozen water and are doing the same. We sit with our legs pressed together and hear the diesel roar of the engine, labouring under the weight of 13 fully kitted soldiers. We are moving back toward Sperwan Ghar, which is only a kilometre away. The turret swings softly from side to side, and we jostle and bounce over the bumps as the carrier moves down the gravel road back home. Over the speaker, I hear 29er informing 2 that we are passing the front gate. I feel my body tilt back as we drive up the hill into Sperwan Ghar, and smile at the thought that the patrol is over.

The LAV door opens to reveal the rocky gravel that covers the top of Sper. Behind the guns and above the HESCO Bastions, the black-blue sky is fading fast, with hints of orange intermingling with it. It is 0430 when we reach our final destination, and already it is dawn. The sound of the LAV door falling open is familiar and I hear it clank on the ground. I am home.

We stand up and awkwardly shuffle out of the carrier as we often have, half stooped so as not to bang our heads against the roof. M72 rocket launchers are suspended from Bungee cords attached to the metal pole that runs the length of the carrier's ceiling; we have to bow our heads to avoid them. We call LAVs "cars," and it sounds like we're talking about our personal vehicle every time someone points one out.

There is a long line of people waiting for their packs at the back of the ANA truck. I walk the 100 metres back to our room, drop my chest rig in the sand, and hang up my flak vest and helmet. The clothes hooks are drilled into a piece of plywood under an awning outside of our Russian compound. The bulldog that we've never named looks out at me as I hang my kit. Inside, scratched into the wall, there is Taliban graffiti that we leave alone. I hang my helmet on the same hook as my flak vest and wonder what it will be like to have a coat rack in Canada. I walk into the room, turn on the light, take off my shirt, grab a Squiggle Coke from the fridge, and sit on the picnic table to have a cigarette. I smoke slowly, and the cold Coke doesn't taste as good as I'd imagined. I have a dull headache, and realize that I'm probably dehydrated. My weapon rests to my left, lying across the picnic table. It is covered in dust and mud. I grab it and make my way back to the ANA truck. The line for kit is much shorter now. My pack sits in a heap some ways back from the truck. A clean-shaven Asiatic ANA soldier smiles at me and stares as I pick it up. I make my way past the mess and the showers back to our room and drop it heavily beside my bunk. A few people in the room have already grabbed breakfast, and the smell of fresh food entices me, so I sling my weapon over my shoulder and go stand in line for breakfast.

It is 0445 and the sun has just broken over the horizon. The cooks have been up since 0330; they knew we were coming back, so they started their morning in the middle of the night to prepare a much-appreciated breakfast for us. I've learned from experience to avoid the pancakes, as they're always heavy and unsatisfying. Instead, the cooks heap scrambled and hard-boiled eggs, beans, thick slices of ham and bacon, and hash browns onto my plate. I go into the mess tent, grab a handful of grapes that we purchased from the village of Sper, a blueberry Otis Spunkmeyer muffin (basically a miniature cake with 20 grams of fat), and a Nescafé 3in1. I then stuff a pear and an apple into my pocket. It's a balancing act trying to make it back to my room, and the pear and apple bang against my leg every step of the way. I make it without dropping anything, and put my food on the table that we usually play poker at. I'm done the meal in about 10 minutes; I hardly breathe as I take in the glorious food. I go outside to smoke, find my Squiggle Coke on the picnic table and finish it. I then go and take off my soiled clothes, unzip my boots, and walk to the shower in my underwear.

As I pass the first mirror I see a stranger out of the corner of my eye, but when I turn to look at him I discover that it's my reflection. I'm covered in dust, my long hair is matted and clumped with dirt, and my stubble has grown out. My face and hands are tanned dark brown against the pure white of the rest of my body. I wash my hands for two minutes straight before jumping into the shower. The water turns brown as it runs off my body.

As the water washes over me, something unexpected happens. I close my eyes and feel a wave overcome me. Tears I didn't know were there come to my eyes. They are tears of exhaustion as much as emotion. The shower is the only private place any of us has in Afghanistan, and maybe that is why it happens here. I convince myself that it is stupid to break down like this, and I turn off the water. When I get out, I realize that I've forgotten my towel, so I put my dirty underwear back on and walk to our room. Then, as I walk, I realize that in Sper we are not allowed to go out in our underwear. It is an army rule that the more comfort one has, the less acceptable it is to act like an animal. In Zangabad, people went days wearing nothing but underwear and sandals. In Sper, we have to wear pants and a T-shirt. In KAF, they have to wear their shirts with the sleeves down and red flags. The sleeves must be unrolled because the powers that be have deemed that to be more tactical.

I grab my ranger blanket, which is still wrapped around the foamie on the outside of my pack, and crawl up into my bunk. I listen to the other 15 guys in my room go through similar motions. My pack sits on the ground, wet with sweat and covered in dirt. Someone turns out the light, and it becomes darker than it was sleeping out under the stars in Mushan. There is absolutely no light in the room and I close my eyes. The bed and pillow are comfortable, my ranger blanket smells of sweat, and I smell of soap. It is 0530 and I sleep for the next 12 hours straight.

The patrol that had begun seven days earlier was over, but my tour wasn't. I spent the next three months in-country. There would be more patrols. The majority were mounted in LAVs; we would roll into an area and either perform a resupply mission or conduct a fighting patrol into a hostile village. On one such resupply mission, I saw my first Taliban die. I was hanging out of the rear air sentry hatch, watching as earth movers tore down the HESCO Bastions in Talukan, when the children that were around our LAV ran away. The next hint that I got that something was wrong were the machine gun rounds pinging off the armour beside me. The 25mm cannon on our LAV fired just as I figured out where the rounds were coming from; it felt like I was getting punched in the head. I watched the Taliban fire a machine gun, then I watched the cloud of dust that used to be him billow outwards. Around me the roar of battle swirled, the sharp bangs of machine gun and automatic rifle fire mingling with the bass thump of mortars being fired.

There was only one other major dismounted patrol that I was part of, called Operation Timis Preem ("lawnmower" in Pashtu, which recalled Optimus Prime, the Transformer). We broke into an Afghan compound north of the river and set up an observation post for a few days while a battle raged around us, just out of our area of responsibility. Allan and I sat on the mud roof of this compound, smoking cigarettes, looking for the enemy. We left our poo bags inside the blown-up door of the compound, and laughed at the neat row.

I drank more coffee and pushed more buttons in the CP. I set up new antennas and new lines, ate ice cream, conducted thousands more radio checks, and counted down the days until I could go home. I handed over to Mike Company, Royal Canadian Regiment's signaller, and endured the final LAV ride between Sper and KAF, dipping and smoking at the same time. There were more games of poker, more cigarettes, more laughs, and more deaths. The world continued to turn.

The story of my tour does not end with this patrol, but something fundamental inside me changed during it. This patrol was my baptism by fire. There was something about the heat beating down on me that day in Mushan, or the leg that would never end in the dark Afghan night, that changed my perception of myself. I no longer wanted to be in Afghanistan, but I had no choice but to be there. Patrols that had once been exciting adventures and opportunities to prove myself became a dangerous game. Many of my friends in the infantry said that they'd rolled the dice enough times. A lot of them wanted to get out after our tour, but most are still in—the army, Afghanistan, and warfare are what they know and what they excel at. I never truly excelled at war, and I never loved it. I think that this patrol was the moment when I had rolled the dice enough times, when I'd taken enough chances.

Growing up in an asphalt big-box-store society, where easy

credit, easy intoxication, and easy pleasure abound, it felt good to do something truly hard. Our society constantly tries to exert a protective hand toward its population: cigarette smoking is discouraged as it causes cancer, highways are barricaded to prevent rollovers, signs point out the safest ways to travel and inform us when a poor decision is made. Every product has been vetted by experts to ensure that it will not harm us. Milk is pasteurized, sharp edges are taken off toys, Tim Hortons coffee is marked "Hot! Be Careful," and for our French friends, "*Chaud! Attention.*" Everywhere the message is the same: follow the rules and you will live a long, happy life; don't follow them and we will inform you of your mistake. We live in a society that has been baby-proofed for adults, and we have come to think that absolute security is our birthright.

Afghanistan is different. There is no way to know which choice will end in safety. There is nothing to prevent you from walking down the wrong road; in fact, you may be ordered to do so. There, you have to make real decisions. There, all you have is your group. Everything that we do in Afghanistan is important, if not for the country or the world as a whole, then at least for us as a group of soldiers. There is no more training, no guiding hand, and there are no more second chances. On the patrol, for the first time in my life, everything was real.

The result is that I'm one of very few people who can say that I chose to risk my life for something that I believe in. Although the act of risking my life was far from comfortable and led to some very serious second thoughts at the time, I still did it, and it was very real. Now when I sip on Starbucks or read *Hustler,* I can say that, for a few brief months, I truly lived.

EPILOGUE

The earth seemed unearthly. We are accustomed to look upon the shackled form of a conquered monster, but there—there you could look at a thing monstrous and free.
—Joseph Conrad, *Heart of Darkness*

I AM NOT SURE she has any idea what she is getting herself into. I am sitting on the tarmac of Edmonton International Airport on board a military commuter plane filled with my chalk of soldiers who are returning home. The customs agent is young and attractive. I don't think she understands the depths that our depravity has reached. Her black hair is held up with pins, showing off her long, thin neck. Her uniform blue shirt reminds us of the uniforms that we wear, and her stab vest reminds us of our body armour. She is identified only by her badge number, which is printed on a tag sewn onto her vest.

"Hey, I already got your number," someone shouts, and everyone laughs. I think that she can feel her authority falling away.

"Hey, beautiful, you feel like supporting your troops?" someone else yells. Some of the soldiers ignore her, and continue to crane their heads out the window or fiddle with their kit before getting off the plane; others use their eyes to undress her as she tries to explain that she just needs our customs cards. She holds them high above her head and points, emphasizing the simplicity of her request. We are tired of filling out forms and being told where to put our paperwork. Instead of listening to her, we go through the familiar routine of fantasizing about our sexual exploits, trying to imagine situations where an encounter might be possible.

"Maybe if she's at the bar after we get off the plane, I could buy her a drink and—" This is the Canadian military; there won't be a bar.

The catcalls continue as she walks up and down the aisles grabbing our cards, and every combat soldier's head turns. We have long since given up the stigma against staring at women; going so long in between sightings of these elusive creatures, we believe it is our right to ogle.

"I would sip from a bowl of her shit," a friend of mine says. Although she ignores the comment, I think that it is loud enough for her to hear. I don't laugh; I just stare. What could she possibly think of us? We've stopped caring about the answer to that question. The customs agent tries to keep some semblance of dignity as she walks off the plane, but she moves too quickly to fool us. Whistles, cheers, and laughter follow her. I still have my customs card in my hand. We have arrived back in Canada.

Between Scotland and Edmonton we watched in-flight movies including Will Smith's *Hancock*; we had already watched a pirated copy purchased at KAF. Generals had recorded messages to run between the in-flight films, telling us what an amazing job we had done, and how proud our nation was of us. They were obviously reading cue cards and were not particularly adept at it. Most of us didn't even take off our iPods. The high point of the journey was when two CF-18 fighter jets took up positions, one on each wing, while their pilots waved at us. I had never seen a fighter jet from the air.

When we finally get off the plane and look out onto the tarmac of

Edmonton International Airport, we see a long line of senior officers and NCMs waiting to greet us. The line stretches from the terminal all the way to the ramp that leads down from the plane. Most wear green CADPAT. Their epaulettes are covered in bars, maple leafs, or the surprisingly garish Canadian coat of arms for the most senior non-commissioned officers. The line is filled with men in uniform who seem past their prime, men who probably still reminisce about the "good old days" of the Airborne Regiment, the old army. Their uniforms are clean and pressed. My uniform is still permeated with Afghan dust, and my pack reeks of sweat. I have waited so long for this day, and amazingly only one emotion is stirred up in me by the sight of Canada, my beloved home: I am consumed with hatred.

I finally make it to the terminal after shaking so many hands that I have images of the after-game routine in children's soccer. I stand incredulous as I watch a line of volunteers giving out Tim Hortons coffee and donuts, asking each person if there is anything they need. When I get to the front of the line, a kind, middle-aged woman asks where I'm from. "Calgary," I reply.

"Oh, that's so close, is someone picking you up?"

"No, I don't think so. I have to go back to Shilo before I can go home."

"Well, do you need to borrow my cell phone?"

"No, I should be okay."

"If you want, I can give you a ride to Calgary right now. We can just leave and you can be back with your family in four hours."

"No, thank you." Although my mind briefly flirts with the idea of going AWOL (absent without leave), I am a bit too institutionalized for that. I am also confused. Why is she being so nice to me? It feels like a trap, as if, were I to say yes, she would take me to her car and hit me over the head with a sock full of pennies. After seven months in Afghanistan I am no longer willing to trust a 40-some-year-old volunteer handing out free coffee.

I sit in the terminal building while those around me hug their families. I watch *Two and a Half Men,* and stew in my own rage, while trying to figure out why I am so angry and how Charlie Sheen keeps getting work. Later, after another plane ride, and another emotional scene in Shilo, I write this entry in my journal.

1 October 2008   *Shilo, Manitoba, Canada*
We were heroes in Edmonton, why? What did we do for those fine folks who gave out Tim Hortons coffee and offered me a ride (and probably the shirt off their back)? Police, firefighters, line after line of officers and RSMs all trying to shake our hands for getting shot at by the Taliban. They have no idea, they have no context. I hate them. That is my overwhelming emotion. It's not like my hatred for those in KAF, but for the fact that they think they've earned the right to talk to me and shake my hand. Mostly, it's because they don't know what I know. They have no conception of the fact that I've hated combat and considered ways to get out of it. They treat me like a hero and I feel like a coward. I hate them for making me feel that way.

But I shouldn't say that. I think pride will come, and I think honour and valour already have. Maybe we were too sweaty, tired and pissed off to realize it at the time.

So tomorrow Calgary, and that unique and heart-wrenching joy of craning my head outside the window of the plane to see my city and my home again. Then smothering by my parents, love with my girlfriend, and stories galore.

Until Tomorrow

Ryan

I am part of a new generation of soldiers, whose formative experiences in uniform were shaped by the explosions of IEDs, the crack of bullets, and the sight of our friends dying. We are the future of the Canadian Forces, and of Canada: we can never allow the things that we know to be forgotten. We must pass on what we have seen to all Canadians, so that they know what we are doing in their name.

In the end, a flag is just a symbol, but it is one that we all wear with pride. It is the only national symbol that escapes the reductive pragmatism of the weary-eyed infantry. I saw it fly proudly above Zangabad, when we should have torn it down as a possible enemy aiming marker. Our efforts have put our mark on Canada's flag. We need others to understand this. "We stand on guard for thee" is something few can claim to have done. But, after looking out over the moondust of Zangabad, waiting to be attacked while the Maple Leaf billowed proudly above us, I can say that we truly did. In the end, I don't know if the Maple Leaf stands more for us than we do for it. Maybe one can truly know Canada only in a far-flung observation post, unwashed, unshaven, and dirty. I am sure that this was where I learned to know myself.

It is almost a year to the day after this patrol began, and I am standing in uniform at the Calgary Stampede. *This is going to be one Gucci go*, I think as I arrive. *Watching the women walk by for a few hours, free food, free admission, and an excuse to be at the Stampede every day.* So I sit at a table in front of a communications truck and answer stupid questions for eight hours a day.

"*So, you're in the army?*"
"*Yes, sir.*"
"*Have you been to Afghanistan?*"
"*Yes.*"

"Have you ever killed anyone?"

"Not to my knowledge, but I can't rule out the possibility."

"Oh, hey, is that a helicopter? Cool! I'm going to go get my picture taken. Hey, son, get behind the machine gun."

. . .

"Is that army food?"

"Yes, it's called an individual meal packet or IMP. They aren't bad."

"Ewwww . . . I would never eat that. Hey, is that a helicopter? Cool! I'm going to go get my picture taken with the big gun."

I watch Canadian society walk past me, as I sit representing the Canadian Forces. For the most part, I see fat people eating fatty foods, ignorant people proud of their ignorance, and loose, drunk women looking to have their self-esteem stroked by a man in uniform. In a gesture of goodwill, someone gives us his tickets to the chuck wagon races, and I feel like I could hug him.

I am walking out of the Stampede grounds, back to my car, and trying to look like a soldier as people turn and stare. I pass a sign that proclaims "Calgary, the friendliest place on earth." I wait at a crosswalk and watch a V12 pickup truck speed through a red light. I then watch a man in a suit run out into the middle of the street to give that pickup both middle fingers and scream, "You fucking asshole!" I wonder if it has all been worth it. I wonder if I can ever truly fit in again.

As time has passed, most of my memories have lost their sting. The sharp edge of experience has been blunted by more experience. I think about going back for one more game of poker, one last cigarette, or one last conversation under the starry Afghan sky. A few days after I got home I told Darcy that if I ever said I wanted to go back, she should punch me in the head repeatedly until I changed my mind. Now as I approach completion of my graduate degree, I think seriously about it. The exhaustion, despair, and danger that were the reality of this patrol have been replaced by memories of the good times. I get e-mails that say that they need qualified signallers for the last rotation, and I fantasize about just one more day, just one more roll of the dice. But there is no such thing as just one more.

The decision not to go back makes me feel I've lost my manhood; it makes me feel like a coward. I didn't know what those words meant until I went; I only learned what it meant to be a man in Afghanistan. I wrote in my journal on the day that I arrived back in Canada that "I think valour and honour will come, but we were too tired, sweaty, and pissed off to realize it at the time." That sounds like a fairly accurate assessment. As time passes, anger is slowly replaced by pride. The growing hatred I felt for the Afghan people after seven months in their country has waned, and I read books like *The Kite Runner* and *The Places in Between* and think about Afghanistan's cultural heritage, which meant little to me when I was on the ground.

I sit in graduate classes where we argue about the nature of security studies and the role of constructivism in shaping international geopolitics. I read Clausewitz, Buzan, Sun Tzu and more academic papers than I could shake a reasonably sized stick at. In my spare moments, I wonder what my friends are doing. When I look around a room filled with eager young scholars debating some obscure academic point, I'm cognizant that they no longer understand me, that I know things my intellectually self-aware peers do not.

I am in Kingston, Ontario. It is almost two years to the day since the patrol ended. Kingston is where signallers do trades training, and learn how much fun it is to party with a group of guys they've never met. The base is separated from the downtown hub by about a kilometre. In between the two is the Cataraqui River, over which is the bridge that I am standing on, naked.

You have to cross this bridge to get from the bars to the base. Every year a group of guys, and ideally a girl or two, take off all their clothes, walk out onto the bridge, and jump into the river. They then surface, put their clothes back on, and try to get out of there before the cops show up.

I am drunk, and decide that it is a good idea to "jump the bridge." I take off everything but my socks (I don't want to cut my feet on the rocks), shimmy out into the middle of the bridge as cars pass over it, and look down. All I see is a black maw. I can't tell where the water starts; it looks like the drop goes on forever. I glance at the people on either side of me, similarly naked and drunk, then look down and realize I can't do it. I don't have the courage. I stand, paralyzed, for a few seconds and then tell myself, *You are not going to jump into the river; you are simply going to step off this ledge.* This sounds plausible, so I will my feet to move forward as if I were simply stepping off a stair. Instantly, I feel the whoosh of air pass my ears and am engulfed in the black water of the Cataraqui, exhilarated as I have almost never been. I swim to shore, cut up my hands on the rocks, see the cops coming, and put on my pants as quickly as possible. (I figure if I am going to go to jail, I should probably have pants on.) An attractive female police officer chastises us—as instructors, we should have known better, she scolds. We walk, tails between our legs, dripping river water and blood, back toward the base.

The feeling of paralyzing fear and the blackness that I saw as I stood, naked and frozen, on the bridge brings back unexpected memories. I remember squatting behind a mud wall in Mushan, heart pounding in my chest while RPGs flew over my head, too terrified to stand up. I remember the complete blackness that separated the two sides of the wadi that I fell into, smashing my face against the ground, and giving myself a bloody nose. But most of all, I remember how to conquer my fear—trick myself into thinking that I am doing something mundane, simple even, then allowing my muscles to carry me through the motion. I think that jumping into the river, drunk and with a group of friends, was the best therapy I could possibly have had—even if it took a little while to sink in.

That is what the army gives you that you can't find anywhere else. It gives you a group that you can trust enough to jump into the unknown with. It fulfills the basic need that humans have for a pack, a pack that is bigger and badder than any other. It gives you the strength to overcome your fears and paralysis, with a little help from the people beside you. On basic training an instructor once told me, "The army can't promise you sleep, it can't promise you food, and it can't promise you water. But it can promise you someone by your side." That is the army's greatest strength.

For seven months in Afghanistan, I had been part of a pack, a group of guys (and one girl) with whom I didn't always get along, but on whom I could rely in the most dangerous situations possible. I was never separated from them for more than 12 hours. When I got home, I was completely cut off from that pack. Although at first, I was happy to see them go and to have time alone whenever I wanted it, as the weeks went by I began to miss them more and more. I wondered if Chris had made it into the Ontario Provincial Police, if Swanny's back had healed, if Mike's girlfriend was cheating on him, or if Dave still played too much World of Warcraft. I missed having people on whom I could rely constantly around, and I missed being in situations where I needed their help. The tradeoff is that I am now no longer in Afghanistan, walking the grape fields and rolling the dice. I have left that country behind and now concentrate on graduate school, building a successful marriage, raising a dog, and partying with my friends. I have traded my pack for another kind of safety, and I doubt that they have given me a second thought. There will always be some eager young signaller waiting for an opportunity to prove him- or herself in combat. I am no longer that signaller.

I wish that I'd liked war more than I did, been braver or less terrified at its darkest points, spent more time shooting and less time ducking. But everyone has fantasies of who they wish they were. I just have to work on being comfortable with the man that came home.

I miss the simplicity of action. In theatre there was us and there was our job, and that was all. I look at the bigger picture, and I'm as lost as anyone else. The bigger picture didn't apply to us except in some abstract way. On the ground, the changes are slow and imperceptible. The military will always be a self-contained organism. Soldiers will always worry far more about food, cigarettes, and women than about geopolitics. In Afghanistan, I went where I was told to go because I was told to go there. I had a tiny box within which to work, and there was a comforting simplicity in that.

It is as if there were two worlds, the one that I study as a grad student and the one that I experienced. I don't know which one is real, and I don't know how I should direct my energy. It's as though, having walked down two paths, I now have to choose which one to accept as meaningful and valid. On the one hand, there are the endless grape fields of Panjway and the drill hall in Shilo. On the other hand, there is school, asphalt, Boston Pizza, and prefabricated happiness available at a price—everything that makes up ordinary life. But this no longer feels real.

I am sitting in front of my computer screen surrounded by empty coffee cups and beer bottles. When I try to link my two worlds, I feel emotion grip my throat, my heart, and push into the corners of my eyes. I type words into the computer in a vain effort to connect these two worlds, but there can never really be a link between those seven days and the rest of my life. It has been a slow but simple process to change back from the person that I was at war. At first, life in Canada didn't feel real, and I felt disingenuous going through the motions of civilian life. But slowly those simple things *became* life. I feel the softness of my wife's skin. I try not to lose my patience with my dog, who refuses to stop pulling on the leash. I forget. I spend my nights in a comfortable Canadian bedroom instead of under the dark Afghan sky. Fireworks are just fireworks. The tears no longer fall.